T0330401

FROM SOCIAL MOVEMENT
TO MORAL MARKET

FROM SOCIAL MOVEMENT TO MORAL MARKET

▮ HOW THE CIRCUIT RIDERS SPARKED

AN IT REVOLUTION AND CREATED

A TECHNOLOGY MARKET ▮

PAUL-BRIAN McINERNEY

STANFORD UNIVERSITY PRESS ▮ STANFORD, CALIFORNIA

Stanford University Press

Stanford, California

Printed and bound by CPI Group (UK) Ltd, Croydon, CR0 4YY

Library of Congress Cataloging-in-Publication Data

McInerney, Paul-Brian, 1970– author.
    From social movement to moral market : how the circuit riders sparked an
  IT revolution and created a technology market / Paul-Brian McInerney.
       pages   cm
    Includes bibliographical references and index.
    ISBN 978-0-8047-8512-9
    1. Social movements—United States.   2. Nonprofit organizations—Information technology—United States.   3. Technology consultants—United States.   4. Consulting firms—United States.   5. Markets—Moral and ethical aspects—United States.
  6. Markets—Social aspects—United States.   I. Title.
  HN59.2.M335   2013
  303.48'40973—dc23   2013040184

Typeset by Westchester Publishing Services in Minion Pro, 10/14

i

CONTENTS

PREFACE

During my teens and twenties, I spent many weekends in punk rock clubs throughout New York City. Though not in a band, the music scene was an important part of my life. I was a member of that community. Things that were important to that community were important to me. Music meant many things to that community. It was entertainment. It was a voice. It gave us rituals around which to form collective identities. The scene was also judgmental. We had codes of what constituted appropriate behavior. If someone fell while slam dancing, someone else picked them up. The touring band always received the biggest cut of the door. Above all, members of the community expected bands to maintain their independence from corporate culture. In practice, this meant recording with small, independent labels. If a band signed a contract with a major label, they were considered "sellouts," ostracized from the community and excoriated by many of its members. In that community, being true to the music was more important than the financial security of the bands that produced it. At the same time, we understood that signing with a major label was often the only way to make a decent living from music.

The punk rock scene of the 1980s and 1990s exposed me to the key social phenomena that have driven my research interests since: How do actors collectively construct and negotiate authenticity while maintaining relevance and growing their ranks? How do groups produce social boundaries and enforce moral codes to ensure authenticity? What happens when those boundaries and codes are compromised or break down? As I became interested in economic sociology, I saw these tensions play out in other social settings. I began studying entrepreneurs in Silicon Alley, a high-tech industrial district in New York City. Throughout my time in the field, I witnessed many entrepreneurs struggle to get their companies off the ground while trying to remain true to the dreams that animated them. They compromised their business plans to attract venture capital funding. When that dried up, they compromised further to attract bank loans and angel investors. Within the market, organizations alternately competed and cooperated. At times, they denounced each others' business plans as laughably untenable. Other times, they applauded the success and decried the injustice of failure when firms seemed to "get it right" according to the new rules of the new economy.

Later on, I had a unique opportunity to combine my interests in economic sociology, social studies of technology, and social movement studies to study a nonprofit technology start-up called NPower NY. At first my research was an ordinary organizational ethnography: examining how one entrepreneurial organization coped when growth outpaced the organization's technical ability to deal with it. However, I soon learned that NPower NY was among the largest members of a much larger organizational field, which itself had a fascinating and contentious history. Contrary to the moral simplicity of the punk rock scene (or of my youth), the organizational field of nonprofit technology assistance providers was morally complex. NPower was at times heralded as the future of technology assistance in the nonprofit sector and at other times called a corporate puppet threatening to homogenize the sector with mediocre technology—often by the same groups. Groups did not fall neatly into one camp or another. The Circuit Riders, who I thought were opposed to NPower, would sometimes collaborate with the organization. Yet, even when a market arose out of the movement, NPower and the Circuit Riders continued to coexist in an uneasy tension.

This book grapples with the moral complexity of markets. As movements increasingly target businesses, markets are becoming morally complex social spaces. Yet, social scientists have few theoretical tools to make sense of such arrangements. In this book, I offer ways to understand how actors manage the ongoing tension produced when contradictory values coexist. I do so by tracking the formation and growth of a social movement that unintentionally creates and shapes a market. Although a small corner of the nonprofit sector, the story of the technology assistance market provides a rare opportunity to simultaneously examine movement outcomes and market creation. In this way, I show how movements imbue markets with certain social values.

ACKNOWLEDGMENTS

I would like to thank the many people who gave their time and knowledge to this project. The executive managers at NPower Seattle and NPower NY, especially Barbara Chang, Joan Fanning, Stephanie Creaturo, and Alison Marano, were extremely generous. Staff members at both organizations let me shadow them in their work sites, making time to answer my questions throughout their busy days. Members of the Circuit Rider technology movement were also extremely generous with their time. Rob Stuart, Gavin Clabaugh, Dirk Slater, Theresa Crawford, and Jamie McClelland guided me through a world of technology activism. Special thanks also go out to the many people who talked with me about their role in technology assistance throughout the years. Their names are too numerous to recount here (see Appendix B for a list of interviewees). Phil Klein welcomed me into his home during my fieldwork in Seattle. Though she was not involved in the project directly, Boo Davis shared her home and dark sense of humor during my fieldwork trips to Seattle.

A number of people were involved in the intellectual development of the project from the outset. David Stark introduced me to economic sociology and kindled my sociological imagination with his innovative approach to theory. He also introduced me to Barbara Chang, which got the whole project started. I spent many hours discussing the minute points of New Institutional Theory and qualitative methods with Nicole Marwell. I am a better theorist and ethnographer because of her. Bill McAllister always welcomed conversation about theory, methods, or sports. Dana Fisher provided an excellent model of research in action. She has also offered invaluable professional and personal support in turning this project into a book. Traveling farther back in time, I owe much to Bill DiFazio, who sparked my interest in sociology in the first place and turned it into a passion. Michael Indergaard gave me my first taste of sociological research and opened the doors to the sociological study of organizations, technology, and the economy. Stanley Aronowitz pushed me to think deeply about the sociology of everyday life.

My editor at Stanford University Press, Margo Beth Fleming, guided me through the world of publishing, in the process helping to transform a rough manuscript into a book. I could not have done it without her or without Brayden King and Fabio Rojas, who each took the time to read the entire manuscript and provide much-needed critical feedback. My colleagues at the University of Illinois at Chicago (UIC), Pam Popielarz and Bill Bielby, read early drafts and helped me better formulate my theoretical concerns. Anna Colaner and Jerry Hendricks also read the manuscript and suggested many ways to improve it. Tünde Cserpes enthusiastically took on many of the less glamorous tasks of research assistance, such as data management and analysis and literature searches. Portions of this book benefited from workshops and presentations I gave at Chuck Tilly's Contentious Politics Workshop, the Workshop on Nonprofit Organizations at Columbia University, the Consortium for the Science of SocioTechnical Systems at the University of Michigan, the Rob Kling Center for Social Informatics at Indiana University, and the Exploring Social Enterprises Conference at the University of California, Los Angeles. I am indebted to the Department of Sociology at the University of Illinois at Chicago for providing the material support and leave necessary for me to complete the book.

This project also benefited from the rich and fulfilling life I have had outside of work. Jennifer Mosley is most responsible for that life. She listened to my half-baked ideas, read drafts, and made sure my work life was balanced with fun and happiness. I am deeply indebted to her for all the professional, personal, and emotional support she has given me over the years. Lola Olivia McInerney has been in my life a very short time, but already she has inspired me to be better at everything I do. David Van Arsdale has been my good friend and cheerleader ever since we met. Arafaat Valiani and Lesley Wood encouraged my development as a scholar, while making sure I maintained a grasp on what is important beyond academics. My family has been a constant source of support and inspiration. My brother Michael has kept me laughing through good times and bad. The rest of my family—my parents, John and Mary, and my brother Chris—provided love, support, and encouragement throughout my life. They left us too soon. I dedicate this book to them.

FROM SOCIAL MOVEMENT
TO MORAL MARKET

INTRODUCTION

The young organic food industry won legitimacy, but only by distancing
itself from its core idea of the connection between soil, food, and health.
(Fromartz, 2006: 29)

In the market for organic food, sellers have found a way to marry social values, such as healthy eating and land stewardship, with economic value, such
as higher margins for their products. This formula works. While the rest of
the U.S. economy contracted following the collapse of its financial markets,
the organic food industry grew unabated. From 2000 to 2010, sales of organic
food increased 438% to $26.7 billion (Organic Trade Association, 2011). Yet
organic food was not always big business. The market began as a countercultural movement in the 1960s. Dedicated to taking back the land from industrial production, groups of activist farmers began buying land to grow fruits
and vegetables according to organic farming principles. Demand for their
produce grew as activists challenged industrial food producers and promoted
organic methods as a healthy, environmentally sound alternative to food
grown with pesticides and synthetic fertilizers. Media accounts about the
dangers of pesticides, like the "Alar scare" of 1989, further stoked the demand
for organic food. Small health food co-ops and stores grew larger. Before long,
mass market organic retailers, such as Whole Foods, were expanding nationally and internationally. Today, consumers can find organic food in just about
any supermarket in the United States. Organic retailers and growers still consider themselves purveyors of healthy food and stewards of the land. However,
as the organic market grew and stabilized, the underlying movement became
less radical. In order to create something economically valuable, market

practices became commonplace and social values were compromised. The Organic Foods Production Act of 1990 signaled the establishment of a legitimate new market. Over several decades, a movement of countercultural farmers was transformed into a state-regulated, multibillion-dollar sector. How did this transformation come about? Put differently, how did a social movement become a market? Did the activists sell out? Did the creation of a new market deliver positive social values to a wider audience? How does the creation of movement-based markets affect producers and consumers?

Social Movements and the Creation of Moral Markets

The creation of markets is a profoundly social process. Even in planned economies, markets are rarely implemented by design (Stark, 1996; Stark & Bruszt, 1998). Rather, markets are shaped by actors and forces beyond the control of any single group. In a seminal article, economic sociologist Harrison White (1981) asks, "Where do markets come from?" His answer takes the form of a technical analysis of producer markets, but provides a key insight: markets come from the interactions of producers as they monitor one another to find specific niches to fill. White's account challenges the stylized neoclassical theory of markets as atomistic, self-interested actors whose activities are coordinated exclusively through price. Building on this insight, economic sociologists have developed several theoretical approaches: Markets are "embedded" in social networks that are marked by trust among buyers and sellers (DiMaggio & Louch, 1998; Granovetter, 1985, 1992). Markets are governed by social institutions, which provide common meanings and rules of interaction for buyers and sellers (DiMaggio & Powell, 1991a; Haveman & Rao, 1997; Lounsbury & Rao, 2004; Thornton, 2004). Markets have cultures; in other words, they have their own systems of meanings and ways of doing things (Levin, 2008; Zelizer, 2010). Finally, markets are performative, which is to say that people in markets enact theories from economics and finance (Callon, 1998; MacKenzie, 2008; MacKenzie, Muniesa, & Siu, 2008). Today these theories are in conversation with one another, helping scholars better understand the social aspects of contemporary markets and explain how markets stabilize over time. However, all have been criticized for not taking into account processes of contention and change in markets (Fligstein, 1996; Fligstein & Dauter, 2007; Fligstein & McAdam, 2012).

To account for contention and change, scholars of markets have begun to study the role of social movements and contentious politics in making and shaping markets (King & Pearce, 2010). Social movements are "collectivities acting with some degree of organization and continuity outside of institutional channels for the purpose of seeking or resisting change in some extant system of authority" (Soule, 2009: 33). While many social movements target states (Tarrow, 2011; Tilly & Wood, 2009), activists are increasingly taking aim at market actors (Yaziji & Doh, 2009). Over the past few decades, social movements have made and shaped markets in the United States and around the world. The "locavore" movement has rekindled Americans' interest in farmers' markets and backyard gardening (McCloud, 2007). The natural foods movement of the 1970s and 1980s gave rise to the multibillion-dollar market for organic foods (Fromartz, 2006; Guthman, 2004). Craft beer brewers organized a movement to gain market share against mass-production brewing companies (Carroll & Swaminatham, 2000). Activist chefs challenged centuries of French cooking tradition to establish nouvelle cuisine (Rao, Monin, & Durand, 2003). Few markets have escaped the influence of the environmental movement, by far the largest and most influential social movement of the contemporary era. The environmental movement has shaped consumer markets for products from lightbulbs to automobiles and has spawned several markets for explicitly environmentally sound products. Pressure from the environmental movement has transformed the waste management industry, turning trash for disposal into a market for recycled materials (Lounsbury, Ventresca, & Hirsch, 2003). The environmental movement has also pressured the energy industry, creating markets for wind and other renewable sources of power (Vasi, 2011).

By way of these studies, sociologists have shown that social movements press market actors to adopt certain values. Yet market rationality does not easily give way to a movement's demands. Otherwise, companies would respond to every group that boycotts or makes some claim against them. Conversely, social movements do not readily accept market solutions to their demands. Activists use the term "greenwashing" to describe market practices disguised as socially responsible acts. When social movements engage with markets, values collide and combine; activists and entrepreneurs come together; and the result is something new. The blending of social and economic values creates what scholars call "moral markets"—markets that coordinate exchange through social as well as economic values (Fourcade & Healy, 2007; Sayer,

2006; Stehr, Henning, & Weiler, 2006). Moral markets are becoming increasingly common as consumers have access to more and better information about the companies they support through their purchases (Stehr, 2008). The market for environmental cleaning products is a good example of a moral market. Consumers pay a premium for products that do not harm the environment, despite the fact that they may receive few direct benefits.[1]

Although all markets have moral bases, what goods and services count as morally correct is contestable and varies across markets, cultures, times, and situations (Anteby, 2010; Prasad, 1999; Zelizer, 1979). Furthermore, the bases upon which morality is judged are multiple and contentious (Boltanski & Thévenot, 1991, 1999, 2006). The same goods and services can be considered morally bad (and therefore illegitimate) in some cultures, places, or times and morally good (and therefore legitimate) at others (Anteby, 2010). Viviana Zelizer's (1979) account of life insurance is a compelling example of how a service once considered morally reprehensible becomes recognized as morally correct. Kieran Healy's (2006) groundbreaking analysis of organ donation shows how the exchange of body parts is morally acceptable (or not) across different institutional arrangements, such as state regulations. Therefore, market values (which express price and exchange) and social values (which express collectivity and solidarity) are analytically distinct moral orders. However, they are often mixed in practice. Actors may express specific social values in market spaces, via cause-related marketing, for instance. Alternatively, actors may express market values in social settings, as nonprofit organizations often do when called upon to measure the economic impact of their services. Therefore, to understand the relationships between movements and markets, economic sociologists have to pay more attention to how different actors combine moral orders and to what ends.

The creation of moral markets forces scholars and managers alike to grapple with many important questions: How do social values become inculcated in markets? Which social values win out? How does the introduction of social values change a market? What are the social and economic consequences? Economic sociologists are only beginning to pay attention to such questions. To contribute to this line of inquiry, this book examines the brief history of a relatively small social movement—the Circuit Riders—that created a moral market for technology services in the nonprofit sector. By focusing on a single movement, this book explicitly traces the process by which a social movement can imbue a market and organizations with social values—and how such activism can lead to unintended consequences.

Theoretically, this book draws on economic and organizational sociology, as well as contemporary theories of collective behavior and social movements. Empirically, it rests on data from a longitudinal ethnography of the Circuit Rider technology movement. Since many readers will be unfamiliar with the Circuit Riders, they will come to this example with fresh eyes. To set the scene, the following section gives a brief overview of the movement and how their activities shaped a market for technology assistance in the nonprofit sector.

A Movement Becomes a Market

Establishing a Movement

During the 1990s, the immense growth and diffusion of the Internet and other computerized network technologies revolutionized how corporations did business (Castells, 1996). However, nonprofit and grassroots organizations remained behind the more technologically advanced business and public sectors (Brainard & Brinkerhoff, 2004; Brainard & Siplon, 2002; Corder, 2001; Saidel & Cour, 2003) for a host of reasons, including a lack of resources (Kirschenbaum & Kunamneni, 2001; Treuhaft, Chandler, Kirschenbaum, Magallanes, & Pinkett, 2007), personnel (Seley & Wolpert, 2002: 75), and access (Robertson, 2001). In response, groups of activists began harnessing the power of information technology to organize a revolution of their own. Calling themselves "Circuit Riders,"[2] these activists were dedicated to using new information technologies to support the ideals of social justice and environmentalism. Their goal was to deliver the promise of the Internet to grassroots and nonprofit organizations, empowering them to change the world. Leveraging support from foundations, the Circuit Riders traveled to organizations across the United States, installing hardware and software and training staff on how to use their new technologies. While the Circuit Riders recognized themselves as a movement sui generis, they mainly identified as environmental and social justice activists, working exclusively with nonprofit and grassroots organizations that shared their ideological commitment to these causes.

The Circuit Riders assembled their revolutionary force quickly. By 1997, the Circuit Riders had swelled their ranks from a handful of activists scattered throughout the country to a technology movement almost 10,000 strong.

They convened meetings and mobilized tech-savvy activists across the United States. Like many movements, they struggled with the consequences of their rapid growth. As more people joined the movement, the meaning of the work began to change. By working with environmental and social justice groups, the Circuit Riders raised awareness among nonprofit organizations and foundations, which began to fund technology projects elsewhere in the sector. Their activities eventually caught the attention of technology companies, such as IBM, Adobe, and Microsoft, which saw the nonprofit sector as an untapped market for their products. As these companies contributed software, technical assistance, financial resources, and legitimacy to the nascent movement, the market for technology services in the nonprofit sector became a reality. Foundations organized conferences around technology assistance. The Alliance for Nonprofit Management, a trade association, created a special section for technology consultants. The Circuit Rider movement was gaining momentum.

A Challenger Rises

In 1999, an organization called NPower was formed with funding from Microsoft. This entity was built as a "social enterprise"—a hybrid organization that applies economic values and business-like practices to solve social problems. Billed as a nonprofit "startup," NPower had close ties to Microsoft as well as other for-profit firms, which also provided funding and technical expertise to the NPower staff. From their for-profit partners, NPower adopted sophisticated time tracking and billing systems, complex metrics for evaluating their work, and a complex bureaucracy to manage it all. Unlike the activist Circuit Riders, NPower more closely resembled a consulting firm.

NPower experienced considerable success in the nonprofit sector, rapidly gaining legitimacy for its particular vision as a social enterprise. NPower's legitimacy was rewarded with increased funding, which allowed it to expand nationally, starting 12 new NPower affiliates in as many cities throughout the United States between 2001 and 2005. NPower's expansion was, at times, problematic because it produced what I call moral ambivalence: tension resulting from the necessary coexistence of competing moral orders within an organization or sector. Blending social and economic values made NPower attractive to socially minded corporations and market-minded nonprofit foundations. However, NPower's combination of social and economic values also made them vulnerable to criticisms from the Circuit Riders, who thought the organization had lost contact with the social values upon which the movement was founded. For example, one Circuit Rider called NPower the "Wal-Mart of nonprofit technology assistance providers." All hybrid organizations that use the entrepreneurial strategy of blending social and market values must find ways to cope with the condition of moral ambivalence. NPower spent much of their considerable resources balancing the social values demanded by their nonprofit clients, foundation supporters, and colleagues with the market values espoused by their corporate board members, partners, and sponsors. For example, NPower developed an elaborate fee matrix that allowed them to charge fees for services on a sliding scale based on a client's budget, while accounting for the complexity of the project. Charging lower fees for clients with smaller budgets allowed NPower to appeal to the social values of the nonprofit sector (e.g., by claiming to help those organizations in need). Charging higher fees for more complex services allowed NPower to appeal to the market ideals of for-profit partners (e.g., by generating higher revenues to offset services provided to less affluent clients).

Whither the Circuit Riders?

As NPower thrived, the Circuit Riders dwindled. Circuit Rider programs and organizations folded, a sign that the activism they espoused was no longer accepted as legitimate in the sector. NPower's business-like practices and social enterprise form had triumphed. It seemed the market had displaced the movement, leading one Circuit Rider to comment via their official e-mail list: "Nonprofit technology assistance has become commercialized and the relationship between nonprofits and technology providers has moved completely over into a vendor-customer relationship. Looking at the successful [nonprofit technology assistance providers], the language, engagement style and basic culture looks a lot more like a consulting company/software company (with a heart) than a nonprofit technical assistance provider. As a sector we have embraced Adam Smith—the market will solve all" (Geilhufe, 2010).

The Circuit Riders had organized and mobilized new practices for providing technology to nonprofit organizations, funneling resources into the nonprofit sector. In the process of building their movement, the Circuit Riders created a demand for technology assistance in the nonprofit sector, allowing NPower to transform their work from social good to economic goods. Work that was once measured in terms of its contribution to social justice was now evaluated in terms of efficiency and cost savings. In the process, social movement activities had become market activities.

Yet the Circuit Rider movement did not die. Their social values had been indelibly imbued in the market that they helped to forge. By creating a demand for technology services to support social causes, they had helped create a moral market. The market was still directed toward helping do-gooders do better through improved use of technology. NPower never became completely dominated by market values. Rather, as a social enterprise the organization combined social and market values as it reconciled competing institutional expectations in a hybrid organizational form. Taking a step back from the exclusivity of the Circuit Riders, NPower and similar technology service providers expanded the market to nonprofit and grassroots organizations of all kinds. As NPower's founder explained, "I have worked for years in direct [social] service delivery, doing domestic violence human services. They are doing social change. . . . I think the agencies working on the ground, working with kids at risk, working with the elderly; they are doing the work of social change" [19].[3] With the help of corporate sponsorship, NPower channeled much-needed money and resources into the nonprofit sector. In this way, NPower continued the Circuit Riders' vision, just not in the ways movement founders intended.

To their credit, the Circuit Riders raised awareness about the technology needs of nonprofit and grassroots organizations. NPower and other nonprofit technology assistance providers (NTAPs) expanded this work. As a result, philanthropic foundations now support the technology infrastructure of many organizations, domestically and abroad. Nonprofit and grassroots organizations are beginning to close the digital divide between themselves, business, and government. One can argue that markets can be more democratic than movements, in a way: In the end, access to services was not limited to organizations that the Circuit Riders deemed worthy; NPower made its services available to any group that could afford them. However, the marketization of technology assistance also reinforced existing organizational inequalities in the nonprofit sector. Nonprofit organizations with large cash reserves or access to foundation funding were better able to avail themselves of technology assistance and could grow larger as a result, leaving less affluent organizations behind. The result was a divided market, in which large organizations grew larger and smaller ones fell further behind. These effects may trickle down to the vulnerable populations served by the nonprofit sector. When the dominant organizing principles of the sector are efficiency and effectiveness, nonprofit organizations are tempted to help the easiest cases first. This reinforces inequality as the most vulnerable find they are waiting in line while the organizations that were once available to help them find themselves without the tools needed to do so.

Markets from Movements

The brief story of the Circuit Riders I have presented represents only an outline of how a movement creates a market. Over the course of this book, I will offer a richer, more detailed history of the Circuit Rider movement and its complex transformation into a technology market. To explain how social movements create markets and imbue certain social values in them, I draw on theoretical insights about the common practices involved in this process: establishing worth, organizing, and coordination. Actors establish worth by making and supporting claims about the value of something and getting others to accept those claims. In markets the thing in question is often a commodity or a service. Movements make claims about the value of things such as the environment or social justice. As I will explain, movements and markets have different bases for evaluating the worth of things, as well as different methods for making and justifying claims about that worth. Organizing stabilizes those claims and measures of worth by creating structures that reflect them. Actors organize fields and create organizations to facilitate shared meanings, for example, ways of expressing value and values. Organizations are formal or informal collective actors that reflect some set of social and economic values in their structure and practices. Finally, market and social movement actors must find ways to coordinate their activities in fields and organizations. Coordination entails setting formal and informal rules about how best to orient toward one another. Conventions of coordination—that is, implicit rules of engagement—emerge over time as actors in and between market and movement organizations alternately compete and collaborate with one another to assert and establish their claims of worth. These concepts reflect the broader themes undergirding the coming chapters. Here, I will explain each concept in a little more detail.

Establishing Worth

Markets and social movements apply different values and practices in establishing what something is worth. Markets evaluate what something is worth through the price mechanism: "reduc[ing] different ways of valuing things to one dimension, measured in money" (Healy, 2006: 5). Social movements mobilize based on the idea that something is worth fighting for. In markets of all kinds, whether production, service, or financial, actors evaluate the worth of exchangeable tangible and intangible assets based on what others are willing to pay for them. Activists argue that the worth of their causes, such as the environment, must be evaluated on principles beyond price, such as the social good (Espeland and Stevens, 1998) . Both seek to elevate the worth of their objects—for example, the speculator takes advantage of different market valuation strategies to maximize profit (Zuckerman, 2012); the environmental activist employs tactics to demonstrate that societies undervalues natural resources, such as clean water. Both pursue ideals predicated on different moral bases, called "orders of worth" (Boltanski & Thévenot, 1991, 1999, 2006).

Actors judge worthiness (or lack of worthiness) based on different values—ideas about what is "right" or "good" that are transposable across situations (Hitlin & Piliavin, 2004). It is important to recognize that social values and economic values are stylized concepts, which I use here and throughout the book as ideal types.[4] In this vein, social values are principles about what is "right" or "good" that are justified by reference to human welfare (e.g., social justice, as well as environmentalism), the civic order (e.g., political participation), the religious order (e.g., church, worship, and sacred things), the family order, and things produced for their own sake (e.g., art, crafts, and music)[5] (Boltanski & Thévenot, 2006). On the other hand, economic values are principles about what is "right" or "good" that are justified in reference to profitability through production (e.g., efficiency) and/or exchange (e.g., buying low and selling high). Though these definitions treat social and economic values as analytically distinct, they are often combined in practice. For example, microcredit finance is a hybrid form that purposefully combines the social values of poverty alleviation with the economic values of lending at a profitable interest rate. Values are predicated on orders of worth, which are moral standpoints on which actors justify their behavior (or conversely denounce the behavior of others) (Boltanski & Thévenot, 1991, 1999, 2006). They help actors reduce uncertainty in social life by supplying guidelines for considering what is right and just in a given situation.

Social movements and markets are different social worlds that privilege different orders of worth in judging the practices of others. As a result, the practices that people consider right or appropriate vary between these two worlds. Profit-making is good in the market world. Equality is good in the social movement world. When social movements challenge market actors, they bring values derived from the moral order of their world to bear on the market world, where things are judged according to a different set of values. The result is a collision of moral orders. How can profit-making coexist with equality as evaluative principles? How can one say which is more important? Such decisions are easy from a single standpoint. However, compromising across social worlds creates challenges for everyone within them. In practice, the social and market orders of worth are rarely pure and separate; social and economic values often intermingle. Principles and how people rank them overlap and intertwine, forcing people to make pragmatic compromises across moral orders. This ongoing process of pragmatic compromise clears a path for hybrid arrangements, such as moral markets and social enterprises.

Though the market has become the dominant organizing principle in the United States and abroad (Boltanski & Chiapello, 2005), social values permeate the economy as well. In the nonprofit sector, voluntary organizations have embraced market values and practices, shifting toward social enterprise as an important organizational model (Bielefeld, 2006; Dart, 2004a, 2004b). Yet even as nonprofit organizations have adopted market practices, many for-profit corporations have paradoxically adopted social practices. And thus, hybrids abound. Starbucks prides itself on providing generous employee benefits, while paying its suppliers a living wage by purchasing and selling fair trade coffee. General Electric has developed innovative environmental products through its "Ecomagination" initiative. Several for-profit companies have made social values part of their core mission. Firms such as Seventh Generation (household products) and Patagonia (sports and outdoor apparel) are inseparable from their commitment to the environment. Entire markets are organizing around social values such as environmentalism. The Chicago Climate Exchange is a stock market in which traders buy and sell carbon offset credits. The express mission of the Exchange is to reduce greenhouse gases through voluntary participation in their market (Chicago Climate Exchange, 2011). Corporations also collaborate with nonprofit organizations to promote worthy causes and contribute solutions to social problems (Austin, 2000; Galaskiewicz & Colman, 2006).

Chapter 1 explains how groups of actors articulate and spread "accounts of worth," stories about the appropriate way to judge value in order to substantiate certain claims of worth and get others to adopt the practices that they justify. This process reflects the need to combine market and social values in different ways, depending on the situation that one faces.

Organizing

Establishing worth is about making claims about the value of things and getting others to accept those claims. To make those claims stick, market and social movement actors organize. Organizing stabilizes relationships among actors and helps them construct common meanings (Lawrence, Suddaby, & Leca, 2009). Market and social movement actors create organizations, which they mobilize to gain access to material and symbolic resources. Both sets of actors organize according to different principles, which are predicated on different claims of worth. Market actors organize based on market principles, which privilege exchange and evaluate worth based on price. Social movement actors organize based on social principles, which privilege solidarity and evaluate worth based on contributions to the social good.

Organizing takes place on different scales. On a large scale, organizing entails groups of actors and organizations assembling into organizational fields. Organizational fields are sets of collective and individual actors that share "a common meaning system" and "interact . . . frequently and fatefully" (Scott, 1994: 207–208). Actors in organizational fields share common cultural frameworks and meanings and are subject to the same formal and informal rules. The concept of fields expresses how sets of actors are subject to similar historical and structural forces due to their relative social positions (Bourdieu & Wacquant, 1992; Martin, 2003; Scott, 2008a). Within organizational fields, individual and collective actors jockey for position as a way to exert their interests and access resources. Resources are unevenly allocated within these fields, which means that dependency relations emerge out of the exchange of scarce resources (Pfeffer & Salancik, 1978). This means some organizations have resources that others need to operate, making the latter dependent on the former. For example, corporations rely on shareholders (potential and actual) for access to money in equity markets. Therefore, corporations depend on shareholders, giving the latter power and influence in corporate America. Such resource-dependent relations give rise to shareholder activism as a means by which social movements attempt to influence corporations. Therefore, organizational fields are considered "arenas of power" (Brint & Karabel, 1991: 335), social spaces in which actors are subject to contention from other actors. As I show in Chapter 2, organizing fields can take place as institutional entrepreneurs act strategically to generate institutional arrangements that are amenable to their interests. Institutional entrepreneurs attempt to configure fields at events such as meetings and conferences, which assemble actors who are also attempting to enact configurations of their own (Lampel & Meyer, 2008). Jockeying among institutional entrepreneurs for position and access to resources shapes organizational fields and creates uncertain outcomes for attempts at strategic action. For the Circuit Riders, this meant the professionalization of their activism and the introduction of market practices into the world of nonprofit technology assistance.

On a smaller scale, actors create formal and informal organizations, which then operate as collective actors. Both market and movement actors create formal organizations to secure legitimacy and flows of resources (McCarthy & Zald, 1977; Meyer & Rowan, 1977; Staggenborg, 1991). Formal market organizations often take the form of a corporation or firm. Social movement organizations can range from informal affinity groups to formally incorporated nonprofit organizations. Organizational forms matter, as certain organizational forms garner legitimacy from and signal authenticity to other actors in the field (Clemens, 1996; DiMaggio & Powell, 1991). For example, both market and movement actors adopt bureaucratic organizational forms over time under pressure to appear legitimate to different stakeholders. Social movement actors may organize as nonprofit corporations to generate donations from individuals, as well as grants from foundations and government agencies. Market actors may organize as for-profit corporations to gain access to equity markets. Chapter 3 explains the process by which institutional entrepreneurs create new organizational forms in nascent fields. In the case of the Circuit Riders, the new organizational form (a social enterprise called NPower) introduced new market practices into a field once dominated by the social values of activists.

Social values implicit in moral markets produce a specific form of uncertainty: moral ambivalence. Moral ambivalence is the condition of uncertainty that arises when an organization's actions are evaluated from multiple and contradictory moral bases. Various stakeholders evaluate an organization's activities from different moral standpoints. For example, shareholders, concerned with maximizing stock price, evaluate what an organization does from the standpoint of profitability. Local activists, concerned with how much a factory pollutes the environment, evaluate the organization's actions from the standpoint of how green they are. Employees, concerned with keeping their jobs, evaluate the organization's action from the standpoint of corporate paternalism. Actors facing moral ambivalence do not know ahead of time who will denounce their activities, which combination of moral bases others will use to evaluate their performance, or whether a dominant moral order will emerge. Moral ambivalence creates complex foresight horizons, meaning entrepreneurs do not know who their allies or enemies will be at any given time in the future (Lane & Maxfield, 1996). Complicating matters further, collaborators at one point in time may become competitors at another. For example, from 1985 to 1992, Microsoft and IBM worked together to produce a computer operating system called OS/2. The organizations soon split as Microsoft created and marketed its own operating system. As the partnership dissolved, IBM continued to develop OS/2 as a competitor to Microsoft's Windows NT platform.

To mitigate the uncertainty of moral ambivalence, actors create hybrid organizations, which assemble diverse elements recognized as legitimate by potential stakeholders. Social enterprises are a good example of such a hybrid organizational form. They are able to bring together market practices and social values by putting forward an organizational identity that balances institutional demands from varied stakeholders (Battilana & Dorado, 2010). As I show in Chapter 4, creating a coherent organizational identity from contradictory elements, while being evaluated from multiple standpoints (orders of worth), challenges entrepreneurs to find ways of reconciling competing demands.

While trying, moral ambivalence can spur entrepreneurial strategy. As David Stark explains, the hallmark of entrepreneurship *"is the ability to keep multiple orders of worth in play and to exploit the resulting overlap"* (Stark, 2005: 5). On this basis, successful entrepreneurs are those who can make their actions sensible to many stakeholders at the same time (Girard & Stark, 2003; Padgett & Ansell, 1993; Stark, 1999, 2001, 2009). For example, while much of the natural foods industry catered to small niche markets and countercultural trends, Whole Foods competed directly with mainstream supermarkets, combining the grassroots social values of the former with the cutthroat competitive practices and market values of the latter. As chief executive officer (CEO) John Mackey explains, "One of the things that has held back natural foods for a long time is that most of the other people in this business never really embraced capitalism the way I did" (Gertner, 2004: 47). Mackey has successfully combined social and market values; Whole Foods created an entire category of grocery store: the natural/gourmet supermarket for the (affluent) masses. Fair trade coffee and grass-fed beef on the shelves tell consumers that Whole

Foods is an ethical organization. The high profit margins these products garner tell investors Whole Foods is a market force.

However, incorporating contrasting values as a strategy poses ideological
and economic challenges to the organization (Johnston, 2008). Mackey's entrepreneurial approach exploits moral ambivalence, which has both pleased and
infuriated various stakeholders at different times: the business press lauds
Whole Foods for its rapid earnings growth (Schlosser, 2006), at the same time
arguing that the company is overvalued (Hogan, 2006). Workers enjoy the
company's team-oriented organizational structure, while the labor movement
denounces their union-busting efforts (Whole Foods Workers Unite!, 2006).
Consumers appreciate the company's commitment to organic produce, while
questioning the wisdom of trucking tomatoes across the country in lieu of
selling local produce (Maloney, 2006; Shapin, 2006). Environmental and ani-
mal rights activists applaud the company's humane treatment standards for
dairy and meat sold in their stores while denouncing Whole Foods as "selling
out" to the cattle and dairy industries (Little, 2004). Exploiting moral ambivalence requires managers to be vigilant about monitoring the moral environment and adjusting their strategy accordingly. At various times, Whole Foods
has had to adjust its adherence to various social and market values to assuage
stakeholders. Over time, these adjustments become structured into the organization itself.

Coordination

Clearly, harnessing moral ambivalence requires coordinating at the organizational level. However, coordination plays a pivotal role at many levels. At
its heart, coordination is about figuring out appropriate modes of orientation
toward other actors. Market producers coordinate to establish the formal and
informal rules of competition (Fligstein, 2001; Storper, 2000; Storper & Salais,
1997). For social movement actors, coordination often entails strategic choices
about appropriate tactics to employ against targets, as well as ways to cooperate with other social movements (Taylor & Van Dyke, 2004). As social movements engage with markets, actors from each side must find appropriate ways
of interacting with one another.

Coordination is a fundamental problem for both market and social movement actors. Economists consider markets a specific mode of coordination
between atomistic buyers and sellers, driven by pure economic rationality.
However, economic sociologists have found that market coordination depends

less on economic rationality and more on the situations in which actors find themselves. For example, the trading pits of the Chicago Board of Trade are an exemplary case of a market, ostensibly coordinated by pure economic rationality. Economic rationality is certainly on display as traders calculate prices and take advantage of differences between where a commodity price is and where they think it should be (MacKenzie, 2008). Entertainment and news media often portray traders as "Gordon Gekko" types, cold-blooded capitalists bent on profit at any cost. However, pit traders rely on social values as well. Social ties permeate the trading floor, including family relationships spanning generations, which affords trust among traders (Baker, 1984). Traders prefer to trade with people with whom they have social ties, even when such trades undermine strict economic rationality. Fearing the loss of these visceral social ties, many traders left the market when physical trading floors were replaced by electronic markets (Zaloom, 2006).

In coordinating activities to pursue their targets, social movements have developed a variety of insider and outsider tactics to protest against nonstate actors, such as corporations (Soule, 2009: 9–19). "Insider" tactics involve activists directly engaging with the corporation. These tactics include purchasing equity in companies to exercise a voice at shareholder meetings. If activists purchase enough stock, they can directly sway the choices of corporate managers and CEOs through shareholder resolutions. Socially responsible investing is another insider tactic that activists can use to influence corporations. By purchasing stock in corporations that share activists' social values, socially responsible investing takes advantage of market valuations to reward or punish certain companies. "Outsider" tactics take many forms. Boycotts, media campaigns, legal actions, advocacy, and protests are examples of outsider tactics activists may use to target corporations. Though expensive, legal actions are the most successful outsider tactic social movements deploy when targeting corporations (Eesley & Lenox, 2006). However, with the right timing and target, protests can be effective at influencing corporate behavior (King & Soule, 2007).

Ultimately, both insider and outsider tactics are attempts by movements to imbue markets with their particular social values, transforming ordinary markets into morally driven ones. Consider activists in Western Europe, who have successfully targeted the biotech industry to raise awareness of the health and environmental problems associated with genetic engineering in agriculture (Schurman, 2004). In doing so, these activists have begun to change the way people think about agriculture. The food supply chain that was once considered industrial commodity production is now treated as an environmental, social justice, and public health issue, transforming an ordinary market into a moral market. However, protests of any sort can be risky. Public sentiment can be fickle. And, aggressive social movement tactics, coupled with a well-funded corporate public relations campaign, can turn public sentiment against activists and increase sympathy for companies. Using hardcore protest tactics, including violent and nonviolent means, radical environmentalists (called deep ecologists) have struggled to contain the logging industry in the Pacific Northwest. Activists from Earth First! have used tactics such as sabotaging tractors and "tree-spiking" to damage logging equipment. Such radical tactics have alienated more mainstream environmental groups and kept them from joining with Earth First! Targeted logging companies have also successfully framed themselves as victims of domestic terrorism (gaining state support for investigation and prosecution). Therefore, social movements' delicate choice of tactics reflects the challenges and uncertainty of coordinating within and across moral standpoints.

Chapter 5 shows how conventions of coordination emerge as actors engage with other actors within organizations and fields. Conventions of coordination reduce the uncertainty of interaction by providing the implicit rules that govern the appropriate ways that individual and collective actors engage with one another. However, conventions of coordination only hold for actors that recognize each other as legitimate members of the same field. Many social movements are extrainstitutional actors, that is, they operate under different sets of shared meanings and rules than the market actors they target. This helps explain why market actors do not always respond to the demands of certain activist groups.

Understanding the moral pressures that social movements put on markets helps scholars to see how and in what ways markets assume social values. In other words, tracing moral markets to the pressures that shape them gives us insight into which social values are likely to temper economic values in any particular market. For example, why do environmental values, as opposed to labor concerns, matter for food production? Locavores aim to lessen their carbon footprint by reducing the distance food has to travel from production to plate.[6] Locavores have developed metrics, like food miles, to express their values in concrete ways. In doing so, they have raised awareness about the importance of reducing food miles among consumers. The effects of their actions can be seen widely from restaurants that contract with local farms for their meats to Wal-Mart, which has instituted a policy to procure vegetables from sources within 100 miles of their stores. As a counter, consider the labor movement. Despite a long and successful history of union organizing efforts among farm workers (Ganz, 2009), the labor movement has struggled to frame food production as an exploitation issue to the public at large. Despite the possible reasons for the success of one movement and the failure of another as they relate to the market, the results are clear. While Wal-Mart promotes regional sources for the produce it sells in its stores, they rarely address the working conditions of pickers and packers on the farm. The same is true for most restaurants. The mixed success of locavores begins to explain why the market for food has adopted certain social values and not others.

The Contingent Outcomes of Moral Market Creation

The processes I have discussed, establishing worth, organizing, and coordinating, take place over long periods of time, in various places, and involve many different actors. This limits the ability of any one person or organization to act strategically and creates uncertain outcomes for movement and market actors. Because of this, it is better to treat any possible outcome as contingent on specific configurations of actors and situations. When social movements establish the worth of their cause, it can lead to successful mobilization, as I will explain in Chapter 1. However, establishing worth necessitates pragmatic compromises. Attracting foundation funding, for example, requires activists to adopt practices legitimate to foundation officers, such as developing performance metrics. Performance measurement introduces market justifications such as claims toward efficiency. Social movements can maintain the purity of their cause by forgoing such funding. However, resources for activism are scarce. Even self-supported social movement organizations face the challenge of "mission drift" and pragmatic compromises to their values (Fisher, 2006).

Similarly, organizing entails pragmatic compromises among orders of worth, which leads to contingent outcomes. Field-level organizing takes place as various collective and individual actors vie for position within the field. Their jockeying takes place as they alternately compete and collaborate for resources and legitimacy. This is particularly true in the nonprofit sector, where organizations are expected to collaborate as a condition of funding, which is often offered through competitive grant opportunities. Fields are the outcomes of these contingent organizing processes on a large scale. They are subject to competition and change, punctuated by periods of stability (Fligstein & McAdam, 2012). Who wins and loses as fields are configured depends on the interplay between historical-institutional arrangements and strategic action. Successful strategic action is coined "institutional entrepreneurship" and results in the reordering of the field to align with the interests of the winner (DiMaggio, 1988). Scholars rarely attend to cases of unsuccessful institutional entrepreneurship. However, as I show in Chapter 2, the structure of competition between institutional entrepreneurs affects who wins and ultimately shapes the outcome of the match. The case of the Circuit Rider technology movement provides an excellent example of both successful and failed institutional entrepreneurship. In this case, the winner was aligned with market actors, which then provided conduits for the introduction of market practices (and justifications for them). Had the activists won, Circuit Riding would have been established as the legitimate model for providing technology assistance to the nonprofit sector.

On a smaller scale, organizations are themselves pragmatic compromises among orders of worth that are structured into organizational form and expressed as organizational practices (Thévenot, 2001). For example, when civil rights protesters targeted university administrators in the late 1960s, the latter responded (bureaucratically) by creating academic departments of African American Studies (Rojas, 2007). The establishment of African American studies as a discipline reflected pragmatic compromises from both sides. In Chapters 3 and 4, I examine the formation and maintenance of a social enterprise, which by its nature reflects pragmatic compromises. Institutional entrepreneurs create new organizational forms by assembling practices and structures from the field into a cohesive whole, which entails making pragmatic compromises among orders of worth. New organizational forms reflect the interaction between the strategic aims of institutional entrepreneurs and the constraints of the organizational field. NPower developed a unique type of social enterprise. Because of its close ties to for-profit corporations, NPower's compromises often meant adopting market practices. The success of the organization further justified the use of market practices among nonprofit technology assistance providers. Had the Circuit Riders been more successful in organizing their movement, they might have mounted more successful challenges to the introduction of market practices into the field. If that were the case, NPower would have shifted closer toward adopting more social move-ment practices, such as working more closely with nonprofit foundations to provide low- or no-cost services to organizations in need.

Yet even with the widespread adoption of market practices, nonprofit tech-nology assistance providers created a moral market—one that combined eco-nomic and social values and market and activist practices. All NTAPs, NPower included, worked exclusively in the nonprofit sector. Within the moral market of technology assistance, NPower and the Circuit Riders alternately competed and collaborated to provide services at reduced rates. Conventions of coordi-nation emerged out of theses interactions as a set of informal rules about when competition or collaboration was most appropriate. Chapter 5 explains how these conventions of coordination emerged. NPower's access to resources and legitimacy meant that they became a pole around which other members of the field organized. Again, had the Circuit Riders been more successful in organizing a movement, conventions of coordination would likely have been more cooperative and less competitive. Circuit Riders organized around a value they called "non-territoriality," meaning that they shared knowledge and practices freely among members of the movement. NPower's market practices exacerbated existing competition, particularly for access to resources such as foundation funding. In Chapter 6, I conclude by discussing what the story of the Circuit Riders has to say about social movement and market outcomes.

A Dialogue About Process

Certainly, this book aims to build on the literature that focuses on how social movements select targets and on the outcomes of their tactics. However, as this chapter has suggested, I take a different perspective. Using a historical-institutional approach with a focus on a rich, extended case, I aim to home in on how social movements infuse markets with values. This book contributes empirical and theoretical material to the new study of strategic action fields, the "mesolevel social orders" that are "the basic structural building block of modern political/organizational life in the economy, civil society, and the state" (Fligstein & McAdam, 2012: 3). Throughout, I build on the theory of strategic action fields to explain how the rules of particular markets come from the ongoing interaction of movement and market actors that participate in them. Understanding how specific values come to matter in specific markets can add considerable richness to the study of strategic action fields by showing the outcomes of contention between business and activists in today's morally complex markets. Moreover, a framework for this careful dance gives us insight into the ways that social movements and corporations coconstruct institutions and change markets over time.

Social movements express social values that people consider important and which may not find voice in other venues, such as markets. Markets are deeply entrenched in our society, which is unlikely to change dramatically in the foreseeable future. And so, a clearer dialogue about the interplay of social movements and market organizations gives us a clearer view of our social landscape and a better chance at sculpting it. By dissecting the social processes by which movements shape and make markets using the curious and fascinating history of the Circuit Riders, this book shows how social and economic values collide; how they are made commensurable in practice; and how pragmatic compromise between the sides is possible. Such a contribution, however humble, is directed toward helping all sides understand one another better. It is my hope that what follows enriches future studies of moral markets, paving the way for more successful transitions from movements into markets that express values beyond profit-making.

1

THE CIRCUIT RIDER MOUNTS

Establishing Worth and the Birth
of a Social Movement

Prologue

A Methodist preacher, when he felt that God had called him to preach, instead of hunting up a college or Biblical Institute, hunted up a hardy pony, and some traveling apparatus, and with his library always at hand, namely, a Bible, Hymn book, and Discipline, he started, and with a text that never wore out nor grew stale, he cried, "Behold, the Lamb of God, that taketh away the sin of the world." In this way he went through storms of wind, hail, snow, and rain; climbed hills and mountains, traversed valleys, plunged through swamps, swollen streams, lay out all night, wet, weary, and hungry, held his horse by the bridle all night, or tied him to a limb, slept with his saddle blanket for a bed, his saddle-bags for a pillow. Often he slept in dirty cabins, ate roasting ears for bread, drank butter-milk for coffee; took deer or bear meat, or wild turkey, for breakfast, dinner, and supper. This was old-fashioned Methodist preacher fare and fortune. (Cartwright & Strickland, 1857: 243)

In the autobiography of a "backwoods preacher," Peter Cartwright wrote these words in 1857 to describe the life of a Methodist Circuit Rider. John Wesley, the founder of Methodism, the first successful evangelical movement, spread his new religion by sending young preachers to villages plotted along a circuit. In the 1990s, a new movement of itinerant activists traveled the country, this time preaching the gospel of information technology and its ability to promote social justice and improve the environment. Calling themselves Circuit Riders, they gave new meaning to the term.

Though avoiding the discomforts of their historical namesakes, the contemporary Circuit Rider movement faced its own set of challenges. Before 2000, most in the nonprofit sector saw little value in information technology. Despite the widespread embrace of technology in the business world, there were few programs and projects dedicated to providing information technology to the nonprofit sector. In general, foundations did not support information technology investments among their grantees throughout the 1980s and 1990s (Robertson, 2001), leaving nonprofit and grassroots organizations without resources to acquire information technologies or the skills needed to use them (Corder, 2001; Kirschenbaum & Kunamneni, 2001; Seley & Wolpert, 2002: 75). Managers in the voluntary sector often failed to recognize the importance of information technology for the work they did (Berlinger & Te'eni, 1999; Stein, 2002). Beyond resource and personnel problems, previous attempts to build technology infrastructure for the voluntary sector had already failed (Mills-Groninger, 2003). It appeared, as many Circuit Riders lamented in interviews, that the people in charge of social progress in U.S. society simply did not "get" technology. As a movement, the Circuit Riders believed that members of the voluntary sector did not understand what technology was worth.

The Circuit Rider movement was not unique in facing such challenges. All social movements grow from inauspicious roots. Social movements are groups of actors (individual people or organizations) that engage in ongoing collective action for or against some institutional actor or arrangement to produce or resist social or political change. Collective action entails those meaningful activities conducted on behalf of a group either by that group or by some claimed representative. In order to engage in collective action and form a movement, organizers must overcome exogenous barriers such as recognizing and taking advantage of political opportunities (Tilly, 1978) presenting one's message effectively (Snow, Rochford, Worden, & Benford, 1986), and mobilizing resources (McCarthy & Zald, 1977) and endogenous barriers such as enrolling and motivating adherents (Olson, 1971) and creating a collective identity (Johnston, Larana, & Gusfield, 1994; Melucci, 1989; Polletta & Jasper, 2001). A key aspect of overcoming barriers to collective action lies in making and justifying claims about what a group's cause is worth. Here and throughout this book, I use the term worth in its social (meritorious, deserving) and economic (having monetary value) dimensions. Establishing worth is a complex social process that begins discursively and relies on the ability of actors to make value claims and get other actors to evaluate such claims using the same criteria (Strauss, 1982: 174–175). People often use worth in both dimensions to describe activities in their everyday lives. For example, when a friend says that a movie she saw recently was not "worth it," she may be claiming that ten dollars is too much money or two hours is too much time to spend on the film.

People express worth through accounts, which are transposable stories actors tell to explain what they do and justify why they do them in a certain way (Mills, 1940; Scott & Lyman, 1968; Tilly, 2006). Harold Garfinkel (1984), an eminent sociological theorist, explains that people make sense of everyday life by giving and receiving accounts. Furthermore, by expecting others to account for their actions, Garfinkel says, actors become "accountable" to one another. People create accounts by turning observations into stories, actively selecting among myriad details to report. Therefore, accounts construct as much as reflect reality (Orbuch, 1997). Stark and Bruszt (1998: 192) note that the term "account" "simultaneously connotes bookkeeping and narration. Both dimensions entail evaluative judgments, and each implies the other." Bookkeeping and narration are forms of justification, which makes accounts of worth "generalizable and relevant for the common good, showing why or how this general claim is legitimate" (Thévenot, Moody, & Lafaye, 2000: 236). In other words, to show how an account extends beyond one's particular experience, one relies on a story, which can be told through various means, depending on the situation and audience. For example, an investment prospectus is a formal account of worth. It describes a company and makes claims that the company is worthy of investors' money. Investors expect such accounts to be expressed in certain ways, for example, to have standard measures of values, such as price-to-earnings ratios and profit statements (accounts of worth as bookkeeping). Alternatively, one explains the value of having a garden by virtue of the aesthetic experience (accounts of worth as narration). One's friend does not expect the justification for having a garden to be expressed in terms of seed costs to productivity, though one could keep the books on a garden as well. When accounts express the value of something—for example, an object, activity, or idea—they are called "accounts of worth" (Stark, 2005, 2009). The moral bases that provide actors with the legitimate justifications they could give for an account are called "orders of worth" (Boltanski & Thévenot, 1991, 2006).

Organizers of social movements employ accounts of worth to mobilize others to engage in collective action. Francesca Polletta (2006) analyzes the stories activists use to get other people involved in protests. Told in the right way, such stories are critical for enrolling adherents into a movement by providing moral authority for collective actions. Attributions of worth link the various kinds of stories she describes. When activists tell stories about grievous injustices and how they sought to rectify them, they are trying to convince others that their cause has value—that it is worth fighting for. Such moral sources of motivation are especially important for successful collective action (Ganz, 2004). They justify one's cause as right and just. Movement organizers often use stories to translate movement interests into moral claims. Rather than saying, "We want X because it is good for us," movement organizers say, "We want X because it is just." John Wesley mobilized early Circuit Riders by invoking God as a cause worth facing inclement weather, sleep deprivation, and bear-meat breakfasts as they rode around the West spreading Methodism. Throughout this chapter, I discuss how early members of the Circuit Rider movement enrolled and mobilized adherents by making moral claims to potential supporters about what technology is worth.

What Is Technology Worth?

Like many conscientious people, Gavin Clabaugh became involved in the voluntary sector to save his soul. Throughout the 1980s and 1990s, he and his colleagues had a small firm that wrote trend analysis software for what he later recognized as "all the bad karma people in the world" [16]. As penance, Clabaugh took his technology skills to the Telecommunications Cooperative Network (TCN), a nonprofit cooperative that purchased communications services for about 4,000 organizations in the voluntary sector. In addition to buying long-distance and other phone services in bulk, TCN began offering technology consulting services for its members. These services, Clabaugh explained, "did not work too well because nonprofits are, by definition, dedicated to mission and if given a choice between a dollar for mission and a dollar for infrastructure, they will spend it on mission" [16]. This attitude reflects why policy analysts found that nonprofit and grassroots organizations lagged behind government and private business firms when it came to information technology adoption and use throughout the 1990s (Corder, 2001). Clabaugh thought of a better way to get voluntary sector organizations to take technology seriously. Rather than wooing nonprofit managers to invest scarce resources in information technology, Clabaugh decided TCN should target the foundations that funded them. By getting foundations to pay for technology, Clabaugh could ensure that the nonprofit and grassroots organizations they supported would follow. The problem was then how to convince foundations technology was worth funding.

One foundation that worked with TCN was the W. Alton Jones Foundation (WAJF), a small philanthropy supporting environmental groups throughout the United States. In 1995, WAJF was about to embark on an initiative to fund about 50 research and advocacy groups working on developing and promoting low/zero emissions vehicles. Clabaugh approached WAJF, claiming that it was in the nature of research and advocacy groups to gather and share information, for which they required technology. Therefore, he argued, information technology was not merely part of a research or advocacy group's infrastructure; it was necessarily their mission. Clabaugh explained the strategy:

> It [approaching WAJF] was very deliberate and, in hindsight, very smart. Foundations do not like to fund general support. This stuff [technology] falls into general support. . . . Foundations fund projects, they fund programs. This [technology for research and advocacy organizations] is program dollars. . . . So we were looking for a way to make a sustainable technical services business model. This was very definitely a business model that said "go where the money is." That is foundations. We will get them to pay for it, then we can support a direct technology service to nonprofits. The only way they are going to pay is if it is program money. [16]

Clabaugh's innovation lay in connecting technology directly with an organization's mission. Bruno Latour, a groundbreaking anthropologist of science, calls this strategy *association* (1986). According to Latour, collective action begins when actors associate two or more previously disconnected things (ideas, objects, events) and successfully convince others to accept the connection between them. As a strategy, the object of association is to get other people to act on behalf of one's interests. Writing about the history of public hygiene in France, Latour (1988b) explains how Louis Pasteur generated support for his theory of disease and mobilized the health ministries and legions of hygienists by associating microbes and disease. In his field experiments, Pasteur demonstrated that microscopic creatures (in which hygienists and public health officials had little interest) caused disease (in which they had much interest), a connection that no one had made before. Once public health officials took Pasteur's association seriously, preventing disease meant attacking the microbes that caused it.

Analogously, Clabaugh associated technology, which was of little interest to foundations, with mission, in which foundations were greatly interested. With his association, Clabaugh was claiming that an organization's information technology and mission are equivalent, a powerful charge in the voluntary sector, where an organization's mission must have taken-for-granted justifications (Clohesy, 2000). Treating technology as a program expense was claiming that nonprofits and the foundations that support them ought to take it seriously. Clabaugh's association said, "Support technology because doing so will support mission." In the voluntary sector, where mission drives organizations, such a claim is a moral one; it says technology support is the right (good) thing to do. In doing so, Clabaugh was constructing an account of worth to support technology in the nonprofit sector.

Drawing on his consulting background, Clabaugh recommended that WAJF hire someone to travel among its portfolio of grantees, installing various information and communications technologies in each and training leaders how to use them. Without fanfare, he and several foundation officers gave a name to the new project, which, Clabaugh recalled, "was about circuits and data" [16]. Evoking itinerant Methodist preachers of the past, they called this method of providing technology to nonprofit and grassroots organizations "Circuit Riding" and the people who did it "Circuit Riders." With that, a new social movement was launched.

Calling the Worthy

The Circuit Rider's job was to travel among the foundation's grantees, delivering general technology assistance. Funded for one year, WAJF's Circuit Rider project had an explicit goal of connecting the 50 environmental advocacy groups to the Internet and thereby to each other. Although information technology was becoming more prevalent and easier to use by the late 1990s, computer networking remained arduous. Nonprofit and grassroots organizations, at the time, would likely be working with only the most basic software applications and computer technologies, more sophisticated stuff being outside of the budget or imagination of most managers in the sector. Having come to the sector to help people, not work with machines (Stein, 2002), nonprofit managers can be suspicious of technology (Berlinger & Te'eni, 1999).

Circuit Riders would therefore need to convince them that technology was worth their time and resources, which would require social as well as technical skills.[1] Clabaugh found this combination of skills in a young public policy advocate living in Washington, D.C., named Jeremy Edes-Pierotti. Before working as an advocate, Edes-Pierotti was an information technology administrator for a small nonprofit in Rhode Island, where he taught himself computer fundamentals. He explained that he was hired to be the first Circuit Rider because of his "understanding of how public advocacy worked":

> They [TCN and WAJF] thought that was a more important skill to have because the Circuit Rider for this particular project was going to be working with environmental groups helping them figure out how to mobilize their constituencies and to use technology for that. *So the technology piece was secondary.* That was the easy part to learn. It would have been much harder if they had decided to hire a technology person and teach them how public policy and advocacy and lobbying and all that stuff works in the United States. You cannot learn that in a couple of months. [18; emphasis added]

From its inception, Circuit Riding was more of a political/social activity than a technical one. Circuit Riders were activists first, technologists a distant second. Edes-Pierotti, who brought years of advocacy and public policy experience to the position, admits that he learned much of the technology he needed to know while on the job. Circuit Riders' activism required a shared affinity with the nonprofit and grassroots organizations they serviced. Another Circuit Rider wrote in an online editorial, "One of the great advantages I have providing this kind of [technology] assistance to environmental groups is that people expect a technical consultant to be a 'propeller head' who cannot speak to the non-computer professional. What they get is someone who not only speaks in plain English, but someone who is interested in their issue and who understands ecology and the environment" (O'Brien, 1999). As a report on WAJF's Circuit Rider project explained, "We didn't want a pocket protector computer geek. No one who saw the world only in bits and bytes. Instead, we looked for someone who understood politics and the political process. Someone who'd be as comfortable in the halls of Congress as in the innards of a software program" (Telecommunications Cooperative Network, 1996: 4). Presenting the Circuit Rider model at a conference in 2000, Clabaugh conveyed the newly formed role on a slide:

What is a Circuit Rider?

- Teacher
- Evangelist
- Researcher
- Facilitator
- Mechanic

What they are not

- Computer geek
- Temporary help

The account of worth Clabaugh produced essentially claimed that technology was worth doing because it produced better social outcomes. The Circuit Riders proved their worth to nonprofit and grassroots organizations through their allegiance to a cause, not a technology. As Clabaugh's slide notes, Circuit Riders are evangelists among the many roles they play. They evangelize for technology to leaders in the voluntary sector to contribute to the greater cause. To be worthy, Circuit Riders had to have a connection to a particular cause. Describing his first days as a Circuit Rider, Dirk Slater likes to tell the following story about evangelizing for information technologies to a conference of women representing grassroots social justice organizations serving low-income mothers:

> The presentation before me, this woman was talking about how organizing women was different. They ate her alive. I am sitting here watching this thing and they are being so nasty to this woman. I am sitting there going, "they are going to eat me for lunch." Here is the little white boy that is going to get up in front of them. It was awful. I was probably the most nervous I had ever been in my entire life. I got up in front of them for my workshop and the first thing I did was I said, "I just have to acknowledge that I am the only guy in the room. The second thing I want to say to you all is that I am the son of a single woman who was on and off public assistance the entire time I was growing up and I just have so much respect for all of you because I know how much my mother was going through just trying to survive and you guys are trying to change things and raise your kids and do all these things to accomplish that." And they all started clapping. I was like, "no, no, no, do not applaud for me." They

were like, "no, honey, we are not applauding for you, we are applauding for your mother." And then, I was seen as a son. I was seen as part of the community. [59]

Slater's story reflects a key component of the Circuit Rider model: a commitment to the cause. He expresses this commitment by forging sympathies with the audience, claiming that he is one of them. Such expressions were important to establishing the worth of technology with managers and leaders of nonprofit and grassroots organizations, many of whom entered the sector to work with people or the environment, not machines (Berlinger & Te'eni, 1999). This commitment to the cause would prove to be a defining feature of the Circuit Rider model.

When the one-year Circuit Rider project with TCN and WAJF ended, Edes-Pierotti left for graduate school. Over the next two years, WAJF turned the project into a program and hired two more Circuit Riders. Because WAJF generally supported environmental groups, the first Circuit Riders came from the environmental movement. Like Edes-Pierotti, both came from policy backgrounds. The next Circuit Rider was Sean O'Brien, a self-taught, reluctant technologist with a PhD in tropical forest ecology. In 1997, he applied for a research position at the foundation. During the interview, O'Brien and a program manager got into a conversation about their PalmPilots, which were novel gadgets at the time. Several days later, O'Brien received a phone call from another program manager at WAJF. The manager was having trouble with his PalmPilot and needed some help. O'Brien explained: "That was the interview right there, the fact that I knew what a PalmPilot was and I was able to figure out the problem over the phone, which is often, as a Circuit Rider, what you do" [17]. Still, O'Brien expressed ambivalence about the position WAJF subsequently offered him. "What a cool thing to do," he recalled. "I think if I had seen the job description, I probably would have been interested in applying, but I probably would have assumed I was not qualified. I might have gone for it anyway, but I do not know that I would have thought this was for me" [17].

As the WAJF Circuit Rider Program continued, the position became increasingly technical. Edes-Pierotti had built much of the technology infrastructure for WAJF grantees. O'Brien continued this work, taking advantage of the rapid pace of change in Internet and networking technologies to provide upgrades. "I was sort of working myself out of a job," O'Brien explained. "By the time the Jones Foundation was looking for a second Circuit Rider, we wanted someone who could program. We wanted someone who had real hardcore experience because it was not a matter of installing modems and convincing people for the very first time they needed a website or e-mail. It was now, 'you have a website, now let us integrate it with your membership database.' It was a whole other level of information and knowledge that was required" [17].

Enter Todd Koym. In October 1999, Koym came across the job posting for a second Circuit Rider on Idealist, a website for nonprofit jobs. He had a background in environmental policy and almost a decade of technology experience. In contrast with O'Brien's ambivalence, Koym expressed confidence:

> I knew that I was the right person for the job and I knew that they were going to know that. They wanted somebody that could work primarily with environmental organizations. They wanted somebody with knowledge of environmental work. And here I am. I had a master's [in public affairs with a specialization in environment and technology] and a couple of years' experience with an organization they funded. They wanted somebody with technology skills. And I had professional experience and I had actually implemented a project with the help of the Circuit Rider Program already, so they knew me and my work. To me it seemed like a good fit and it seemed like a good fit for them, too. [72]

As Circuit Riders, O'Brien and Koym had a great deal of freedom. Circuit Riding was organized as a permanent program of WAJF, rather than a department in the foundation. The Circuit Riders received internal grants over which they had almost complete discretion. O'Brien and Koym met regularly with foundation trustees to discuss organizations they wanted to work with and projects they would like to undertake. This structure made the Circuit Riders independent from the foundation. It also meant that Circuit Riding remained amorphous and depended on the people who occupied the position to provide structure and meaning to the activity. In other words, the Circuit Riders were organized as foundation-supported activists rather than as foundation officers. Having independence from the formal structure of the foundation allowed the Circuit Riders to continue their activism without many of the constraints that a formal position within it would impose on their activities. Organizational forms are expressions of social movement ideals: how a group organizes reflects their collective identity and strategy (Clemens, 1996). As it was forged, the Circuit Rider model took on the form of a loosely structured movement. Circuit Riders considered themselves connected to the cause.

As noted above, it was the commitment to the cause that trumped organizational affiliations for Circuit Riders. When I asked Jamie McClelland about his organization's relationship to other nonprofit technology assistance providers, he explained, "We do not see ourselves as a service organization. We see ourselves as a political organization. For that reason, we are much more strongly aligned with the social justice community" [49].

Pioneers' Tales

As the first Circuit Rider, Edes-Pierotti traveled across the country, visiting each of WAJF's grantees and providing information technology services such as connecting them to the Internet. In total, the project cost $122,300 and served all 50 environmental organizations by the time the pilot year ended in 1996. As the contract between TCN and WAJF was about to expire, the two organizations collaborated on a report. Entitled "Circuit Riders: Pioneers in Non-Profit Networking," the report described the Circuit Rider project in detail and heralded their success delivering Internet technologies to a portfolio of grantees (TCN, 1996). The document is sprinkled with puns and plays on technology terms and features cartoons of cowboys (alluding to their early Methodist namesakes) in various policy-work settings. For example, at the end of the report, the cowboy is shown delivering a stack of documents—presumably the output of the environmental organizations involved in the project, which have been vastly improved by better information and communications technologies—to the U.S. Capitol.

WAJF circulated the report widely and it is considered "one of the early milestones"[2] of the Circuit Rider movement. In writing it, Clabaugh and his colleagues told the story of Circuit Riding. As such, the Circuit Rider report was a formal account of worth. The WAJF report explained Edes-Pierotti's activities as a Circuit Rider and provided justifications for why he did them that way. Clabaugh explained the challenge he faced: "Trying to describe what you do and justifying it is difficult, especially in the foundation world. Most foundations do not like to fund that stuff [technology assistance]. It is not really that sexy" [16]. As an account of worth, the report was both "narrative" and "bookkeeping" (Stark & Bruszt, 1998: 192). The narrative aspect of the account described the Circuit Rider pilot program: what Edes-Pierotti did, at which organizations, and the basic outcomes it produced. This helped enroll and mobilize legions of activists, as I will explain in the remainder of the chapter. The bookkeeping aspect expressed the dollar amount spent on the number of agencies in question: $122,300 on 50 nonprofit and grassroots organizations. This demonstrated the economic worthiness of Circuit Riding, which appealed to other foundations, which I will explain below and in the next chapter. Both aspects combined to provide a multivalent account of worth, which would mobilize multiple audiences simultaneously. In this way, accounts of worth in the nonprofit technology world were simultaneously social *and* economic.

As an account of worth, the report connected Clabaugh's original association (technology and mission are equivalent) with Circuit Riding as a prescription for acting on it. There are many possible ways to deliver technology to nonprofit and voluntary sector organizations. The report presents Circuit Riding as "best practice" for delivering technology to nonprofit and grassroots organizations. "Best practice" is a management concept describing the technique that is most effective at accomplishing a certain goal or objective. "Best practices" spread not because they are actually "best" but because organizations in a field borrow practices and structures from others that they see as successful (DiMaggio & Powell, 1991b). By presenting their model of Circuit Riding as a set of "best practices" for delivering technology services to voluntary sector organizations, WAJF and TCN were connecting a claim about a specific set of activities (Circuit Riding is the best way to deliver technology) to an association (that technology is equivalent to mission). The connection between Clabaugh's association and the idea of Circuit Riding as best practice formed an account: Technology is worth the same as mission; Circuit Riding was the way to ensure nonprofit and grassroots organizations were getting the technology they needed to be effective. Figure 1.1 shows how the account of worth was fashioned. The Circuit Riding account begins with an association designed to mobilize resources. It creates a narrative that says that if foundations care about mission, they should support technology and Circuit Riding

$$\left\{ \left\{ \begin{array}{c} \text{Technology and mission are equivalent.} \\ \text{(Association)} \end{array} \right\} \left. \begin{array}{c} \text{Circuit riding is the best way to} \\ \text{deliver technology to nonprofit and} \\ \text{grassroots organizations.} \\ \text{(Prescription for Action)} \end{array} \right\} \right.$$

Account

FIGURE 1.1. Fashioning an account

is the best way to support technology in the voluntary sector. Together, the account of worth provides a model for action that is transposable and a justification for that model.

Practicing What They Preached

Following the success of the pilot project, WAJF decided to turn Circuit Riding into a long-term program. As Pete Myers, then the director of WAJF, explained in a video made at a nonprofit technology conference: "The foundation decided to step in and bring new resources and hopefully some new thinking that would allow experiments to play out about how the Internet and a variety of new uses of electronic communication could be brought to bear to achieve programmatic goals" (O'Brien, 2000). By committing additional resources to Circuit Riding, WAJF was endorsing Clabaugh's initial account of nonprofit technology and its connection to Circuit Riding as a model of achieving its vision. Aside from the material resources WAJF pledged to the program, Circuit Riding gained the symbolic resources that came with the endorsement, such as support and legitimacy for the moral claims associated with the account. With material and symbolic support from a major foundation, technology began to gain importance among powerful actors in the nonprofit field.

Spreading the Circuit Rider Account

With the Circuit Rider Program, WAJF was following a capacity-building trend in philanthropy. In addition to cash grants, foundations were increasingly providing technical support to grantees, which often took the form of management assistance (Light, 2000). During the late 1990s, groups such as Grantmakers for Effective Organizations began to convene foundations in the interest of supporting capacity-building efforts among their grantees. Pete Myers explained WAJF's interpretation of this trend in the Circuit Rider video: "Our experience with Circuit Riding has been enormously rewarding. I am convinced that the vision we had early on was that this was going to be an important investment rang true, emphatically true. We hope that other foundations realize that building the capacity within the community of grantees that they serve, to make the most effective use of technology, is one of their obligations as a grantor" (O'Brien, 2000). Still, for most foundations technical support meant management, fund-raising, marketing, and other organizational development skills.

Beyond its commitment to running their program, WAJF developed a philosophical attachment to the idea of Circuit Riding and looked to enroll other foundations in creating Circuit Rider programs of their own. Sean O'Brien explained: "The model that we worked on was the foundation made a grant to itself, essentially to start the Circuit Rider Program to support its specific set of grantees, but also to support the concept of Circuit Riding, to build that concept. So I had a double mandate" [17]. O'Brien's second mandate was to spread WAJF's account of Circuit Riding in the foundation community. To fulfill it, he wrote articles about Circuit Riding for various online outlets. WAJF continued to distribute the Circuit Rider report.

From Program to Movement

As the WAJF Circuit Rider report spread, it crossed the desks of many foundation officers. Among them was a foundation fellow at the Rockefeller Family Fund named Rob Stuart. Though no one knew it at the time, Stuart would become responsible for transforming Circuit Riding from a foundation program into a full-fledged social movement. Acting as a movement organizer, Stuart would change Clabaugh's account of Circuit Riding into something that would appeal to a larger audience and spread that account to enroll legions of activists into the Circuit Rider movement.

Stuart worked as a state- and national-level lobbyist at public interest advocacy organizations for ten years before becoming an advocate for technology. He met Edes-Pierotti in 1995, while working as the executive director of a small nonprofit in Vermont, and was intrigued by the idea of Circuit Riding. A year later, Donald Ross, a program manager at the Rockefeller Family Fund, offered Stuart a fellowship at the foundation, under the auspices of the newly created Rockefeller Technology Project (RTP). While at RTP in 1997, Stuart came across the WAJF Circuit Rider report. Clabaugh recalled: "I got a call from Rob Stuart who said 'Hi, my name is Rob Stuart and I am working with the Rockefeller Family Fund and I want to be a Circuit Rider. Can I come talk to you?'" [16].

With support from RTP, Stuart established a Circuit Rider program at the Rockefeller Family Fund. The foundation recognized the worth of Circuit Riding by virtue of the economic values expressed in the Circuit Rider report. Yet, Stuart's Circuit Riding program was not an exact copy of WAJF's. The diffusion of organizing models is rarely an act of pure emulation (Campbell, 2005). Rather, actors "translate" ideas and models according to their interests (Callon, 1986; Latour, 1987). In this case, Stuart "translated" Clabaugh's and WAJF's account of Circuit Riding (see Figure 1.2). Instead of technology being

$$\left\{ \left\{ \begin{array}{l} \text{Technology and mission are equivalent;} \\ \text{social justice is our mission; therefore:} \\ \text{technology is a force for social justice.} \end{array} \right\} \left. \begin{array}{l} \text{Circuit riding is the best way to} \\ \text{deliver technology to nonprofit and} \\ \text{grassroots organizations.} \end{array} \right\} \right\}$$

(Extended Association)   (Prescription for Action)

Account

FIGURE 1.2. Translating an account

equivalent to mission, which appealed to foundation officers and managers in the nonprofit sector, in Stuart's revised account technology was about promoting social justice. Stuart directed his account of worth at mobilizing activists. "I am an organizer by training," Stuart noted in an interview. "I was interested in organizing this [Circuit Rider] community around . . . making social change organizations more effective" [14].

Stuart's translation of Clabaugh's account to include a social justice component created the ideological conditions to enroll legions of activists into the movement. Extending Clabaugh's association, Stuart was connecting technology, in which few activists had an interest, with social justice, which legions of activists sought to promote. By taking on a social justice component, the Circuit Rider movement was able to tap into networks of social justice activists throughout the country for members. Stuart described the people he sought to attract as "hav[ing] a mission to serve social change or do-gooder organizations" [14]. As he explained, "W. Alton Jones had coined the term and what I did was promote it, in terms of my work [as a Circuit Rider]. But after a year, my fellowship [at the Rockefeller Family Fund] turned into a program and I was able to get additional resources from other foundations. I began to do a variety of projects" [14]. Chief among those projects was building a social movement.

Like Clabaugh, Stuart took the Circuit Rider metaphor very seriously, noting in an interview with Michael Gilbert (1998), "Evangelism is a very important part of the job." However, Stuart turned his evangelizing efforts toward building a movement. In order to enroll others in the movement, accounts of worth must be mobile. Calling himself a "Circuit Rider's Circuit Rider," he spent much of his time as the director of RTP traveling around the country, spreading his modified account of worth (i.e., technology as a force for social justice) and its mode of expression in Circuit Riding. With his community organizing background, Stuart charged himself with building the movement by targeting two groups: politically progressive computer activists, who he could get to identify as Circuit Riders, and foundation directors and managers, who could provide financial and symbolic resources.

To give the Circuit Rider account mobility, Stuart developed a communications infrastructure, beginning with an e-mail list. Stuart said he was motivated to start an e-mail list by an experience he had traveling to visit environmental groups in Baton Rouge to discuss the importance of information technology. His lecture was sparsely attended, because Edes-Pierroti had been there only two days earlier. "So I was struck by that," he recalled, "and said there has got to be better coordination and communication between the few of us that are actually doing this work. That actually gave me the incentive to start the Circuit Rider LISTSERV because I figured at least we can talk to each other about where we are going to be, so we wouldn't compete and confuse folks" [14]. Stuart began the Circuit Riders e-mail list in 1997 with about 25 members. Beyond advertising their locations, the e-mail list provided an online venue to share knowledge and stories, in other words, accounts. As Stuart described the situation, "There were oftentimes lone missionaries doing great work but not having a set of peers to reflect with and bounce ideas with and to strategize with" [14]. Most of the early messages on the LISTSERV consisted of shared stories justifying their work interspersed with technical questions about problems they encountered in the field. By 2001, the e-mail list had grown to over 2,000 names, becoming a vital part of the virtual community and uniting the diffuse Circuit Riders. It is important to highlight the use of e-mail lists as an organizing tool for the Circuit Rider movement. Scholars of social movements have found that the use of Internet technologies increases the importance of individual movement organizers over traditional forms of organizing (Earl & Schussman, 2003). By initially organizing the Circuit Rider movement online, Stuart also reinforced his leadership position in the movement.

Forging a Collective Identity, Building a Movement

As mentioned in the introduction to this chapter, a key barrier to collective action is mobilizing adherents. However, before adherents can be mobilized, they have to recognize themselves as members of a movement (Gamson, 1991). Collective identity is the sense of connection to a group that one acquires through sustained interaction with it. According to Polletta and Jasper (2001: 284), collective identity is "an individual's cognitive, moral, and emotional connections with a broader community, category, practice, or institution. It is a perception of a shared status or relation, which may be imagined rather than experienced directly, and it is distinct from personal identities, although it may form part of a personal identity. A collective identity may have been first constructed by outsiders (for example, as in the case of 'Hispanics' in this country), who may still enforce it, but it depends on some acceptance by those to whom it is applied." One does not identify oneself as an activist and then seek out opportunities to mobilize. Collective identity formation is a social process. Just as one acquires an identity through interaction with the social world (Mead, 1995), collective identities emerge out of interaction with members of a particular social movement (Munson, 2008). For activists to accept them, they must recognize such collective identities as legitimate (Wry, Lounsbury, & Glynn, 2011), which requires an association to an account of worth.

Gavin Clabaugh coined the term "Circuit Rider" to describe a particular way of delivering technology to voluntary sector organizations. To enroll adherents in the movement, Stuart developed a collective identity out of Circuit Riding. Collective identities connect people's actions with basic understandings of who they are. Forging a collective identity helps movement organizers enroll and mobilize movement adherents (Johnston, Larana, & Gusfield, 1994; Melucci, 1989; Polletta & Jasper, 2001). Many of the early Circuit Riders with whom I spoke identified Stuart as the person who enrolled them in the movement. Richard Zorza, who started his nonprofit technology career in the mid-1980s, noted: "When Rob [Stuart] came in and started to build a network that was much more about transformation [i.e., information technology and progressive social change], then the network started to build. . . . What has happened is so organic that you cannot point to any particular thing. But if you pull Rob out of the picture, I think it [the network] does collapse though" [60]. Clabaugh agreed: "To a large extent, it was Rob [Stuart] who built the movement. . . . We [WAJF and TCN] came up with a model and did some of the initial stuff, but he was the one who expanded it and pushed it forward" [16].

With his account of technology as a force for social justice, Stuart traveled the country subscribing people to the e-mail list and getting politically progressive technologists to recognize themselves as Circuit Riders. Along the way, Stuart turned Circuit Riding from what people did to who they were. Making Circuit Riding into a collective identity brought people into the fold, as they came to see themselves as part of a larger movement. According to Stuart, with his background in community organizing on the left, the strategy was intentional: "One of the reasons I think the movement grew was we were very quick to help people identify themselves as Circuit Riders. They had never called themselves that before. They were maybe consultants or they did not know what they were. Giving them a name . . . helped to establish [the] Circuit Rider [movement]. We began to grow as actual numbers and in fact have more formal Circuit Rider programs being supported" [14]. Marshall Mayer, another leading figure in the movement, explained how he and others came to identify as Circuit Riders:

> Most of us . . . had been doing Circuit Riding. In my case, I had already been doing it for ten years. I just never called it that. I did on-site technical assistance for nonprofits since 1986. It was not my full-time job, but I was doing it. Many of us were the same way; we just had not called it that. Literally, by just calling it that, we created a methodology and a buzz that went along with that methodology that actually raised more money for each of our programs because we had, in essence, a consistent message to give to funders. *So they could see an industry being born and they wanted to be a part of it.* [11; emphasis added]

Collective identity provides structure, reasons to join, and rules for participation, especially for members of loosely connected or geographically dispersed social movements (Haenfler, 2004). By creating a collective identity, Stuart provided such structure and helped enroll myriad activists into the ranks, quickly building a movement of Circuit Riders. Within five years (1997–2002), the movement grew from a handful of activists to a legion reportedly 10,000 strong. Furthermore, with numbers the Circuit Riders were considered as legitimate by independent foundations in the nonprofit sector. As Clabaugh reflected in an interview:

> CLABAUGH: It has become more legitimate.
> INTERVIEWER: What has become more legitimate?
> CLABAUGH: The phrase itself, Circuit Riding. I have seen other foundations and I have seen people within my own foundation who would have never have thought about it, put through a proposal that said "we are going to do this, we are going to [hire] a Circuit Rider to provide support to X people to do graphical information systems." So it has become a descriptive, recognized term, hence more legitimate, more fundable. And I think it has become a recognized approach to providing technology support. [16]

Contested Identities

With the rapid growth of the movement, the collective identity of Circuit Riders came to be contested. As Clabaugh and WAJF originally envisioned it, Circuit Riding was foundation-supported technology assistance to nonprofit and grassroots organizations in a specific mission area. Clabaugh described Circuit Riding in a memo to the C. S. Mott Foundation in 1998 as "an approach to grantee technical assistance pioneered by the W. Alton Jones Foundation and TCN (a not-for-profit technology assistance provider). Circuit Riders are usually issue focused, and provide assistance across a number of projects and/or grantees." At the same time, Rob Stuart was spreading his own account of Circuit Riding to enroll adherents from the social justice community. As he wrote in a 1998 magazine article, "In the 19th century, the original Circuit Riders were itinerant traveling preachers. Modern-day Circuit Riders travel the country 'evangelizing' for the use of new communications technology—particularly the Internet—and teaching nonprofit leaders the skills necessary to make the most of these new tools" (Stuart, 1998). Stuart's definition was picked up in a *Nonprofit Times* article (Batchilder, 1998) and was used by its authors to describe organizations such as Online Networking for the Environment (ONE) Northwest in Seattle and the IT Resource Center in Chicago, which had little resemblance to Circuit Riding as it was originally conceived.

As the movement grew, the meaning of Circuit Riding became increasingly ambiguous. For Stuart, this was part of the strategy to build the movement: "Originally, I was coming from the [Rockefeller] Family Fund and we had a particular focus on advocacy organizations, loosely defined as social change organizations. When we were reaching out and looking to engage Circuit Riders and grow Circuit Riding programs, there was a focus on those organizations" [14]. However, Stuart compromised his account of worth (based on social justice) as he sought to grow the movement: "To build a big tent, we opted to engage and involve folks that were actually more focused on helping the traditional organizations, like the IT Resource Center and Management Assistance Program in Minneapolis" [14]. The move highlights the tension within social movements between maintaining strict boundaries of insiders and outsiders (those who are worthy and those who are not) (Gamson, 1997; Hunt, Benford, & Snow, 1994) and accommodating ideological diversity within the movement (Reger, 2002). In either case, the tension around boundary maintenance and expansion challenges the stability of collective identities (Robnett,

2005). For the Circuit Riders, this meant changing the meaning of their work from social justice and the environment to other social problem arenas and shifting the model to accommodate members of the movement who were not peripatetic activists supported by foundation programs.

Some movement members, like Edes-Pierotti, O'Brien, and Koym, were Circuit Riders in accordance with the original model, supported by foundation programs, like WAJF and the Rockefeller Technology Project. Some were affiliated with nonprofit organizations, such as the Low Income Networking and Communications (LINC) Project, which was the Circuit Riding program of the Welfare Law Center in New York City. Others joined together to develop stand-alone Circuit Rider organizations, such as ONE Northwest, Project Alchemy, and Media Jumpstart, which worked directly with nonprofit and grassroots organizations, but mixed foundation support with fees-for-service. Still others were self-employed, what one Circuit Rider called "NPIs," or nonprofit individuals, who served as independent technology consultants in the voluntary sector. Clabaugh observed in an interview: "It [Circuit Riding] has really morphed and changed. When I get up and give a speech about the Circuit Rider business model, there are few people in the room that actually meet the criteria for the business model, but yet they call themselves Circuit Riders" [16].

Historical sociologists have explained the ascendant power of Cosimo de Medici (Machiavelli's Prince) by his strategic use of ambiguous statements, which, like horoscopes, were vague enough to be interpreted by various others, yet sufficiently focused for each recipient to consider them apropos (Padgett & Ansell, 1993). Called "multivocality," the strategy relies on the polysemic nature of language as a social lubricant. Allowing terms such as "Circuit Rider" to be interpreted in many ways, Stuart was able to convince actors to identify as Circuit Riders, even when they did not subscribe to its original definition. Padgett and Ansell (1993: 1263) explain the phenomenon: "Multivocal action leads to Rorschach blot identities, with all alters constructing their own distinctive attribution of the identity of ego."[3] In other words, Stuart's multivocality allowed many potential adherents to see themselves and those around them as Circuit Riders. As a strategy to grow a social movement, multivocality can have drawbacks. According to sociologists, modes of organizing are as important as collective identities for social movement adherents (Clemens, 1996; Reger, 2002). Elisabeth Clemens (1997: 50), a political sociologist, writes, "The answer to 'who are we?' need not be a quality or a noun; 'we are people who do these sorts of things in this particular way' can be equally compelling." For the movement, that "particular way" was being called into question by the proliferation of individuals identifying as Circuit Riders, but following very different models.

Within a few short years this trend resulted in the term Circuit Rider losing much of its original meaning. Trabian Shorters, a one-time Circuit Rider for the Rockefeller Technology Project and director of Technology Works for Good, wrote in an essay, "Nowadays we apply the term Circuit Rider to any person deployed to help a group of nonprofits to integrate information technology. The research for Technology Works [a fledgling technology assistance organization] revealed that there are at least seven models around the United States for doing this" (Shorters, 2001: 3). With the development of a trade association, the Nonprofit Technology Enterprise Network, came attempts at creating an official definition: "A Circuit Rider is someone who provides technology assistance to the nonprofit sector. . . . Part technology cheerleader, evangelist, and skilled technologist, Riders come in many forms. In some cases, foundations fund several Riders to service their grantees. Riders sometimes are housed within existing technology support provider organizations. Many Riders operate as independent consultants and in some cases a community of nonprofits might pool resources and hire a Rider. The Circuit Riding community grew out of the U.S. progressive social change and environmental movements, as well as other technology assistance efforts" (Osten, 1999).

As late as 2001, Circuit Riders still lacked a standardized job description, leading one Circuit Rider to lament publicly that "when I started as a Circuit Rider, I wished that someone had taken a moment to give me some reference materials on the particulars of my actual job. Such documents did not exist as far as I could tell" (Shorters, 2001: 1).

Although sociologists have studied the response of activists when their collective identities clash with their personal identities (Robnett, 2005), few have examined how the negotiation of identities within a movement produces unintended contention. The particular meaning of Circuit Riding mattered for the future of the movement. As accounts of worth, the narratives that developed around Circuit Riding articulated and justified the activity to actual and potential adherents. By justifying an activity, accounts explain why it has value and how that value should be measured (e.g., by narrative or bookkeeping). Narrowly interpreting an account means the movement risked attracting few members because too few potential adherents would fit the description. For example, a narrowly interpreted account would consider only those working with social justice or environmental groups to be true Circuit Riders. Broadly interpreting an account meant attracting more adherents, but risked alienating the original constituency, including diehards who were particularly active in the movement. To this core group, more inclusive interpretations of Circuit Riding threatened to undermine the movement's core values. A broadly interpreted account of Circuit Riding would include independent contractors and other technologists working in the nonprofit sector, regardless of their commitment to a particular cause.

Like any movement, authenticity was important to Circuit Riding's collective identity. As such, Circuit Riders justified their work as meaningful based on its contribution (and their allegiance) to the cause. Michael Ward, an early RTP Circuit Rider explained, "There was the dot-com stuff going on. As it progressed, you always [wonder whether] I should jump ship and go work for a dot-com. . . . I opted to stay [in the movement] because my real passion was the political advocacy stuff" [64]. Here, Ward recognizes the temptation of leaving the movement to make more money in the dot-com boom of the late 1990s. Instead, he remained a Circuit Rider, committed to his political ideals. French sociologists Luc Boltanski and Laurent Thévenot (2006) contend that such justifications are anchored to what they call a "civic" order of worth. People justify their actions in many different ways. Boltanski and Thévenot have found in their research a limited number of "orders" in which people can make claims of worth. A civic order of worth entails appeals to collective interests and thinks of relations in terms of solidarity and equality. By justifying their account of Circuit Riding under a civic order of worth, members of the movement are effectively claiming that the collectivity counts, as well as its borders.

Dilution of the collective identity was an endogenous threat to the movement. The Circuit Riders' collective identity also faced exogenous threats from the movement's ideological competition, a competing nonprofit technology assistance provider called NPower. NPower's New York director of consulting explained his identity in an interview: "It's [our work] not just a server going here or whatever. It is not just the technical talk, but it is actually doing something useful for society. There is a whole layer of technologists that are doing this, Circuit Riders, which we consider ourselves amongst. . . . We call ourselves Circuit Riders and our claim to fame is being able to bring technology to people" [21]. I will explain the growing threat from NPower in Chapters 3 and 4. For now, it is important to understand that NPower would come to

threaten the Circuit Riders' livelihood by attracting foundation and corporate support to a competing model of technology assistance. More important, NPower challenged who the Circuit Riders were and the "particular way"
they did their work. Unlike the Circuit Riders, for whom political activism
and social justice were a critical component of their "authentic" identity, NPower
was concerned almost exclusively with making nonprofit organizations more
efficient. Instead of organizing like a movement, NPower incorporated as a
501(c)(3) nonprofit. Yet NPower did not simply usurp the Circuit Riding mon-
iker. To help build the movement, Stuart had actively engaged NPower's leaders to call their consultants Circuit Riders as part of his multivocal/multivalent
strategy. Some, like the NPower affiliate in New York, did so at first. Later,
however, all the NPower affiliates simply referred to their employees as consultants, as was written into their formal job descriptions. As Stuart recalled,
"NPower has gotten very big and while their consultants are in large part Circuit Riders, they are not called Circuit Riders. They are called consultants and
that has kind of sucked some of the spirit out of the Rider movement" [76].

The geographic and temporal dispersion of the Circuit Riders challenged
their ability to form a cohesive sense of who they were as well as how and why
they were doing it. Beyond leading to several interpretations of Circuit Riding, their lack of a coherent collective identity stymied attempts to articulate
consistent claims of worth. Without a consistent message, the Circuit Riders,
as a group, had difficulty securing material resources from foundations and
other groups. Instead they had to go it alone and write individual grants in
collaboration with potential client organizations. To remedy this set of problems, movement leaders organized meetings, called the Riders Roundups, to
assemble the Circuit Riders and stabilize their collective identity. However, in
trying to balance building a big tent and maintaining an authentic identity,
the Circuit Riders created a structural opportunity in the nonprofit technology assistance field for external threats, such as NPower, to gain power and
attract resources.

Associations, Accounts, and Collective Identities

To gain support and succeed, all social movements have to prove the worthiness of their cause. They do so by making associations, producing accounts of
worth, and forging collective identities. Actors make associations to get others
to recognize the value of what they want to do by connecting it to something

valuable to others. Accounts of worth encapsulate associations, turning them into transposable narratives that explain and justify actions, which can be used to attract potential supporters and adherents to the movement. Movement organizers can strategically construct collective identities out of accounts, which create networks of people who do things a particular way.

This chapter highlights the importance of associations, accounts, and collective identities for collective action. The founding of the Circuit Rider movement illustrates how movement organizers establish the worthiness of their causes, a necessary component of collective action that many scholars overlook. To organize a movement of politically progressive technologists, the Circuit Riders needed to convince foundations and potential adherents that information technologies were vital to the future of the voluntary sector and part of the larger social good. In other words, the Circuit Riders had to prove the worth of information technology as part of their goal of helping nonprofit and grassroots organizations to achieve their missions more effectively. Ultimately, the Circuit Riders believed that the distribution of information technologies throughout society would lead to greater social and economic equality as the poor and disenfranchised would be empowered with new tools. In other words, by facilitating a technology revolution, the Circuit Riders worked toward fostering a social revolution. Associations establish the worthiness of things by claiming their equivalence to something of value. Gavin Clabaugh spawned the first Circuit Rider program with his initial association, drawing equivalence between technology and mission, effectively sending a message to foundations: if mission is important to you, support technology. Working with the W. Alton Jones Foundation, Clabaugh developed Circuit Riding as a model for delivering technology to the voluntary sector.

Accounts convey the actions people took to realize the potential of the association and, in doing so, justify those actions as the "right" or proper way to do them. The pilot program and subsequent report forged a link between Clabaugh's association and Circuit Riding as a means of realizing its promise. To activists, the report expressed social values: Circuit Riding helped do-gooders do better. To foundations, the report expressed economic values: Circuit Riding was a cost-effective way to help nonprofit grantees achieve their missions. Circuit Riding now had an account, that is, a story that simultaneously explained and justified action. Rob Stuart, a foundation fellow at the Rockefeller Family Fund, modified the account to include a social justice component and began organizing a movement of like-minded technologists.

Movement organizers build collective identities out of these accounts to enroll adherents for whom doing things a certain way is important. Developing a social-justice-oriented collective identity from the Circuit Rider account, Stuart was able to attract legions of politically progressive computer enthusiasts into the movement. However, his collective-identity strategy had unintended consequences. By engaging in a multivocal strategy to "build a big tent," Stuart allowed others to broaden the definition of Circuit Riding. This increased the number of people who identified themselves as Circuit Riders, but it also undermined the authenticity of Circuit Riding and alienated the core members of the movement, those who were committed to social justice ideals, a process that will be explained in greater detail in the next chapter.

Despite threats to their collective identity and the resultant struggles they faced, the Circuit Riders established the worth of technology in the voluntary sector, and leaders accepted their account as legitimate. The movement continued to grow through the sustained efforts of Stuart and other movement organizers. In the next chapter, I will explain the process of movement growth and mobilization in greater detail by showing how Stuart convened two sets of meetings to bring adherents and resources into the fledgling movement. The Riders Roundups convened Circuit Riders from across the country to share individual accounts of their work, enroll new members, and help solidify their collective identity. The National Strategy for Nonprofit Technology assembled technology leaders, reporters, foundation officers, and corporate sponsors in an attempt to produce an institutional framework for the movement while soliciting material and symbolic resources for it. Both initiatives attempted to establish the Circuit Riders as harbingers of technology as a force for social good. Meetings for these twin efforts became the loci of contention in the Circuit Rider movement as adherents struggled to assert their collective identity and the particular forms of activism associated with it.

2

ORGANIZING FOR CHANGE

Conferences, Meetings, and the Configuration of Fields

Social movement mobilization begins when organizers establish the worth of their endeavors and the worthiness of their collective identity. To establish the worth of technology assistance, organizers of the Circuit Rider movement developed and deployed an account that associated their model of action with the goals of other activists as well as elite actors in the field, such as foundation officers. The success of their account gained early Circuit Riders access to adherents and resources. New adherents to the movement translated the work for their local contexts, which changed the meaning and collective identity on which Circuit Riding was originally built. Despite (or, more accurately, because of) the multiple meanings and identities that emerged, Circuit Riding grew to represent a recognized set of practices in the nonprofit sector, supported by mainstream foundations and enrolling legions of activists and technologists. Although these activities mobilized a first wave of adherents, leaders soon found that sustaining a movement required organizing and organization. Organizing the Circuit Riders into a cohesive movement took place at conferences and meetings throughout the late 1990s and early 2000s.

Conferences and meetings, such as those described in this chapter, are a kind of field-configuring event, "temporary social organizations . . . that encapsulate and shape the development of professions, technologies, markets, and industries" (Lampel & Meyer, 2008: 1026). Field-configuring events provide times and places for the spread of new practices (Meyer, Gaba, & Colwell, 2005).

By assembling stakeholders, field-configuring events, such as meetings, allow movement actors to tell stories and provide narratives, which contribute to the creation of shared meanings, collective action frames, and collective identities (Chesters & Welsh, 2004), which contributes to stability and institutionalization (Anand & Watson, 2004). At the same time, by bringing together competing actors, field-configuring events provide the context for contentious situations to arise, which brings about instability and institutional change (Garud, 2008; McInerney, 2008).

In this chapter I explain the role of meetings in the creation of fields, highlighting the contradictory nature of field-configuring events as loci of both stabilization processes (leading to institutionalization) and contention (leading to institutional change). I present two concurrent sets of meetings: the Riders Roundups and the National Strategy for Nonprofit Technology (NSNT). Beginning in 1997, the Riders Roundups were a series of annual conferences that were designed to accomplish several goals: share tactics among existing Circuit Riders, strengthen their collective identity, and enroll new adherents in the movement. The NSNT was a series of three meetings taking place in 1998 with the goal of enrolling elite patrons, such as mainstream foundations and technology companies, to support the Circuit Rider movement by providing resources and legitimacy.

Configuring a Professional Field at the Riders Roundups

Beginning in 1997, the Circuit Riders organized an annual conference called the Riders Roundup. The Riders Roundups were a deliberate attempt to transform a cadre of technology activists into a coherent movement. The meetings enrolled activists into the movement by providing training grounds and inculcating them into the culture of Circuit Riding. This culture, as I showed in the last chapter, was based on a collective identity and a shared account of technology as a means of promoting social justice and environmentalism. Stuart spread the cultural ideals of the latter-day Circuit Riders with the evangelical zeal of their namesake. For these ideals to take root, Stuart would need more than an e-mail list and brief visits with potential adherents. He would have to convene the masses and get them to recognize one another as participants in a larger movement.

As noted in Chapter 1, collective identity construction is tricky. Defined too narrowly, it appeals only to the most ardent supporters and risks undermining broader enrollment and mobilization efforts. Defined too broadly, collective identity attracts many more adherents, but risks diluting the ideals and values of a movement. The Riders Roundups were an attempt to walk the line: to control the message through selective enrollment while ensuring that the movement mobilized a good number of supporters. By maintaining control over the collective identity of the Circuit Riders, early leaders were also attempting to gain legitimacy for the movement by ensuring that it remained true to its founding ideals. However, this plan became difficult to execute. As the Circuit Riders increased their ranks, new adherents translated the meaning of their work into terms that aligned with their interest in growing a profession. To attract foundation support (and the money and legitimacy that came with it), some in the Circuit Rider movement thought it necessary to tone down their more radical rhetoric and embrace a professional ethic.

Leveraging Position to Mobilize Resources

Stuart's post at the Rockefeller Family Fund (RFF) gave him access to key resource holders as well as a pool of material and symbolic resources. At the time, the RFF was a major donor to social justice organizations. According to resource mobilization theory, leaders of social movements must acquire various types of resources (e.g., money, volunteer time, knowledge, moral support) to build the infrastructure necessary to enroll activists and get them to act collectively (Edwards & McCarthy, 2004; McCarthy & Zald, 1977). As a fellow at the RFF, Stuart was able to capitalize on resources to create the Rockefeller Technology Project, a Circuit Rider program modeled on the one developed by the W. Alton Jones Foundation. The Rockefeller Technology Project hired several staff members to do the work of Circuit Riding for the RFF's social justice grantees. As activists and evangelists, staff was also charged with growing the movement. One strategy for doing so was convening a set of movement meetings—the Riders Roundups.

In a memo to RFF trustees requesting financial support to convene the Circuit Riders, Stuart presented what he saw as the movement's primary problem: disconnectedness. "Circuit Riding is a somewhat lonely experience," he wrote, "with a few exceptions. . . . , the 'riders' do not have peers to regularly compare notes with or to learn from; they generally are the ones doing the teaching. Given the combined experience of these folks, a loosely structured meeting would provide an excellent opportunity for new peer to peer discussion, networking and skill building to occur."

With his account of Circuit Riding as promoting social justice, Stuart convinced the RFF to underwrite the cost of the entire event, including airfare, accommodations, and food for all attendees. His ability to convince the RFF to fund the event was evidence of Stuart's social skill as a leader and of his ability to exploit his positional capital to access and mobilize material resources, mainly money (Battilana, 2006; Fligstein, 1997; Fligstein and McAdam, 2012). Stuart explained in an interview: "We [the RFF] funded the whole thing, bought people plane tickets. It was a small group, but it was all-expenses paid for first-class treatment, which was really great for folks, because these were folks who were oftentimes running on a shoestring budget" [14]. Michael Ward, a Circuit Rider for the Rockefeller Technology Project who worked with Stuart to organize the event, further explains the meeting's appeal to potential attendees:

> There was a big subsidization [of the early meetings, from the Rockefeller Family Fund] that I think was a critical catalyst in building the Circuit Rider movement. The meetings were all free for people to attend, including their flight, their food. It was like a big party. It was like a junket for these people who are usually stuck in dingy offices working ridiculous hours. The technology at the time was imperfect, so you needed to work ridiculous hours to get it to work. The Rockefeller Family Fund would subsidize the event so the nonprofits did not have much to lose except some staff time. [64]

Money is only one type of resource social movements need to gain and to mobilize adherents (Edwards & McCarthy, 2004). Beyond supporting the event, the Rockefeller Family Fund's contribution to the Riders Roundups bestowed legitimacy on Stuart's efforts, reinforcing his position as movement leader and shoring up the Circuit Rider account he worked so diligently to advance. The RFF's support tied the foundation to the movement and gave Stuart the moral authority to approach additional foundations for support. In other words, the RFF's support further reinforced the fact that Circuit Riding was worth doing.

Stuart also mobilized key personnel in the movement by handpicking the invitees to the inaugural Roundup. He explained how he found them in the memo cited above: "In the course of my travels and the development of the 'Circuit Riders' LISTSERV I have identified about a dozen 'Circuit Rider' type efforts nationwide. I am confident that there are probably several more projects that would be easy to find. In addition to foundation-supported models, there are numerous nonprofit/profit consultants working with nonprofits in this area." Stuart invited 15 adherents to the first Riders Roundup, including members of organizations not generally recognized as Circuit Riding. For example, Tim Mills-Groninger was invited to the initial meeting, largely because his organization, the IT Resource Center, in Chicago had worked for almost a decade providing technology assistance to nonprofits in the Midwest. Although incorporated as a nonprofit, IT Resource Center sprang from the management-support organization field in the late 1980s and thus resembled more of a consulting or traditional technical assistance firm than a Circuit Rider organization. IT Resource Center also had resources it could contribute to the movement. Aside from technical knowledge about providing technology services to nonprofit organizations, IT Resource Center had conference rooms in its office that Stuart could use to convene the first Riders Roundup. With a location secured, Stuart turned his attention to organizing the meeting's topics.

Evangelizing the Evangelists

In his memo to RFF trustees, Stuart described the objective of the first Roundup simply: "get them together and allow good things to happen." The first meeting was loosely structured. The 15 attendees had much free time to become acquainted with one another. The brief agenda for the two-and-a-half-day meeting included a plenary session entitled "Elements of a Successful Circuit Rider Program," and ended with a scheduled discussion called "What We Can Do to Promote Our Work." Stuart intended the Riders Roundup to be a locus for spreading the Circuit Rider account that he had sanctioned. It was also an opportunity to strategize about building the movement, with sessions dedicated to mapping existing programs and discussing the barriers to developing more Circuit Rider projects.

In June 1998, the second Roundup was hosted by the C. S. Mott Foundation in Flint, Michigan. In the year since he began the first Circuit Rider Program with the W. Alton Jones Foundation, Gavin Clabaugh took a position with Mott. From Mott, Clabaugh was able to funnel additional resources to Stuart and the Circuit Riders. In a memo to Mott, Clabaugh described the objective for the second meeting along similar lines to Stuart: "strengthen[ing] a network of information specialists who provide technical assistance— exclusively in the area of information technology—to a broad range of nonprofit organizations." To that end, the meeting focused on collaboration among

Circuit Riders and ways to forge a collective identity. In an e-mail to Stuart after the second Roundup, one Circuit Rider commented: "I think you guys have done a lot to create a 'Circuit Rider' culture and community. There was a real 'quality' to the people attending with the depth of skills and commitment. The relationships I began to develop at the conference were as important to my work as the content of the workshops" (Slater, 1998). Stuart recalls: "They did not think anybody else was doing it, so when they would actually find and be invited to a community of peers, it was like Nirvana, like, 'Oh, my gosh, I found my home'" [14].

When I spoke with Circuit Riders, many recalled the early meetings fondly, describing how strongly they sympathized with each other's efforts. Denise Joines, one-time executive director of a leading Circuit Rider organization called ONE Northwest, described her experience: "We got together and we had so much fun and it was so generous and everyone was sharing all the things they were learning and wanting, really truly wanting, the whole sector to grow" [39]. Sean O'Brien explained: "We really developed a serious bond among that young group after just that one weekend together. We all felt this intense connection. I am not a terribly 'huggy' person, but those are the kind of friends that when you see them again, you hug them" [17]. Dirk Slater, who was hired by the Welfare Law Center in 1998 to run its Circuit Rider program, the Low Income Networking and Communications (LINC) Project, described those early Roundups as "people identifying each other as 'we have something in common, we can help each other do this'" [59]. Upon returning from the second Roundup, he wrote in a memo to the Welfare Law Center that "[t]he movement for a stronger use of technologies by nonprofits is well underway."

By the third Roundup, the Circuit Riders had largely forged a collective identity around social justice and the environment and were steadily growing their ranks. Michael Ward, who worked at the RFF and helped organize the first Roundups, explained: "That core group [of supporters] initially was more about politically progressive policy advocacy. W. Alton Jones did a lot of political advocacy funding. So did the [Rockefeller] Family Fund. And then, ONE Northwest worked with environmental groups. . . . That is how we differentiated Circuit Riders from other technology people is that we had a mission that we were trying to achieve, that it was not just about the technology. It was around progressing certain ideals" [64]. Collective identity is key to developing a movement and enrolling adherents (Clemens, 1996; Polletta & Jasper, 2001; Reger, 2002; Robnett, 2005). By 1999, the movement had a loyal core. To enroll new adherents, the Roundup planners decided to locate the event in new territory. The third annual Roundup took place in Minneapolis, a city with a strong nonprofit sector (Galaskiewicz & Bielefeld, 1998) but without ties to the Circuit Rider movement. The event enrolled members of the Management Assistance Program (MAP), a management-support organization with a fledgling technology component. Stuart explained that this was intentional, "Wherever we would do the Roundup, we would do focused outreach to ensure that folks from those communities came. . . . MAP did not have a Circuit Rider program before the Roundup in 1999, when we went to Minneapolis. Subsequent to that meeting, Sheldon Mains organized a program. Now, they have four Circuit Riders and they come to the Roundup" [14]. In terms of content, Dirk Slater, who attended both, reports that "Flint and Minneapolis were very similar events" [59].

The End of the Beginning

The fourth Roundup took place in 2000 in Kansas City, home of the Kaufmann Foundation, which is known to support market-based solutions to social problems. The Kansas City Roundup was a turning point for several reasons. First, it was the first roundup organized by a professional event organizer, hired by Stuart and Clabaugh. The organizer booked a conference hotel for the Roundup and developed a formal agenda, which was distributed in a binder. This represented a significant step toward formalization of the larger movement. Second, admission was open to the wider public for the first time. As a result, attendance spiked, tripling the previous year's. Although nominally open, earlier Roundups were invitation-only events in practice. One needed to be a part of a network to hear about the Roundups.[1] Third, open admission at a conference hotel meant people had to pay their own way to, from, and during the meeting—the "junket" was over. As Michael Ward from the Rockefeller Technology Project explained, "We [Rockefeller Technology Project] completely supported Chicago and Flint. They [Rockefeller Family Fund] gave us the grants to do that and we did the fund-raising for it. We did Chicago, Flint, Minnesota. I think all those were free. I think Kansas City was the first year where it was not completely free. We gave scholarships to anyone who could not pay their own way" [64].

The change that would prove most important in shaping the future of the Circuit Riders was the shift in focus away from movement ideals, tactics, and strategies toward professional development and the technical aspects of consulting. Two forces drove the shift. First, social enterprise, which sought to implement market-based solutions to social problems, was increasing in popularity and legitimacy (Bielefeld, 2006; Dart, 2004b). Tapping the Kaufmann Foundation for support connected the Circuit Riders to this growing trend. Second, by opening the meeting to all and charging for admission, the Roundup organizers had to attract a wider audience in order for the meeting to cover the costs of hiring organizers and renting conference space in a hotel. Conference organizers understood that not many people would pay to attend a movement meeting centered on esoteric activist topics. However, consultants to the nonprofit sector are interested in learning professional skills they can deploy in their own businesses, especially when such skills provide them access to new markets. Funding from the Kauffman Foundation, as well as the addition of professional consultants, introduced market practices into Circuit Riding, though in subtle ways at first.

The Circuit Riders recognized that their activism was being tempered. Sheldon Mains, a Circuit Rider from Minneapolis attending his second Roundup, noticed: "One of the other early controversies in Kansas City was 'are we just people who help left-leaning organizations or are we open to anyone?'" [58]. The debate split the Circuit Riders into politically progressive and politically agnostic camps, reflecting the conventions of activism and professionalism, respectively. Mains reported that those with the attitude "'we are helping all nonprofits' seems to have won out" [58]. In other words, politically agnostic Circuit Riders and professional consultants came to dominate the Roundup, shifting the movement toward market principles and away from progressive political action. The meaning of Circuit Riding was beginning to change as the account by which Circuit Riders demonstrated their worth shifted from social justice and environmentalism to efficiency and capacity building.[2]

The emergence of professional ideals was reflected in the topics discussed at the meeting. Conference organizers assembled information packets for newcomers including essays written by Stuart and other leaders in the field. One essay, "What is Circuit Riding?," provided a basic description of the WAJF/RTP model. Conference materials described the Roundup as "a three-day professional development conference that unites Riders from around the country who serve diverse constituencies in order to discuss strategy, to train, to network, and build relationships and to develop joint projects and outcomes. Through the Roundup, Circuit Riders create and maintain the informal network that solves many of the issues related to our individual geographic isolation, and takes key steps to developing our overall trade." In addition to staple Roundup sessions such as "Lessons from the Field," and "Where Do We Go from Here," new sessions appeared on the agenda, such as "Client Management," "Organizational Effectiveness," "Evaluation," and "The Digital Divide." Conference materials, while giving a nod to the past, shifted the account of Circuit Riding from activism to professional activity. Just as Paul DiMaggio explained in his examination of the museum field (DiMaggio, 1991: 268), "The price of acceptance was the mobilization of a constituency, including professionals and social reformers, with interests that diverged from those of the founding elites." In this case, professional technology assistance meant the movement was no longer beholden to activists and patrons focusing exclusively on social justice and environmental issues. Rather, Circuit Riding as a profession could potentially gain access to funding from the new capacity-building movement within philanthropy that was emerging at the time. Such funding was driven by a growing spirit of social enterprise in the nonprofit sector (Young, 2003).

The configuration of a professional field was reinforced at later Roundups. By 2001, the fifth Riders Roundup attracted over 100 people to a hotel in Denver. The event was cohosted by TechRocks, the outgrowth of the Rockefeller Technology Project, and the Colorado Environmental Coalition. If the Circuit Riders sowed the seeds of professionalization in Kansas City, those seeds took root in Denver. Many of the topics discussed at earlier meetings, such as building a movement and defining Circuit Riding for new adherents, were overshadowed by panels on professional consulting, database design, and computer standards. The new agenda also featured short biographies of presenters, describing the formal credentials of each. Early Roundups were small and intimate, making bios unnecessary, as Circuit Riders knew the presenters, often personally. Slater explained that "the best part of [early Roundups] was when it was really informal and people just got what they needed and had informal relationships" [59]. A member of Media Jumpstart, a social justice Circuit Rider group, told me in an informal interview that the Roundup in Denver featured too many sessions about helping for-profit consultants make the transition to the nonprofit sector. Whereas panels at earlier Roundups were about sharing information, panels at more recent Roundups were about "getting on the agenda" and increasing exposure in order to expand the market for consulting businesses (Fieldnotes 7–24–2003).

The Roundup in Denver signaled a formal shift in the movement. In planning documents included with the 2001 Roundup Agenda, TechRocks publicly rescinded its position as community organizer, passing that role to a trade association in formation, the Nonprofit Technology Enterprise Network (NTEN). Stuart wrote in the planning documents that "TechRocks is moving out of the role of the coordinating organization for the Circuit Rider Community. An alternative to hiring a coordinator would be to work with NTEN to take over support of the Circuit Rider Community as a part of its broader mission of promoting technology in the nonprofit community" (Planning Committee, 2001). With prescience, Stuart also warned that, with this shift, the Circuit Rider movement was losing "its unique identity" as well as "control of its future." Others considered the shift the end of the Circuit Rider movement. Dirk Slater later recalled in an e-mail to the Riders e-mail list: "I was so heartbroken that day in Denver when the Riders Roundups' fate got sealed into NTEN's hands, you could see it coming. Didn't want the movement [to] end, but knew with how quickly things were changing and growing that it was inevitable. I'm glad I was there then—wouldn't have missed it for the world. I'm glad the Riders movement was there when it was, because it showed me what was possible and it got me started down this path" (E-mail to Riders list, 4–12–2010).

The Market for Professional Technology Assistance

The Riders Roundup took place in Orlando the following year. TechRocks had fully yielded their organizing responsibilities to NTEN. Ed Batista, NTEN's executive director, wrote in a welcoming statement included with the agenda that one of the goals for the meeting was "[to] insure a smooth transition from TechRocks to NTEN" (Batista, 2002). For the first time, planning and managing the Roundup was entirely out of the Circuit Riders' hands. Dirk Slater explained: "My sense was that people were frustrated that there had been five Roundups up until Denver and there was the LISTSERV and that was it. There was not any sort of infrastructure for the community at all. I think people were really like, 'NTEN has some money and they have staff. If they take it on, we can do it.' Practically, I can see that as being a very wise thing to do" [59]. Slater's comments reflect the resignation many Circuit Riders expressed toward the formalization of the movement. Stuart had relied on principles of self-organization for the movement, following his logic of "get them together and allow good things to happen." Such logic evoked a do-it-yourself ethic espoused by many grassroots social movements. The organizational form reflecting the principles of self-organization was a loosely configured network. However, foundations and other resource holders would support a loosely configured network of technology activists only for so long. In order to solicit more resources, many Circuit Riders recognized that the movement had to organize formally as a way of signaling that their cause was worth continued material and moral support, especially in a world that increasingly valorized market-based solutions to social problems (Moody, 2008; Young, 2003).

In only a few years, the Roundups, which started as movement meetings, evolved into conferences for professional nonprofit technology assistance providers. The politically progressive message of the Circuit Riders, articulated in Stuart's account of technology assistance as promoting social justice and environmental stewardship, gave way to an account of technology assistance as capacity building in the nonprofit sector. As Michael Ward explained, the Circuit Riders "had a mission that we were trying to achieve. It was not just about the technology. It was around progressing certain ideals . . . it has definitely moved into different places" [64]. Foundations and corporations endorsed the new professionalized account and the market practices that accompanied it. Professional consultants found that the rhetoric of capacity building resonated with foundations as well as nonprofit organizations seeking to tap them for funding.

With NTEN at the helm, attendance at the Riders Roundup grew exponentially. The Roundup in Orlando assembled twice as many attendees as Denver had the previous year. The number crossed a threshold. According to Stuart, "As [the Roundups] have gotten larger, some of the overriding themes have been lost, because it gets too big. . . . I actually advised them not to go over 150 [attendees]. I believe that once you get over 150, people will not meet each other. And it is totally true. There were people at that roundup [in Orlando] that I never met. Whereas even in the Denver, when we had 100, everyone met each other" [14]. Many of the new attendees represented a new wave of nonprofit technology assistance providers—consultants who were either independent entrepreneurs or employees at one of the newer NTAP organizations that had been springing up across the country.[3] Circuit Riders considered themselves different from consultants. Circuit Riders considered consultants hired guns—working with nonprofit organizations because the sector represented an untapped market, not because they were committed to its ideals. Todd Koym, one of the original Circuit Riders at the W. Alton Jones Foundation, explained: "There is a difference [between consultants and Circuit Riders]. It is usually mission-specific. [Circuit Riders] are doing it because they care about that issue; it is what they can do for that movement. They care about the issues and the people that are working on them" [72]. With the influx of more entrepreneurial and business-like NTAPs at the meetings, politically progressive Circuit Riders felt "the sense of 'we are going to change the world' and 'how are we going to work together to change the world' was gone" [59].

The Beginning of the End?

In 2004, NTEN drew over 600 people to the meeting in Philadelphia. The trade association decided to change the name of the Riders Roundup to the Nonprofit Technology Conference (NTC). Figure 2.1 charts the rapid growth in the Riders Roundups from 1997 to 2004. Due to the high turnout, fewer than half of the people in attendance at the NTC had attended earlier Roundups. Newcomers consisted of internal information technology (IT) staff at nonprofit organizations and for-profit technology vendors. As the dominant collective identity moved from activism to professional consulting and the meaning of their work changed from promoting social justice and environmental stewardship to building capacity in the nonprofit sector, the Circuit Riders felt increasingly alienated. Rob Stuart told me in an interview: "the devolution of community started with the decision to, in Orlando, expand the number of people who attended to over 150. . . . Once you get over 150, people are compelled to pull away and get into smaller groups. That happened for the first time in Orlando. It was totally replicated again in Oakland with a dual conference. Then, it was totally manifested in Philadelphia. You know, it [the meeting in Philadelphia] was with the generic Nonprofit Technology Conference" [76].

Following the Nonprofit Technology Conference in Philadelphia, several Circuit Riders posted nostalgic essays on the Riders e-mail list, yearning for the earlier days when the meetings were about collective identity building and changing the world through technology. Tim Mills-Groninger, associate executive director of the IT Resource Center in Chicago and host of the first Riders Roundup, wrote an article about the history of Circuit Riding for the

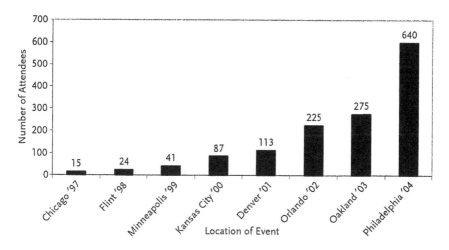

FIGURE 2.1. Riders Roundup attendees by year

Nonprofit Times, lamenting that NTEN and the Nonprofit Technology Conference had strayed too far from their movement roots (Mills-Groninger, 2004). Dirk Slater posted the following message to the e-mail list:

> In that huge accomplishment [an unprecedented 640 attendees at the conference], there was a piece that left me very sad. The Circuit Rider community seemed non-existent. It is clearly no longer our event. While I am happy to see the NTC shift and become focused on Non-Profit IT, Circuit Riding is still a very important and integral part of the Non-Profit IT environment. There are still plenty of groups out there that cannot afford their own IT staff and still plenty of us still in the saddle working with communities of groups and helping to build their capacities through technology. So when the event ended on Saturday, I had a very different sadness than I usually do. Where were the Circuit Riders that this event had been formed around? (E-mail to the Riders list, 3–31–04)

Todd Koym, an early WAJF Circuit Rider, said that early Roundups had a politically progressive feel to them. From my fieldnotes dated 3–26–2004: "[Koym] said that there was an implicit progressivism in the room in the early days. He said that at this [the 2004] conference and at some earlier ones, even that is gone. The [nonprofit technology] sector has been pushed into more moderate territory." Beyond lamenting the shift, the Circuit Riders began organizing an alternative movement. During the Nonprofit Technology Conference in Philadelphia, several core members of the Circuit Rider movement were convening across town under the banner of free and open source software at a meeting they called "Penguin Day."[4]

Configuring a Field of Professionals at the Riders Roundups

Movement organizers, such as Stuart, thought they could work with foundations and corporations while maintaining the authenticity of the Circuit Riders movement, as embodied in the group's collective identity and articulated in their account. However, gains in access to resources and legitimacy came with a loss of control over the movement. The rapid growth of the Circuit Rider movement enrolled new actors with different ideas about the role and meaning of information technology in the nonprofit sector. These new actors considered information technology a part of the capacity-building project in the nonprofit sector, one that should be dedicated to enhancing the efficiency and contributing to the fiscal sustainability of nonprofit organizations. Ultimately, the growing focus on market principles undermined movement ideals, such as social justice and a commitment to protecting the environment.

Within the movement, forces of professionalization began to take hold. Professionalization is a process by which members of an occupational group draw boundaries around a set of practices and establish criteria for inclusion, often represented as credentials (Abbott, 1988). In this case, the professionalization of Circuit Riding meant shifting the focus from social values to market practices, as reflected in the changing agendas of the meetings. Professionalization made sense to many in the movement. Professionalization among activists had helped sustain social movement groups and organizations in other areas. For instance, professionalization was responsible for the maintenance of the pro-choice movement throughout the 1970s and 1980s (Staggenborg, 1988). However, once the movement began moving in this direction, the forces of professionalization became difficult to stop. Key resources, especially money and legitimacy, became tied to professional ideals. Professional consultants were concerned with creating a market for technology. The shift was reflected on the Circuit Riders LISTSERV, which began as a crucial organizing and mobilizing tool for activists. Michael Ward, who worked with Stuart as a Circuit Rider for the Rockefeller Family Fund, said, "The tone [on the Riders LIST-

SERV] has changed and the mission part of it has been dropped. . . . It is definitely more often about the technology now" [64].

Moving toward professionalization meant a change in the Circuit Riders'
account of worth. A long-time Circuit Rider reflected about the changes in an
e-mail to the LISTSERV in 2010:

> Like many movements, things get professionalized. It wasn't going to last,
> anyway, NTEN or not. The funding for circuit riders per se dried up, technol-
> ogy changed, organizations hired in, circuit riders became "nonprofit techies"
> of all stripes: consultants, developers, strategists, some joined companies,
> some dropped out, because NTC didn't provide them with what they need for
> one reason or another. I hold the "circuit rider" legacy seat on the NTEN
> board (kinda sorta), and once I go off early next year, I doubt that anyone like
> that will replace me, since for the most part folks don't identify that way—
> even if they do the same work. (Murrain, 2010)

The worth of Circuit Riding was established on its ability to facilitate social
movement goals. The professional consultants or nonprofit technology assistance providers, as they called themselves, predicated their worth on being
able to facilitate much smaller goals, such as capacity building and efficiency
at the organizational level. From 1997 to 2004, Circuit Riding was transformed
from activism to consulting and from a social movement to a fledgling market
for technology assistance in the sector. Market principles took hold.

The changes that took place across the Riders Roundups reflected larger
social forces shaping the nonprofit sector in general. The nonprofit sector was
experiencing a commercial transformation (Tuckman, 1998; Weisbrod, 1998).
Nonprofit organizations were adopting more entrepreneurial practices (Young,
2003). Nonprofit foundations were encouraging market-based solutions to
social problems (Moody, 2008). This trend took place throughout the late
1990s and gained momentum in the early 2000s with the rise of social enterprise (Bielefeld, 2006; Borzaga & Defourny, 2001; Dart, 2004b). The bases for
worth in the sector shifted toward the market, as nonprofit organizations increasingly pursued sustainability and efficiency, which were measured through
financial metrics, such as earned revenues. With their commitment to volunteerism and activist ideals, the Circuit Riders saw such metrics as expressions
of market values, which undermined the goals of their movement.

Configuring a Market at the National Strategy for Nonprofit Technology Meetings

Over several months in 1998, Stuart convened a separate, more intimate, set of meetings under the banner of National Strategy for Nonprofit Technology. The NSNT assembled select leaders of the Circuit Rider movement and nationally recognized NTAPs with officers from major foundations, including Ford, Rockefeller, and Surdna, and executives from Microsoft and IBM. The stated goal of the NSNT meetings was to produce a planning document, also called the National Strategy for Nonprofit Technology, which would articulate a standardized set of technology assistance practices to guide future funding decisions in the nonprofit sector. If successful, the NSNT would provide elite support and resources to further establish the activism of Circuit Riding as a legitimate enterprise.

Assembling the Elites

Entitled "Technology Leveraging Change," the first NSNT meeting took place in Atlanta, Georgia, on July 20–22, 1998 to correspond with the Alliance for Nonprofit Management conference. Stuart began the meeting with a Power-Point presentation, explaining that its 24 attendees were "an expanding network of creative and collaborative leaders committed to using technology to leverage social change." According to planning documents for the meeting, the express goal of the NSNT was "to increase the Third Sector's capacity to use technology so that it can better protect, preserve, and extend the social values entrusted to it, while serving our communities and our country as a new economy emerges" (Partners, 1999). Planning documents also articulated the NSNT's core values: "reciprocity, fair compensation, continual learning, and open standards."

In expressing these ideals to foundations and other elites, the NSNT was an attempt to secure the legitimacy of the Circuit Rider model by associating the social values expressed in the account with the ideals of the "Third Sector." Stuart's hope was that his account, once inscribed in the NSNT, would establish the Circuit Rider model as *the* way to provide technology assistance to the nonprofit sector. Once backed by powerful actors in the field, such as the foundation officers who could provide material support and legitimacy to the model, the justification underlying Stuart's account would become taken for granted. Stuart's position in the field, in relation to his work as a fellow with the Rockefeller Family Fund, afforded him the ability to mobilize resources toward this end.

The second NSNT meeting was strategically held in Monterey, California, in October 19–21, 1998. A new consortium of foundations, called Grantmakers for Effective Organizations, was convening their inaugural conference there at the same time. This provided Stuart access to new funders already interested in capacity building[5] in the nonprofit sector. Stuart invited Barbara Kibbe, who had worked at the Packard Foundation and now headed Grantmakers for Effective Organizations, to join the NSNT initiative. She brought her former employer into the fold and provided Stuart access to an entirely new group of funders. A discussion of how best to support information technology was already on the capacity-building agenda for Grantmakers for Effective Organizations. However, Stuart recognized the opportunity to shape the way grants for technology capacity were made.

According to planning documents, the vision for the NSNT meeting in Monterey was to "apply knowledge and lessons learned to enable the Third Sector to transform itself through information technology and the Internet." This vision drew heavily on Stuart's emancipatory rhetoric within the Circuit Rider movement, based on a civic order of worth, meaning that claims made in the NSNT presupposed that the collective good would take primacy over individual desires (Boltanski & Thévenot, 2006: 185). In practice this meant that Stuart's account of Circuit Riding was still about contributions to social justice and the environment, not the efficiency or capacity of particular nonprofit organizations. Stuart's strategy at Monterey was to mobilize elite foundation officers in support of Circuit Riding, as opposed to other models of technology assistance in the nonprofit sector. Once accepted by the powerful actors present at the meetings, the NSNT would help institutionalize the practice of Circuit Riding.

Rhetorical Devices of Mobilization

The catchphrase—and rhetoric—Stuart espoused for the meetings was "chaordic," a term the NSNT founding members borrowed from a Fast Company article about Dee Hock, the founder of the credit card company Visa. "Chaordic" ostensibly described a new set of organizing principles, based on "the promise of a shining synthesis of chaos and order" (Waldrop, 1996: 75). The NSNT organizers linked to an electronic copy of the article on their website, providing a bridge between accounts proffered in different fields. The term "chaordic" expressed the radical nonhierarchical network principles that reflected organizing principles associated with the Internet boom. It also coincided with

the organizing principles of the Circuit Rider movement. To the NSNT organizers, especially Stuart, "chaordic" reflected the "revolutionary power" of
information technology, that is, the order that ostensibly emerges from the
anarchy of the Internet. The term also reflected the hope that the NSNT would
provide the scaffolding for an emergent order for the otherwise anarchic Circuit Riders. The Circuit Riders understood information technology as revolutionary in two senses of the term: (1) technology would radically alter the way
nonprofits worked and (2) fundamentally change the way society was itself
organized. In an interview, Stuart told me, "My approach or vision for Circuit
Riders was to reach the leadership [in the nonprofit sector], get them to realize
the transformative power of this [technology] stuff" [76]. By "transformative,"
Stuart meant radical organizational and social change. Elsewhere in the interview, Stuart refers to the Internet as a "transformative political tool." Here,
Stuart was attempting to align technological and social revolutions by associating the meaning of Circuit Riding (as promoting progressive social
change) with its organizational form (radically nonhierarchical, loosely coupled network).

Showdown at Kykuit

The turning point for the Circuit Rider movement came at the third NSNT
meeting, held December 3–6, 1998. By then, Stuart had spent nearly a year
working on the NSNT initiative, enrolling foundations and leaders in the nonprofit sector. He invited 20 foundation officers and corporate representatives
to the Rockefeller Estate and conference center in Kykuit, New York, to unveil
the latest version of the National Strategy for Nonprofit Technology. A page
on the Rockefeller Family Fund website announced the event: "The Camp will
feature presentations about the National Strategy as it has been developed to
date, as well as engage you in discussions about how to make technology assistance even more responsive to the burgeoning technology needs of the
nonprofit sector. Since the National Strategy is nearing completion, your in-
put now will have the greatest influence on how the technology capacity of the
nonprofit sector is developed in the next several years" (Stuart, 1999). Stuart
reasoned that by bringing foundation officers together before the plan was
completed, he could give them a stake in the process and therefore the outcome. According to Stuart's strategy, this would make the foundations more
likely to support the Circuit Rider movement, materially and symbolically.

Through his position at the Rockefeller Family Fund, Stuart was able to reserve the Pocantico Conference Center at the Rockefeller Estate for the three-day meeting. The meeting assembled leaders from the Circuit Rider movement, foundation officers, representatives from technology companies, and the heads of several newly founded nonprofit technology assistance providers. Some of the foundation officers had been involved from the outset, such as those from the Rockefeller Family Fund, the Rockefeller Brothers Fund, the Charles Stewart Mott Foundation, and the W. Alton Jones Foundation. Representatives from Microsoft, though having come later to the initiative, were present as well. New to the initiative were foundation officers from the W. K. Kellogg and Surdna Foundations; the Open Society Institute; Merrill Lynch Philanthropic Financial Services; and the Beldon Fund. Representatives from IBM and Hewlett-Packard were also new to the initiative.

Also in attendance was Joan Fanning, who was in the process of starting a new NTAP in Seattle. Microsoft had hired Fanning in 1998 to write a white paper about how to improve their software donation program. The white paper recommended creating a new kind of professional NTAP organization to help nonprofit organizations select and deploy software solutions more effectively. Following the recommendation, Microsoft provided Fanning with financial, in-kind, and technical support to start the NTAP she envisioned in her white paper. She called it NPower.

Fanning considered the moral basis of Circuit Riding, that is, working exclusively with social justice or environmental groups, overly exclusionary. She created NPower's model of technology assistance as a response. As Fanning explained, "I have worked for years in direct service delivery, domestic violence, human services, they are doing social change. It [the Circuit Riders' exclusivity] felt like this real judgmental thing. I think the agencies on the ground working with kids at risk, working with the elderly, they are doing the work of social change" [19]. Rather than focusing on ideological niches and a civic order, like the Circuit Riders, NPower would rely on the democracy of the market, working with any nonprofit who could afford its services, as we will see in Chapter 3. This meant forgoing certain sources of philanthropic support, like the third-party-payer model of the Circuit Riders. Rather than a movement, Fanning envisioned technology assistance as a market. And, in New York, Fanning, Stuart, and other key players gathered for an unanticipated collision of ideals.

A Political Opportunity Arises out of Conflicting Orders of Worth
The meeting at Kykuit began auspiciously, but dialogue degraded quickly. Many of the foundation officers did not respond well to the NSNT's rhetoric of "chaordic" systems and technological revolutions. By the end of meeting's first day, several foundation officers simply left. Others were threatening to leave. Joan Fanning described the reactions of foundation officers:

> A number of funders thought that it was a bit of a fiasco. . . . Rob [Stuart] and Richard Civille [another social justice activist involved in the NSNT] were just talking about nonconcrete and interesting things like "chaordic" systems. How do you make this work? You have this group of foundation officers that are there for three days. They want to leave with an actionable agenda. It blew up. The Ford person left on day one. A number of funders at the time, Ed Skloot [an officer at the Surdna Foundation] were against funding anything in the field [of nonprofit technology assistance]. I started to get agitated too. [71]

Vince Stehle, who worked at the Surdna Foundation, explained: "There was some high-level participation and the invitation sounded like there was going to be something to sign off on. And their experience of it was much more like a brainstorming kind of thing. I remember quite distinctly the feeling on the part of senior folks that this is not fully cooked. I think it might have been my boss [Ed Skloot] who said, 'You do not invite people of our rank to a brainstorming session'" [78].

Fanning recognized a political opportunity in the discord: the foundation officers and corporate executives, while ostensibly open to Stuart's account of nonprofit technology, did not accept its civic moral basis. She thought foundation officers and corporate executives might be more open to the market approach she espoused in NPower's organizing principles. In practice, this would mean technology assistance should be available to any nonprofit organization that could afford the service, with prices set according to market principles—affordable to the client, but sustainable for the provider. Fanning argued that such an arrangement would make technology assistance self-sustaining, rather than dependent on foundation support.

Fanning took control of the meeting and used it as an opportunity to present the NPower model: framed properly, her account might be viewed as a more viable alternative to Stuart's "chaordic" vision, and therefore more appropriate for the nonprofit sector. As Fanning explained, "I could really understand where they [the foundation program officers] were coming from and so I started to play a facilitator role, like 'OK, it sounds like the path this meeting was going was not working. What can we do?'" [71]. Having attracted the attention of the foundation officers and corporate executives in the room, Fanning shifted the conversation from "chaordic" organization to what she called "concrete, actionable" agenda items. With her pragmatic approach, she presented an alternative account about how to provide effective technology assistance to the nonprofit sector.

Unlike the Circuit Riders, whose progressive and revolutionary accounts were justified by social values, Fanning's account venerated efficiency, competency, and financial measures of success. Her pragmatics resounded with the foundation officers, who themselves were in the midst of overseeing a transformation in the nonprofit sector toward adopting market practices and performance metrics (Dart 2004a, 2004b; Rojas, 2000; Weisbrod, 1998). As such, foundation officers were predisposed to market-based approaches, because they had come to value such practices in their grantmaking activities. Within the brief time and confined space of a single field-configuring event, Fanning became an influential institutional entrepreneur because she recognized a political opportunity during which she was able to align her account with shifting moral orders in the foundation world (Hwang & Powell, 2005; Rao & Giorgi, 2006). Whereas Stuart was locked in to treating technology as promoting social and organizational revolution and the Circuit Rider model as a way of expressing this account throughout the NSNT planning process, Fanning had no stake in the prevailing "pattern of value commitments" (Greenwood & Hinings, 1996: 1035) and could frame her account to take advantage of the political opportunity presented to her.

After Kykuit

By the end of the weekend at Kykuit, foundation officers pledged to support the NSNT only if Fanning led the initiative. Deborah Strauss, the director of another leading NTAP in the field, said to me: "There were pretty strong differences of vision among the leadership. . . . Joan Fanning basically stepped in and pulled the [NSNT] document into shape and carried it further, and . . . she was the savior" [57]. After the meeting, Fanning rewrote the NSNT vision statement over the next several months before handing it over to a colleague for completion and execution. She then turned her attention to raising funds to build NPower.

Since Fanning wrote her white paper, Microsoft had been providing monetary and technical resources to the fledgling NPower. With the connections she made at Kykuit, Fanning attracted additional start-up funding. "For me and for NPower, that meeting [at Kykuit] was very, very helpful," Fanning recalled [71]. NPower launched in 2000. By 2001, the organization had an operating budget of over $1.5 million. With subsequent funding from NSNT supporters Microsoft and Surdna, NPower continued expanding its operations, establishing 12 affiliates in as many cities over the next two years.

In an interview, Stuart described the Kykuit meeting as "'difficult' . . . a big bump in the road for organizing the funding community to back this thing [his account of Circuit Riding] as it goes forward" [76]. He blamed the outcome of the meeting on the foundation officers in attendance who failed to grasp "the transformative stuff." A journalist for the Philanthropy News Network reported:

> The National Strategy has big plans mixing visionary ideas with practical solutions to help nonprofits put technology to productive and innovative use. One idea would be to create a barter system to exchange tech skills, tools and know-how. Another would be to create a nonprofit mega-site on the Web.
>
> At Kykuit, some of those loftier ideas ran into tough scrutiny. "The goal was engagement," says Rob Stuart, a National Strategy partner who organized the retreat and directs the Rockefeller Technology Project of the Rockefeller Family Fund. "We did not get there." (Cohen, 1999)

As Fanning and a colleague rewrote the final version of the NSNT, "one of the steps was to have a process with providers . . . to have a formal way to share promising practices, coordinate the field, and accelerate the impact" [71]. That "formal way" was the creation of a trade association for NTAPs, including the Circuit Riders, called the Nonprofit Technology Enterprise Network. In rewriting the NSNT document, Fanning inscribed the same market values in NTEN's organizing principles as she had in NPower. The NTEN planning document came to resemble NPower's business plan more than the original NSNT planning document. For example, the original NSNT planning document made no mention of membership, opting instead for universal inclusiveness. In contrast, the NTEN planning document presents a tiered membership model much like the one articulated in NPower's business plan. Richard Zorza, who was involved in the NSNT planning, explained: "Ironically in a way, if you look at the ideology of the National Strategy [for Nonprofit Technology], it has got values and principles and so on. There is more of a match between how NPower operates [with] those values, notwithstanding the fact that Microsoft's money is there, than the way the [Circuit] Riders operate" [60]. The NSNT's original guiding principles—transparency, open systems, fair exchange, and fair compensation—remain in the final text, though they are buried in the middle of the document and presented in a smaller font.

As a condition of support, foundations supporting the initiative charged NPower with establishing NTEN and overseeing its finances. As Fanning explained, "He [Vince Stehle of Surdna] was pretty much at the time only comfortable with NPower being the fiscal agent because we had a reputation for following through and getting stuff done" [71]. Fanning was thus able to leverage her success at Kykuit into shaping the entire field of nonprofit technology assistance and the direction institutionalization took. NPower capitalized on its position as financial overseer of NTEN. Fanning took a board position, as did Jane Meseck from Microsoft and Vincent Stehle from the Surdna Foundation. Rob Stuart would later claim in an interview that NPower often received funding that should have gone to NTEN [76]. For example, in 2003, NPower and NTEN competed for a large grant from telecommunications giant SBC. NPower was awarded the grant (Business Wire, 2003).

A Shifting Field

To determine how the meeting at Kykuit altered the funding landscape of the field, I analyzed Internal Revenue Service filings (990 tax forms) for all NTAPs that filed in the years from 1998 to 2003 (n = 11). The year 1998 serves as a baseline, because it represents the year before the NSNT meetings took place. It is also the first year any of the organizations in my sample filed 990 tax forms. My analysis shows that philanthropic funding for technology assistance increased in the aftermath of Kykuit and the rise of NPower. However, the majority of philanthropic support went to large NTAPs, which resembled NPower's model, rather than Circuit Rider organizations. In 1997, before NPower or the NSNT meetings, the IT Resource Center and Compumentor were the two largest stand-alone NTAPs in the country (measured by budget). They each received $350,000 in donations in that year. After Kykuit, the largest two NTAPs, now NPower and Compumentor, raised over $1 million in donations in 2000 ($3 million and $1.4 million, respectively). IT Resource Center, which predated NPower and served as a model for NPower's service delivery, raised $.5 million in 2000 and $1.4 million in 2001. Stand-alone Circuit Rider organizations, such as ONE Northwest and Project Alchemy (both headquartered in Seattle), also witnessed increased donations, though not as large in absolute or relative terms. ONE Northwest raised $700,000 in 2000 and $757,000 in 2001. It is important to note that ONE Northwest was started in 1996, but the organization's budget was less than the minimum required to file a 990 form with the IRS until 2000. Project Alchemy, founded in 2000, received $150,000 that year and $248,000 in 2001. This evidence suggests that NPower did make the funding pie for nonprofit technology bigger. It also took a larger piece.

In the years following Kykuit, several Circuit Rider organizations folded as funding shifted toward NPower's market model of technology assistance. Project Alchemy closed its doors in 2004. A board member cited the reason as a lack of a "significant funding stream dedicated to capacity building for social justice" (Cohen, 2004). TechRocks, a spinoff of the Rockefeller Technology Project, operated for two years before closing for good in 2003. The LINC Project managed to operate until 2006, largely due to being housed in the Welfare Law Center. One Circuit Rider organization, Technology Works For Good, joined the NPower Network, changing its name to NPower Greater D.C. Region.

The NSNT did have the intended effect of creating a national field of nonprofit technology assistance providers. Before the meetings, most NTAPs were isolated in local areas, such as Seattle, San Francisco, and New York. There was no national dialogue and little recognition that NTAP organizations were members of a field prior to the NSNT. After the NSNT and with the establishment of NTEN, nonprofit technology assistance providers went from an uncoordinated population of organizations into a recognized organizational field. Daniel Ben-Horin, the executive director of Compumentor, explained: "I think NSNT was frustrating on some levels, but without it there would be no NTEN and there might not be a TechSoup [a Compumentor program]. We were very local at that time, but once NSNT was around, we thought we ought to be there and that brought us back out into the field. So it was a good thing" [81]. The unintended consequence of the NSNT was how it changed the landscape of nonprofit technology assistance providers. Large, established NTAPs became important players in the organizational field, often displacing the Circuit Riders at events such as the Riders Roundup and in dialogues such as those on the Riders LISTSERV. Large NTAPs, especially NPower, were able to attract foundation funding as well as direct payments from clients. Within a few years, NPower had grown to be the largest and most influential NTAP in the country. Exactly how is the topic of Chapters 3 and 4.

Organizing for Change

Meetings, such as the Riders Roundups and the NSNT, afford insight into the processes by which fields are organized. By assembling heterogeneous actors, such events provide a time and a place for critical situations—fateful moments of interaction among actors within fields. In the case of the Riders Roundups, changes in conference attendees over time led to the professionalization of Circuit Riding. In the case of the NSNT meetings, a critical situation provided an opportunity for an institutional entrepreneur to advance a market account to a group of elites. These meetings allowed entrepreneurs to plant the seeds of a market in the space previously reserved for a social movement. This became a critical step toward creating a market for technology assistance in the United States. Both sets of meetings demonstrate the limits of strategic action in organizing fields. Rob Stuart's institutional entrepreneurship was under-mined by larger forces driving organizations in the nonprofit sector to adopt market practices and principles.

The Riders Roundups were organized to enroll and mobilize new adher-ents into the movement. However, as attendance at the Roundups grew, meet-ings that started out as informal movement gatherings became professional conferences. This happened as the mix of people at the meetings changed. Whereas early adherents were technologically oriented activists, new entrants saw Circuit Riding as a career opportunity and nonprofit and grassroots orga-nizations as an untapped market for professional consulting. Over time, the collective identity of the Circuit Riders shifted from activist to professional consultant. Professionalization provided a new set of practices justified on ef-ficiency gains and capacity building for nonprofit organizations, rather than their contribution to movement goals. Working with entrepreneurial founda-tions, such as Kauffman, and technical assistance organizations, such as the Management Assistance Program, reinforced the professionalization of the nonprofit technology field.

The meetings around the NSNT were designed to mobilize support and resources from elites. However, by assembling elite actors and movement leaders, the NSNT created a tournament for competing accounts. Stuart's account of Circuit Riding, which sparked the movement, was criticized as unsustainable for its reliance on revolutionary organizing principles, such as "chaordic" systems. This provided an opportunity for Fanning to act as an institutional entrepreneur and offer an alternative account, one justified with market principles. With market principles more widely accepted in the nonprofit sector, especially among elite members such as foundation officers, Fanning's account gained legitimacy.

The organizational outcome of the two meetings was the creation of the Nonprofit Technology Enterprise Network. The kernel of NTEN was described in the original NSNT document. The original purpose of NTEN was to be a coordinating body for the Circuit Riders, allowing them to share information, best practices, and providing them access to financial resources from foundations. However, with the growing influence of professional and market-based practices and principles from new entrants in the field, NTEN emerged as a trade association. As a trade association, NTEN aggregated knowledge, published reports on nonprofit technology, coordinated local and regional efforts, and organized the annual Nonprofit Technology Conference (formerly the Riders Roundup).

The introduction of professional and market practices and principles transformed the basis of worth on which Circuit Riding was predicated. The account that established Circuit Riding as a legitimate activity claimed that it was worth doing because it helped achieve the goals of the social justice and environmental movements. After Kykuit and the transformation of the Riders Roundups into the Nonprofit Technology Conference, this justification for Circuit Riding no longer held. Nonprofit technology assistance was now worth funding because it contributed to the efficiency and capacity of nonprofit organizations. At the same time, the model of Circuit Riding—that is, third-party payer, activists working with activists—was criticized as unsustainable. The new model of market-based nonprofit technology assistance providers, that is, first-party payer, staffed by consultants with formal credentials, was touted as the future of technology assistance in the nonprofit sector.

The literature on resource mobilization has long identified and explained the importance of organizations like foundations in providing such support for social movements (McCarthy & Zald, 1977). Foundations also shape social movements by supporting professionalization projects within them (DiMaggio, 1991; Jenkins & Eckert, 1986). Beyond such roles, more recent studies have shown how foundations shape social movements more fundamentally by constructing and shaping organizational fields, that is, the relations among social movement organizations and their targets (Bartley, 2007). However, foundation field-building projects are not imposed from the top down. Rather, in the events described in this chapter, they emerge from the organizing efforts of movement leaders and institutional entrepreneurs, such as Rob Stuart and Joan Fanning. Foundations help shape fields by rewarding and legitimating certain organizing models and principles while shifting resources away from others (or not supporting them in the first place). Thus, foundations are not merely power brokers. Rather, they are ensconced in field-level dynamics and are constrained by the strategic activities of movement organizers and institutional entrepreneurs whose activities they may choose to condone. Fields are political arenas in which collective and individual actors jockey for position as they attempt to advance their interests by stabilizing meanings and collective identities (Fligstein & McAdam, 2012). As I will explain in Chapter 5, the interaction among these actors as they compete and collaborate shapes the "rules of engagement" on which future interactions are based.

For now, I next turn to the rise of market principles as manifested in Fanning's new organization, NPower. Chapter 3 explores the role of institutional entrepreneurs, such as Joan Fanning, in building new organizational forms and ultimately shaping markets.

3

INSTITUTIONAL ENTREPRENEURS
BUILD A BRIDGE

Connecting Movements and Markets
Through Social Enterprise

In Chapter 2 I showed how the Riders Roundups and NSNT meetings provided loci for both evolutionary and revolutionary changes in the Circuit Rider movement. The breakdown of the NSNT meetings, which climaxed at Kykuit, along with the professionalization taking place at the Riders Roundups, which culminated in their renaming as the Nonprofit Technology Conference, signaled a crisis for the Circuit Rider movement. In the aftermath of the two sets of meetings, technology assistance in the nonprofit sector shifted away from the Circuit Rider movement and toward a legitimized organizational field of professional technology consultants. The crisis afforded an opportunity for Joan Fanning to critique the account of worth on which the Circuit Rider movement was built. In its place she offered an alternative to Circuit Riding: a social enterprise based on a combination of market practices and movement principles. In order to advance her new model, Fanning had to take the role of an institutional entrepreneur—an individual or organization empowered to challenge extant institutional arrangements and advance the development of new institutions.

Fanning's ability to take an institutional entrepreneurship role was based on her competences and position, which she leveraged to create advance a new account of worth. She was helped by the fact that the nonprofit technology assistance field was nascent and therefore had yet to be settled. According to Fligstein and McAdam (2012), fields become settled when arrangements within them become taken for granted as the status quo. In settled fields, institutions are realized, which provide actors with rules and scripts as well as ways to evaluate whether others are acting appropriately. A wider variety of actions are permissible in less settled fields, since the bases for evaluating the legitimacy of actors and actions are not yet in place. Such conditions provide opportunities for institutional entrepreneurship. Fanning's competence includes her ability to recognize a political opportunity at Kykuit as well as her ability to convince foundation officers to accept her account of worth. Her position in the field is as both an insider and an outsider: an insider by virtue of being invited to the NSNT meetings; an outsider because she was not a member of the Circuit Rider movement. These factors allowed Fanning to develop a new nonprofit technology assistance provider, NPower, that combined aspects of the Circuit Rider account while taking advantage of a new organizational form—social enterprise[1]—to gain legitimacy among important actors in the nonprofit and for-profit sectors. By combining elements of Circuit Riding and market principles into a legitimate organizational form, a social enterprise, NPower successfully bridged movement and market worlds. In this chapter I demonstrate the important role of institutional entrepreneurship in bridging movements and markets. By establishing the legitimacy of new organizational forms and practices, institutional entrepreneurs help create and shape new institutions, especially in unsettled fields. In the case presented in this chapter, Fanning created a new organizational form by assembling existing elements from the environment with unique contributions (organizational innovations). She then worked to establish the legitimacy of her new organizational form by relying on legitimate organizational elements as well as appeals to powerful actors in the field, for example, nonprofit foundations and for-profit corporations. Such appeals were expressed through market practices, such as branding strategies and the construction of performance metrics, which produced a market-based account for NPower. Her choice of social and market values to adopt and reject would prove to have important, though unintended, consequences for how nonprofit organizations received technology assistance. Although Fanning did not intend to create a market for nonprofit technology assistance, one took shape out of the legitimacy and proliferation of NPower's design.

In this chapter I explain the role of institutional entrepreneurs in bridging movements and markets. The sociological and management literatures on institutional entrepreneurs describe the conditions necessary for successful institutional entrepreneurship as well as the characteristics of institutional entrepreneurs. I begin this chapter by reviewing how scholars have conceptualized institutional entrepreneurs as actors and institutional entrepreneurship as action. I illustrate the significance of institutional entrepreneurs by describing the work of Joan Fanning in organizing NPower, first into a free-standing social enterprise and ultimately into a national network of NTAPs. Fanning was recognized and respected as an institutional entrepreneur by many members of the Circuit Rider movement, because she was able to produce a multivalent account that appealed to the movement as well as to the market. And she had the social skill, that is, the competence and position, to make her account stick. As one Circuit Rider mentioned in an interview, Fanning was "absolutely fantastic" [51].

Institutional Entrepreneurs and Entrepreneurship

Institutional entrepreneurs are actors that challenge existing institutional arrangements and create and establish new institutions that align with their interests. As a concept, institutional entrepreneurship emerged to explain actor-driven institutional change (DiMaggio, 1988). Institutional entrepreneurs establish new accounts of worth by taking advantage of their competences and structural position. Organizations help institutional entrepreneurs transform accounts of worth into new practices, which they can then institutionalize in the field.

As noted in Chapter 2, Fanning arose out of Kykuit as an institutional entrepreneur, proposing an alternative model of technology assistance to the nonprofit sector. She built on this success to establish an organization that embodied the new account of technology assistance she promoted at Kykuit. As an organizational entrepreneur, Fanning assembled elements from the existing environment, combined with her own innovations, to produce a new organizational form. As an institutional entrepreneur, Fanning secured the legitimacy of her new organizational form with other actors in the field—for example, Circuit Riders, nonprofit foundations, and for-profit corporations—which then provided a new model for organizing NTAPs. In theory, establishing a new organizational form as legitimate has the potential to reconfigure organizational fields. However, the process by which this happens is complex, contingent, and uncertain.

Institutional Entrepreneurship as the Exploitation of Competences
Institutional entrepreneurship is the employment of competences toward establishing new accounts of worth. By competences, I mean the skills and awareness actors bring to particular social situations. My conception of competences is based on Pierre Bourdieu's (1990: 66) notion of practical sense, which he describes as a "feel for the game." I build on this idea by conceiving of "the game" as a social situation rather than as an abstract field. All actors have a practical sense based on their understanding of "the game." They have a theoretical understanding of their social worlds. Similarly, all actors have competences with which they are equipped as they enter social situations.[2] The relative advantage afforded by a competence depends on the situation. For example, Fanning's competences enabled her action at Kykuit. Fanning recognized that foundation officers were not getting what they wanted from the NSNT meeting. Because she had already prepared a white paper on nonprofit technology assistance for Microsoft, she was equipped with the knowledge necessary to offer an account amenable to their interests.

A key component to the competences of institutional entrepreneurs is what Fligstein (1997: 398) calls social skill, "the ability to motivate cooperation in other actors by providing those actors with common meanings and identities in which actions can be undertaken and justified." Social skill is about aligning the interests of others by providing an account of worth that gives them a stake in the endeavor, which transforms them into stakeholders. At Kykuit, Fanning was able to ply her social skill by convincing foundation officers that NPower would provide the information technology assistance that nonprofit organizations needed to use grants more efficiently and effectively.

Institutional Entrepreneur as Structural Position
In the most abstract sense, fields are social arenas in which specific forms of interaction take place and specific forms of capital are meaningful (Bourdieu, 1986, 1990). Take the art world for example. The art world is a field in which actors interact through artwork (which is ideally produced for its own sake) and in which knowledge about cultural codes (such as knowing the difference between abstract impressionism and fauvism) matters (Bourdieu, 1996). Fields are governed by institutions, the formal and informal rules that actors must follow if they are to be considered legitimate members of the field. Institutional entrepreneurs are actors that are enabled by their position in fields to challenge institutions (Battilana, 2006; Wright & Zammuto, 2012). An actor's

position in the field determines their access to important resources as well as opportunities to establish new rules, which is why actors jockey for position in fields.

Both outsiders and insiders can act as institutional entrepreneurs, depending on the situation. Research shows that outsiders are able to challenge institutions due to their position, which renders them unconstrained by existing stakeholders or rules (Maguire & Hardy, 2009). As shown in Chapter 2, Fanning's move at Kykuit is a good example of this type of institutional entrepreneurship. Outsiders can also act as institutional entrepreneurs by importing practices into organizational fields, that is, by transposing them across institutional boundaries (Boxenbaum & Battilana, 2005). Insiders can act as institutional entrepreneurs as well, particularly when they are situated either at the edge of a field or in a position to cross institutional boundaries (Greenwood & Suddaby, 2006). Using social network models, Burt (2004) shows how actors at the periphery of social boundaries are more likely to produce good ideas. Similarly, Vedres and Stark (2010) show how occupying spaces of overlap among group affiliations gives rise to entrepreneurial opportunities. Such positions enable institutional entrepreneurship by affording access to new practices or the ability to exploit multiple identities.

As both an insider and an outsider, Fanning had a unique position vis-à-vis the Circuit Riders. Fanning was an insider by virtue of being invited to the NSNT meetings, which were ostensibly for the central figures in the Circuit Rider movement. She was an outsider because she was not a member of the movement. Rather, she was pulled into nonprofit technology assistance through Jane Meseck, the director of community affairs at Microsoft, who knew Fanning from graduate school, commissioned her to write a white paper on technology in the nonprofit sector, and sent her to the NSNT meetings. Richard Zorza, who worked alongside Circuit Riders from the beginning of the movement, explained Fanning's multiple affiliations: "I think Joan [Fanning] is an exceptional person. She was supported by the National Strategy [for Nonprofit Technology] network and by the ideas that she and we developed as part of that and by her relationships with people including Microsoft. I think the unusual combination of Microsoft resources and reputation behind her innovative capacity and personal skills [contributed to her success]" [60]. In this instance, Fanning's affiliation with the NSNT reflects her position as insider and her connection to Microsoft reflects her position as outsider.

The Situatedness of Institutional Entrepreneurship

Institutional entrepreneurs are actors that are empowered to challenge extant institutions and, when successful, change them. The concept explains certain forms of actor-driven endogenous institutional change. Powell and Colyvas (2008: 277) note that not all institutional change is actor-driven, adding that theories of institutional entrepreneurship are problematic in their focus on actors as either "heroes" or "cultural dopes." Furthermore, scholars have argued that institutional entrepreneurs are treated as superhuman in the literature, based on their ability to supersede powerful actors or remove themselves from the social structure that constrains their action and conditions their rationality[3] (Green & Li, 2011).

A solution to this problem is to shift the focus away from individual actors and toward interactions (Hallett, 2010). In line with this solution, I treat institutional entrepreneurship as an action and institutional entrepreneur as a role. With the right alignment of competences and position, actors can take advantage of certain situations to become institutional entrepreneurs or exercise institutional entrepreneurship. Fanning is not an institutional entrepreneur by virtue of any innate qualities. Rather, she had the relevant competences and occupied a key position at a particular historical moment in which both were important. This chapter attempts to explain actor-driven institutional change by situating institutional entrepreneurship in times and places, focusing on the work of establishing a new account of worth and building an organization to stabilize relations around it. In this case, institutional entrepreneurship bridged movements and markets.

The process by which Fanning and NPower arose followed the trajectory of the Circuit Riders' rise to prominence. As noted above and in Chapter 2, Fanning took advantage of a political opportunity in the Circuit Rider movement. She identified a contradiction between the Circuit Riders' revolutionary rhetoric and resource holders' (i.e., foundation officers') dispositions toward certain accounts. To take advantage of this political opportunity, Fanning had to establish the worth of her alternative account, which took the form of a design for a new way of delivering technology assistance services to the nonprofit sector.

Fanning had a head start establishing the worth of NPower. Her business plan had already convinced Microsoft of NPower's value, as evidenced by the software firm's start-up funding and continued support for the NTAP. Microsoft's endorsement helped secure funding and support from Boeing and Starbucks, each of which donated money and took seats on NPower's board. However, securing the support of multinational corporations is not the same as gaining foundation support. To gain the endorsement and financial support of the latter, Fanning's account had to combine the market practices that endeared NPower to corporate sponsors with the social values important to actors in the nonprofit sector. As noted in Chapter 2, Fanning's work at Kykuit leveraged the Circuit Rider account to convince independent foundations that technology assistance was worth their investment. Building on her success at Kykuit and her relationship to Microsoft, Fanning organized groups of stakeholders to create NPower, which then worked to establish the worth of their model of technology assistance in the nonprofit sector.

How Organizational Forms Matter to Institutional Entrepreneurs

Organizing is a central task of institutional entrepreneurship. Whether building networks or creating organizations, institutional entrepreneurs require stable structures to establish new accounts. Since Fanning leveraged her role as an institutional entrepreneur to build NPower, I will focus on the organization-building aspects of institutional entrepreneurship throughout this chapter and the next.

Institutional entrepreneurs assemble existing organizational elements from the environment into an organizational form (Tracey, Phillips, & Jarvis, 2011). Choosing particular organizational elements and assembling them in certain ways is itself an entrepreneurial strategy. In the case of NPower, Fanning brought together aspects of the Circuit Rider model, rejecting other aspects, along with elements of commercial nonprofit organizations as well as for-profit corporations, to create a social enterprise. As an organizational form, social enterprise reflects the entrepreneurial spirit in some parts of the nonprofit sector (Bielefeld, 2006).

Repertoires of organizational forms exist in and reflect institutional environments. Yet, organizational forms do not exist prêt-à-porter. Rather, entrepreneurs assemble the preexisting building blocks of organizations, combining them with unique elements. In a classic piece of organizational literature, Meyer and Rowan (1977: 345) write that "the building blocks for organizations come to be littered around the societal landscape; it takes only a little entrepreneurial energy to assemble them into a structure." Even when ready-made organizational forms appear to exist, entrepreneurs must "translate" models for local contexts (Czarniawska, 2008; Sahlin-Andersson, 1996). Entrepreneurship is an act of bricolage. Business entrepreneurs combine and reconfigure existing resources to create new economic value (Baker & Nelson, 2005). Social entrepreneurs do the same to create new social value (Di Domenico, Haugh, & Tracey, 2010). When successful, entrepreneurs of either stripe create organizational forms that mobilize adherents while providing access to institutional resources (Clemens, 1996).

Choice of organizational form is important for several reasons. Certain organizational forms are considered legitimate among members of an organizational field (DiMaggio & Powell, 1991b). Choice of organizational form also makes a powerful statement about the identity of the organization and what its leaders want to accomplish. Elisabeth Clemens, scholar of organizations and social movements, notes that "the adoption of new organizational forms is not purely a response to environmental conditions and technological requirements—it is also a political and symbolic act" (Clemens, 1997: 46–47). In other words, choice of organizational form is not simply a technical decision, for example, incorporating as a nonprofit to ensure tax benefits. Organizational forms are political and symbolic representations. The Circuit Riders network form made a statement against hierarchy, reflecting the ideology of social movements from which they came. Fanning's choice of a social enterprise reflected a pragmatic compromise among the social values of many nonprofit and grassroots organizations, the market values of corporate partners, and the value of industriousness favored by many foundation officers that is often expressed as a desire for financial sustainability. In other words, Fanning's social enterprise—and therefore her institutional entrepreneurship—bridged markets and movements.

Fanning could have organized NPower according to any number of logics along the spectrum of movement and market. NPower could have developed a version of a Circuit Rider program, by toning down the activist rhetoric enough to compete successfully for clients and foundation funding. Alternatively, NPower could have organized as a for-profit consulting firm with clientele selected exclusively from the nonprofit sector. Such a move would have rendered NPower ineligible for tax-deductible donations, but it would have given the organization access to equity markets and other forms of capital investment, for example, venture capital. By organizing a social enterprise, a form that bridged movement and market worlds, Fanning created a model of nonprofit technology assistance that helped shift activism toward the market. However, because social values remain a key element of social enterprise, NPower's organizational form signaled that the market for nonprofit technology assistance ought to have certain social values as well.

Social Enterprise as a New Organizational Form

Social enterprise is a relatively new organizational form that applies market solutions and business-like practices to social problems[4] (Bielefeld, 2006). Much of the research on social enterprise has focused on taxonomies (Roper & Cheney, 2005; Thompson, 2002; Weerawardena & Mort, 2006) or normative accounts of such organizations in action (Dees, Economy, Emerson, & NetLibrary Inc., 2001; Dees, Emerson, & Economy, 2002; Emerson & Twersky, 1996). Scholars are just beginning to pay attention to the theoretical and practical implications of social enterprise as an organizational form (Lounsbury, 2004; Nicholls, 2006; Ziegler, 2009). Social enterprise connects entrepreneurship in the general sense with institutional entrepreneurship, as leaders of social enterprises must engage in institutional work on multiple levels (Tracey, Phillips, & Jarvis, 2011; Vasi, 2009).

Although many social enterprises are incorporated as nonprofit organizations, there are no conventions for legal status. For example, Kiva and the Grameen Bank are both social enterprises in the microcredit field. Kiva is nonprofit; Grameen is for-profit. Both are subject to similar evaluative criteria: whether the loans they make help alleviate poverty. Social enterprises are designed to be self-sustaining. Even though nonprofit social enterprises can receive donations from individuals and foundations, such donations are often made based on the organization's potential sustainability. Based on values adopted from the market, sustainability takes on specific meaning as fiscal sustainability, that is, can the organization continue to meet its social mission while relying minimally (or not at all) on donative revenue? Within their deontic system, social enterprises ought to generate all the revenues necessary to achieve their social mission. However, many social enterprises operate in markets for social goods that make such a goal exceedingly difficult to achieve.

The social enterprise form afforded NPower key revenue advantages relative to the Circuit Riders. Whereas the Circuit Riders debated the moral aspects of charging clients fees for services, NPower's social enterprise model embraced such market practices. Charging clients offered NPower a scalable revenue source—the more clients they secured, the more revenue they had to provide services. Due to their revenue model, the Circuit Riders faced near-constant resource problems: the more successful they were at evangelizing for technology among nonprofit and grassroots organizations, the more stretched their budgets became.[5]

The Institutional Hybridity of Social Enterprise

The number of social enterprises in the United States and abroad is growing rapidly (Austin, Stevenson, & Jane, 2006). The institutionalization of social enterprise as a legitimate organizational form reflects the acceptance of certain market values in the voluntary sector (Dart, 2004b). Social enterprise reflects a shift in the moral bases that justify accounts in the nonprofit sector. Definitions of social enterprise remain contested, which allows social entrepreneurs considerable latitude in creating organizations and generating accounts (Nicholls, 2010). Because social enterprises blend values and practices from different institutional domains—for example, from both the market and voluntary sectors—they are considered hybrid organizational forms (Battilana & Dorado, 2010; Cooney, 2006; Hasenfeld & Gidron, 2005; Tracey, Phillips, & Jarvis, 2011).

The institutional hybridity of social enterprise challenges organizational leaders to manage multiple and contradictory institutional expectations (Battilana & Dorado, 2010; Hasenfeld & Gidron, 2005). This challenge also provides opportunities for innovation (Hargrave & Van de Ven, 2009; Jarzabkowski, Matthiesen, & Van de Ven, 2009; Zilber, 2011). In this way, introducing social enterprise into a field and establishing it as a legitimate organizational form is itself already a form of institutional entrepreneurship. The next section of this chapter explains how Fanning assembled existing organizational elements with new innovations in organizing NPower as a social enterprise. The act of combining elements from the institutional environment is called bricolage (Baker & Nelson, 2005; Garud & Karnoe, 2003). Social enterprises are engaged in bricolage insofar as they create social value out of the combination of social and market values (Di Domenico, Haugh, & Tracey, 2010; Swedberg, 2009).

Organizing NPower

The idea for NPower was spawned in the Community Affairs Department at Microsoft. Although Microsoft's business model is to produce and market computer hardware and software, especially its Windows platform and Office programs, the corporation formed a philanthropic arm in 1983. From early in its history, the Community Affairs Department at Microsoft has overseen software donations to the nonprofit sector. With the rise of Circuit Riding in the late 1990s, Microsoft witnessed a sharp rise in requests for software donations. As nonprofits asked for more software; they also asked for more expensive and powerful software. Before long, small, volunteer-driven organizations were requesting enterprise-level database products, leading staff in the Community Affairs Department to wonder whether their donations were being used effectively [15].

To find out, Jane Meseck, the manager of Community Affairs, enlisted Joan Fanning to conduct research about the state of technology use and knowledge in the local nonprofit sector, the Puget Sound area in Washington. Meseck knew Fanning from graduate school at the University of Washington, where they both earned master's degrees in public administration (MPA). Originally from the Midwest, Fanning earned a bachelor's degree in business with a minor in information technology management from Washington University in Saint Louis, Missouri. She worked at a software company for several years before moving to Seattle and enrolling in the MPA program at the University of Washington. Fanning's MPA focused on public policy and information technology. After earning her MPA, Fanning worked in the nonprofit sector for a decade, mostly with domestic violence organizations, helping with service delivery but also setting up computer labs for them. With Meseck, Fanning helped conduct focus groups of Microsoft grantees and eventually took over the research, which culminated in a white paper. In her white paper, Fanning described a need among nonprofit organizations in the region for better knowledge about technology. Fanning made a diagnosis: nonprofits were asking for software they did not need because they lacked sufficient technical knowledge about information technologies. To solve this problem, Fanning suggested that Microsoft start an organization to help nonprofits acquire and deploy technology. Microsoft agreed and provided Fanning with funding to write a business plan for such an organization.

Fanning began drafting her business plan in 1998. Writing the business plan for NPower was an act of bricolage. In it, Fanning assembled elements of existing NTAP programs with her experience working in the nonprofit sector to create a social enterprise. As noted in Chapter 2, Fanning participated in the National Strategy for Nonprofit Technology. From her involvement with the NSNT and attendance at the Riders Roundups, Fanning understood the Circuit Riders and the world of nonprofit technology assistance, which allowed her to draw from existing organizational and service-delivery models in formulating a new NTAP. The experience equipped her with competences relevant to the NTAP field. Her business plan cites several organizations that inspired NPower: IT Resource Center, Compumentor, Fund for the City of New York, ONE Northwest , and the Support Center for Nonprofit Management. Fanning selected certain elements of each, discarding others, creatively selecting and recombining organizational traits from the institutional environment to create something new. As she explained, "I chose pieces of their [other NTAPs] models that I think worked really well, which was working with nonprofits. I also did the opposite of things that I thought really were not doing a favor to the nonprofits" [19].

Competences in Action: Making Markets out of Movements

Fanning created NPower as a response to the Circuit Rider movement. In particular, Fanning was responding to what she called the Circuit Rider's "niche market" strategy. Framing the Circuit Riders' approach to technology assistance in such terms already introduces a market ideology into the field of NTAPs. The problem with this strategy, according to Fanning, was the "self-righteousness" by which organizations were considered worthy of Circuit Riders' help:

> I have worked for years in direct [social] service delivery, doing domestic violence human services. They [organizations involved in direct social service delivery] are doing social change. It [Circuit Riders' exclusivity with social justice organizations] felt like this real judgmental thing. I think the hardest work is the doing. I think the agencies working on the ground, working with kids at risk, working with the elderly; they are doing the work of social change. They might not be advocating; they might not be lobbying; but they are doing the hard stuff. So, leading off with 'we will only work with those doing social change,' I just thought it was really patronizing quite honestly. [19]

Fanning used terms such as "judgmental" and "patronizing" to describe the Circuit Riders' attitude toward which organizations are doing the work of social change. Fanning understood the Circuit Riders' methods of achieving social change as narrow and misguided. The problem went as deep as their definition of "the good" and what it means to be worthy. The Circuit Riders' notions of worth rested on radical social change and far-left politics. Upon such a basis for evaluating worth, Circuit Riders considered only organizations that align with their ideals, such as environmental or social justice groups, worthy of their services. In other words, some missions were more worthy than others of support.

Fanning challenged this ideal, moving to introduce more liberal notions of the market to the nonprofit technology assistance field. Fanning expressed her market ideals in an organizational form by designing NPower to work with any 501(c)(3) organization. As she explained: "Many of the [Circuit] Riders would just pick and choose [which organizations] were progressive social change organizations. I thought, 'how do you define who is doing that?' That requires labeling the organization, what they are doing. . . . I recoiled against that. I thought, 'we [NPower] are going to be open to any 501(c)(3) public charity, because they are all doing really good stuff'" [19].

NPower's prospectus stated the organization's mission: "The mission of NPower is to help nonprofit organizations in Greater Puget Sound use information technology in delivering their services more effectively and efficiently. In pursuit of this mission, NPower will provide clients with a continuum of technology assistance services that are anchored in knowledge of the nonprofit industry, and are affordable and of the highest quality" (NPower, 1998: 2). Contrary to the Circuit Riders, NPower claimed to be agnostic about the mission of a nonprofit organization. Fanning explained the mission at a meeting of executive directors of NPower Affiliates, "First of all, we are about serving the nonprofit sector. So it is that passion for helping nonprofits make a difference in their community that drives our work. It really is about that impact. Because of our work, are lives being improved? Are communities stronger? What is the impact? That is our mission: to help nonprofits have the tools to really serve their communities" (Fieldnotes 10–16–2002).

On the surface, Fanning's rhetoric recalled the Circuit Rider's account. However, differences arose in its justification. NPower would assist in making nonprofit organizations more effective and efficient. Terms such as "effectiveness" and "efficiency" reflect a different moral basis than those used to justify the Circuit Riders' account. Whereas Circuit Riding was justified based on its contribution to social justice and environmentalism, NPower justified its practices based on contributions to efficiency and effectiveness in the nonprofit sector. Although Circuit Riders worked exclusively with organizations whose missions aligned with their own, NPower judged the worthiness of prospective clients based on the democracy of the market, that is, on an organization's ability to pay.

Beyond ideology, Fanning's critique of the Circuit Riders had consequences for NPower's ability to create a market for technology services in the nonprofit sector. NPower's *Prospectus* contains an analysis defining NPower's principal market as "the approximately 1,360 501(c)(3) public charities with annual revenues between $100,000 and $5 million in King, Pierce, and Snohomish Counties" (NPower, 1998: 6). Although ostensibly a small market, the NPower *Prospectus* notes that none of the prospective competitors in the nonprofit technology assistance market in Seattle works with all types of nonprofit organizations. Each operates within a specific niche. ONE Northwest, for example, works exclusively with environmental groups, which represent only 3% of nonprofit organizations in Washington State and 3.3% of the sector nationally, accounting for only 1.2% of the sector's assets (Weitzman, Jalandoni, Lampkin, & Pollak, 2002: 134). In contrast, NPower was willing to work with any 501(c)(3) organization, which offered a considerably larger market. Additionally, NPower made geography part of its mission. This meant that they would also cut the overhead associated with the Circuit Riders' substantial travel budget. Beyond saving money, defining their potential market geographically within driving distance meant that NPower's consulting staff could serve more organizations in less time.

Practically, Fanning borrowed elements of professionalized NTAPs in organizing NPower. For example, Fanning took the practice of charging fees for services from the IT Resource Center, a long-standing NTAP based in Chicago, as Fanning explained:

> The IT Resource Center had some interesting business models [such as various] fee-for-service [models], although I chose a different one, and the membership. But you know, honestly, IT Resource Center felt a bit soulless. They did not have that passion, you know, they are more traditional, and I do not mean to label them, but it felt more like traditional capacity building where it was this professionalized field focused on their work and then they give it to the nonprofit. It was not 'we believe so passionately in what nonprofits do that we want to help them.' It just felt like it [IT Resource Center] had lost a bit of that. [19]

Fanning organized NPower as a rejection of certain elements of Circuit Riding, particularly the moral basis of activism and the niche-based approach to the market for technology assistance. In its place, Fanning organized NPower around market-based principles and practices, such as making services available to all nonprofit organizations that could afford them and charging clients fees for services. However, NPower was also critical of overly professionalized NTAPs, which felt "soulless" to her. The result was a strategic selection of key elements from the organizational environment, some of which came from the Circuit Riders.

Movements Shape Markets

NPower was not a wholesale rejection of Circuit Riding. As a social enterprise, the organization combined market values with social values gleaned from the Circuit Rider movement. However, taking on elements from the institutional environment entails translation (Callon, 1986; Latour, 2005; Sahlin-Andersson, 1996). This means that entrepreneurs interpret meanings and alter structures from the institutional environment, adapting them to the local context and circumstances of the organizations they are assembling. Applying her competences at Kykuit, Fanning recognized that certain values were more legitimate than others. When she found expressions of those values in existing organizational elements, she adopted them for NPower.

The Circuit Riders had been successful in attracting resources and adherents to build a movement. Fanning found value in parts of the Circuit Riders' model and adapted some of their practices for NPower. In her research for NPower, she spoke with members of ONE Northwest, which prides itself on working exclusively with environmental groups throughout the Pacific Northwest, from Northern California through Alaska, including coastal British Columbia. Jon Stahl, a consultant with ONE Northwest since 1997, explained their mission: "It leans very clearly toward the environmental community. Our job is to serve the environmental community. Our success and our mission is determined by how good a job we do by that community" [36]. Based on her earlier quote, one expects that she would consider ONE Northwest "judgmental" and "patronizing." Instead, Fanning admired their "100 percent unwavering commitment to the mission of the organizations they work with. They care. Everything they do is informed by 'will this help the environment?'" [19].

Fanning articulated her admiration for ONE Northwest's commitment to the mission of the organizations they served by including a membership component to NPower. Membership was Fanning's attempt to organize a community of organizations around NPower. In exchange for an annual fee, nonprofit organizations could become members of NPower. For clients, the primary benefit of membership was discounted consulting services.[6] According to some, membership was a self-serving interpretation of the Circuit Riders' commitment to the mission of the organizations they served. As the director of one NTAP told me, "We believe that their motivation [with] membership is basically building a market, building market loyalty" [32].

In creating NPower, Fanning borrowed selectively from the traditional Circuit Rider model. For example, in this quote she echoes Jeremy Edes-Pierotti, the first Circuit Rider hired by the W. Alton Jones Foundation (see Chapter 1, excerpts from interview [18]): "I structured the organization [NPower] and the staff who we hired so that, first and foremost, I looked for an intimate understanding and experience in the nonprofit sector" [19]. Fanning went on to explain that "the biggest value you could bring to your customer was understanding their business, and then you would be cocreating with them. . . . So that was one thing I pulled from the [Circuit] Riders" [19]. Fanning translates the Circuit Riders' affinity for social movements in which they were members into an affinity for the business of the nonprofit sector. It is important to note that part of the translation entailed a move from understanding what the movement was trying to accomplish to "understanding their [i.e., a singular nonprofit organization's] business."

Fanning also borrowed other features from the Circuit Rider movement in organizing NPower. As mentioned in Chapter 2, Fanning took over finalizing the National Strategy for Nonprofit Technology planning document. Over six months, she also helped transform that planning document into the Nonprofit Technology Enterprise Network, the trade association for NTAPs. Several of NPower's "core values" are taken directly from the NSNT planning document. The value of knowledge sharing is a good example, as Fanning explained at a conference for NPower affiliates called the NPower Summit: "[NPower] is a mission-based organization. While we are focusing on services, we want to frame that in values and how we are going to operate. And so even at the local level we committed to free sharing of information. That free sharing of information would be tools and products that we create for nonprofits. We share with other nonprofits as well as our internal learning [with NPower affiliates]. So from day one, we committed to free sharing of information" (Fieldnotes 10–15–2002).

The "free sharing of information" was a core value of the NSNT from its foundation in the Circuit Rider movement. In planning documents for the first NSNT meeting in Atlanta, Stuart articulated the organizing principles of the initiative, one of which he called "reciprocity": "By sharing knowledge we have learned through hard-won experience, we can insure our access to others' knowledge." In an interview, Stuart explained how NPower adopted certain ideals of the Circuit Rider movement: "The irony is that NPower has actually realized the original vision of NSNT. It [the vision] is a set of standards from Atlanta [the first NSNT meeting]. It is in all these strategic places and it is very network-centric. There is learning. There is knowledge sharing" [76].

What appears on the surface as inconsistency actually demonstrates the competence of institutional entrepreneurs qua bricoleurs. The basis of entrepreneurial competence is the ability to select among moral orders to evaluate and justify your work and the work of others. Yet, entrepreneurial competence is limited by the small number of institutionally appropriate moral orders, meaning that there are only so many ways that entrepreneurs can justify their behavior and still make sense to other actors in the field. To be considered legitimate, entrepreneurs must appear sensible (rational) to other actors in the field (Ashforth & Gibbs, 1990). Doing so requires institutional entrepreneurs to balance innovation with existing practices. For Fanning, this meant creating NPower as a social enterprise that blended the social values of the existing field—that is, those of the Circuit Riders—with the market values that appealed to current and potential corporate and philanthropic supporters.

Besides providing the claimed inspiration for the membership model, the Circuit Riders' philanthropic model of remuneration constrained NPower's market-based approach to service delivery. In the original and pure model, the Circuit Riders' services were funded exclusively by philanthropy (a third-party-payer model). Fanning adapted the model for NPower's model of social enterprise: "Membership dues and fees-for-services are expected to supply approximately 25 to 30 percent of NPower revenues. The balance of operating and capital expenses will be raised from philanthropic underwriters" (NPower, 1998: 1). The result was a blending of market practices (e.g., charging fees for services, adopting the language of professional consulting, developing market metrics, and collaborating with for-profit corporations) with social values (e.g., serving nonprofit organizations exclusively, charging below-market fees, and subsidizing services through philanthropic support). However, in doing so, Fanning also adapted the meaning of philanthropic support for the context of social enterprise.

Institutional Entrepreneurship as Position: Leveraging Relationships to Fund NPower

Incorporated as a 501(c)(3), NPower raised money primarily from corporate and foundation donors. However, the organization was business-like even in its fund-raising. A case study about NPower written for the University of Washington notes that NPower's board "will guide major organizational decisions based on the social venture capital model" (Salm, 2000: 8). Fanning explained the partnership with Microsoft as based on such a model at a meeting of NPower affiliates: "I firmly believe that Microsoft is really a model of what venture philanthropy looks like when it works well. Not very many people represent that. How do I define venture philanthropy? Really, you have an equal partner at the table. You both come together because you have the same mission. You bring different resources and tools and then you work together in a complete partnership to achieve that mission. And Microsoft has done a great job modeling what successful venture philanthropy looks like" (Field-notes 10–16–2002).

Venture philanthropy models align well with the libertarian brand of capitalism that dominated the high-tech sector during the dot-com boom (Borsook, 2000; Indergaard, 2004; Rifkin, 2000). Venture capital funding was central to the creation of many high-tech start-ups throughout the period. Many high-tech parvenus applied venture capital values and practices to help transform the world of philanthropy (Moody, 2008). Paul Brainerd, a venture philanthropist who made his money in the high-tech boom, was a leader in that movement.[7] Brainerd established an eponymous foundation and organized Social Venture Partners, a consortium of venture philanthropists. He explains the principles of the model: "invest in people and their ideas," "take risks and manage a portfolio of investments," "take a long-term approach in terms of our funding," "measure outcomes to a much greater degree than has been done in the nonprofit world in the past," and "develop deeper, more engaged relationships or partnerships with the nonprofits" (1999). Venture philanthropy translates the traditional values and practices of philanthropy into expressions of market principles. As the legitimacy of venture philanthropy grew, its ideas permeated traditional foundation approaches, particularly its commitment to standardized performance metrics and the intervention of funders qua investors (Frumkin, 2003).

NPower benefited from the rise of venture philanthropy as well as its proximity to the high-tech boom in Seattle, which featured defense contractors such as Boeing as well as independent technology firms such as Microsoft, both of which were major funders for NPower. Corporate foundations tend to support organizations in cities where their headquarters are located (Galaskiewicz & Bielefeld, 1998; Useem, 1987). NPower was not the first NTAP established in Seattle. However, Fanning embraced venture philanthropy from the outset and employed its rhetoric in enrolling corporate partners into supporting NPower. Social venture entrepreneurship employs the values and practices of venture capitalism for altruistic, and generally nonprofit, activities.[8]

NPower received founding grants from corporations (Microsoft and Boeing) and foundations (the Seattle Foundation and Medina Foundation). By the end of 1998, NPower had raised $1.7 million in donations from philanthropic sources. Of this sum, $1 million came from independent nonprofit foundations and $500,000 in cash and $200,000 in in-kind donations came from corporations and corporate foundations. In comparison, the largest competing NTAPs in the country, Compumentor and IT Resource Center, raised approximately $500,000 and $230,000, respectively, from such philanthropic sources in 1998. In 1999, NPower's donated revenue dropped to just over $1 million. However, the organization raised $3.5 million in 2000 to fund operations as well as a national expansion of the model.

NPower supplemented its philanthropic support with earned revenues from membership and fees-for-services. In the NPower *Prospectus* (1998: 1), Fanning projected earned revenues of between 25% and 30% of NPower's operating budget. In practice, NPower earned $161,000 in 1999, its first year of operation, which represented only 8% of its operating budget. Earned revenues increased significantly in subsequent years. Table 3.1 shows NPower's projected and actual revenue breakdown for the first four years of operation. As the figures show, NPower exceeded projected donations and earned revenues each year from 1999 to 2003. Although donations fluctuated from year to year, NPower continued to increase its earned revenue each year, roughly maintaining the projected percentage of the total operating budget from that source.

TABLE 3.1
NPower Seattle revenues, 1999–2003

	Donations		Earned		Total operating	Percent
Year	Projected	Actual	Projected	Actual	budget	earned
1999	$531,882	$1,739,600	$53,959	$161,417	$1,901,017	8
2000	$486,339	$1,089,467	$108,977	$539,632	$1,629,099	33
2001	$537,716	$3,501,651	$126,960	$721,342	$4,212,803	17
2002	$631,429	$1,979,764	$143,219	$751,568	$2,718,612	28
2003	$609,258	$2,483,290	$190,422	$897,552	$3,458,910	26

SOURCES: Projected: NPower Prospectus, p. 18; Actuals: IRS Form 990, years 1999–2003.

For NPower, embracing social enterprise meant combining the values of the NTAP field (e.g., working with nonprofit organizations) with those of its partners in the business world (e.g., financial stability, competitiveness, and growth). The combination was intentional. Jane Meseck called NPower "a high-tech start-up in the nonprofit world" [15]. Nikki Roberg, who coordinates NPower's national program, explained the difference between her organization and a typical nonprofit: "We are more entrepreneurial, first of all. We are pretty business-oriented" [24].

Generating Market Accounts

Like Stuart, Fanning created an account in order to establish the worth of NPower's approach to nonprofit technology assistance. Fanning offered her initial account to foundation officers at Kykuit as an alternative to the Circuit Riders. Fanning's account was predicated on a business-like model of nonprofit technology assistance, grounded in market principles, expressed in a business plan, and justified by a claim that it would be financially sustainable while providing services to many more nonprofit organizations. The success of Fanning's challenge to the Circuit Rider account at Kykuit provided her with access to resources with which to construct an organization. The NPower account continued to evolve beyond this initial stage. In this next section, I explain the construction and ongoing evolution of NPower's account through the creation of metrics—quantitative measures designed to evaluate the performance of organizational practices. Like all accounts, those based on metrics selectively represent organizational realities, focusing stakeholders' attention on particular aspects of its performance (Anderson, 1997). However, unlike more narrative accounts, accounts based on metrics are designed to appear objective (Desrosières, 2001; Hägglund, 2000; Rottenburg, Kalthoff, & Wagener, 2000). Metrics provide a very specific language with which to express worth in organizational fields. In doing so, they create as much as reflect reality. Therefore, creating metrics is itself a form of institutional entrepreneurship in nascent fields (DeJean, Gond, & Leca, 2004). In NPower's case, creating market-based metrics meant that Fanning's institutional entrepreneurship measured movement practices on market principles—bridging movement and market.

Metrics Matter

Metrics express values in a form amenable to calculation and comparison (accounts as bookkeeping). They are heuristics that allow actors to judge the worth of accounts and the practices they describe using quantitative tools. Metrics entail translating social and market values into numbers, which allow stakeholders to compare the performance of different organizations across social worlds, such as those inhabited by foundation officers and the NTAPs they fund (Czarniawski, 2000; Rottenburg, 2000). The social process underlying the creation of metrics is commensuration, that is, making different things comparable with a common measure. Commensuration is a social process involving setting up and agreeing on systems of measurement and equivalence (Boltanski & Chiapello, 2005; Espeland & Stevens, 1998). However, as things are measured, systems of commensuration also focus attention on what is important about those things: "Commensuration can be understood as a system for discarding information and organizing what remains into new forms. In abstracting and reducing information, the link between what is represented and the empirical world is obscured, and uncertainty is absorbed. . . . Everyday experience, practical reasoning, and empathetic identification become increasingly irrelevant bases for judgment as context is stripped away and relationships become more abstractly represented by numbers" (Espeland and Stevens 1998: 317).

Many organizations develop metrics to evaluate and account for their performance. For-profit organizations often rely on legitimated or standardized metrics to give accounts of their performance, such as price-to-earnings ratios and return on investment. What makes them legitimate is that they are widely accepted as representing some underlying performance. Organizations in the nonprofit sector have long struggled to create legitimate metrics (Herman & Renz, 1997, 1999, 2002). Much of the challenge in creating and legitimating metrics in the nonprofit sector has to do with the difficulty in developing quantifiable measures for social goods (Kanter & Summers, 1987; R. Young, 2006). At the heart of this problem is relating metrics to the mission of an organization under conditions of uncertainty. For example, Feeding America is a nationwide network of food banks whose mission is "to feed America's hungry through a nationwide network of member food banks and engage our country in the fight to end hunger" (Feeding America, 2012). Figuring out how well Feeding America is achieving its mission is a challenge and not just a technical one. Furthermore, organizations are accountable to multiple stakeholders (Donaldson & Preston, 1995). Nonprofit organizations, such as Feeding America, are accountable to foundations and individual donors, the people they serve, local governments, and the communities in which their food banks are located. As a result, many nonprofit organizations rely on what they call process measures (e.g., the number of meals served), rather than outcome measures (e.g., the number of people who are no longer hungry) of performance (Forbes, 1998; Holland, 1988; Light, 2002; Murray & Tassie, 1994).

Hybrid organizational forms, such as social enterprises, are said to be subject to the "double bottom line" of proving social and market effectiveness (Dart, 2004b; Emerson & Twersky, 1996). The double bottom line complicates accountability for social enterprises. Social enterprises that rely too heavily on market metrics may be accused of sacrificing social values for market values. Borrowing too many social impact metrics from the nonprofit sector may undermine the ability of social enterprises to make claims of financial sustainability. Social enterprises and the foundations that fund them have experimented with Social Return on Investment (SROI). SROI attempts to reconcile social and market effectiveness and meet the demands of the double bottom line with a single metric. SROI compares the achievement of concrete social goals against the amount of money spent to achieve them, allowing investors or donors to evaluate how well their money was spent. The approach to evaluation has been successfully applied to microfinance, where microcredit loans are specified in currency and produce businesses whose valuation can be determined by the amount of income they bring to the borrower as well as how much money they contribute to the local economy. However, social enterprises have struggled with using the metric in domains less amenable to quantitative measurement, such as the arts and homelessness (Quarter, Mook, & Richmond, 2003; Quarter & Richmond, 2001; Rotheroe & Richards, 2007; Ryan & Lyne, 2008; Young, 2006). This challenge is particularly acute with nonprofit technology assistance providers, whose performance is based on improving the performance of other organizations.

Metrics at NPower

Beyond the complexity of performance measurement for social enterprise, technology assistance metrics were especially problematic. Richard Zorza, who worked alongside the Circuit Riders, explained: "We were having a research group discussion and I ended up saying that I was interested in research that shows 'is it a difference that makes a difference?' Most of the people who are engaged with most technology innovation in the nonprofit sector really see it in efficiency terms. 'So we used to communicate with ten people, now we are communicating with 50 or 100.' Rather than does this actually change the relationship between the helping and the helped, does this change the institutional role that antipoverty organizations can play in a poor community?" [60]. In other words, NTAPs were stuck employing process measures (the change in number of people reached), rather than gold-standard outcome measures ("the difference that makes a difference").

Early on, NPower set to work on the problem of performance metrics for technology assistance. Solving it would give NPower two key advantages in the field. First, performance metrics provide legitimacy to accounts. As Berger and Luckmann (1966: 61) point out, "the institutional world requires legitimation, that is, ways by which it can be 'explained' and justified." In the nonprofit and business worlds, performance metrics justify the activities of organizations (Meyer, 1994; Meyer & O'Shaughnessy, 1993). The WAJF Circuit Rider program gained credibility and helped establish the worth of Circuit Riding when the foundation was able to show that it provided working Internet access to 50 organizations for $122,000. Quantitative metrics reflect the calculative rationality embraced by businesses (Miller, 2001), which was also favored by prospective corporate sponsors as well as similarly inclined independent foundations. Second, the creation of performance metrics is a form of institutional entrepreneurship (DeJean, Gond, & Leca, 2004). By creating and legitimating a set of metrics, institutional entrepreneurs can establish appropriate ways of judging the actions of organizations in the field. Having systems in place to evaluate organizational activities offers institutional entrepreneurs and their organizations a competitive advantage in the market for legitimacy.

According to managers at NPower, technology assistance is ultimately about bolstering the performance of the nonprofit organizations it serves. For an organization such as NPower, which serves nonprofit organizations with various missions, comparing an intervention with an arts organization with that of a homeless shelter is extremely difficult, as Joan Fanning explained:

> Ultimately, if the agency does not measure their mission impact in quantifiable ways, you are stuck with agency self-reports as well as some observation. What we are doing right now is self-reports. We have done some case studies and observation. Hopefully we are on the right path, but we do not have anything completely quantifiable. Our last [evaluation] report, lots of agencies said, 'yeah, we think it has helped our mission, but we do not know by how much.' That is where we are trying to slowly get to. To really measure impact on mission, you have to have some sort of proxy measures. [19]

In this quote, Fanning expresses the challenge of producing outcome measures for technology assistance providers. Since the client organizations do not have quantitative performance measures themselves, it becomes difficult for NTAPs to know whether they have made a difference, especially one that "makes a difference." Instead, like many nonprofit organizations, NPower turned to process measures to demonstrate their effectiveness. Jane Meseck, who helped start NPower from her position at Microsoft, explained the institutional environment of data collection among NTAPs: "In my research, I found that not a lot of metrics and measurement was being done by peer organizations. If you ask one of the peer organizations, 'what is your earned income?,' they did not know. 'Oh, we do not get more than 30%. Maybe it is about 30%.' But none of them had done a lot of data gathering in the past. We were going into a lot of unknown [territory]. No one knew how to provide any of that. They gave us best guesses, but they did not have any actual data" [15]. One of the first metrics NPower began to track was its level of earned income, broken down in several ways, including by service as well as by client characteristics. Earned income metrics served as a proxy "Return on Investment" metric for corporate sponsors and independent foundation donors. As a 501(c)(3), NPower could not distribute excess earnings to these parties (Hansmann, 1980). However, demonstrating earned revenues expressed success with clients that key resource holders rewarded with additional donations. As Jane Meseck explained: "NPower Seattle actuals [reported metrics] blew away everyone's best guesses, including earned income. So, right away, NPower jumped kind of ahead of [all other NTAPs]. Maybe it was because they did better data tracking" [15].

However, by developing metrics such as earned income, NPower contributed to the creation of a market reality. In practice, "better data tracking" at NPower meant quantitative performance metrics. Many Circuit Riders had a tenuous relationship to performance metrics. Most kept track of client satisfaction, which was often expressed as narrative or by virtue of the fact that the client returned for additional services. The larger Circuit Rider organizations published case studies about how their interventions helped client organizations. However, for most Circuit Rider groups, performance metrics were not a key focus of their work. As one Circuit Rider told me: "We do not spend $100,000 a year on evaluation. Resources are limited. There is always more we would like to know, but it costs a lot of money" [36].

NPower dedicated significant resources to developing and implementing quantitative performance metrics. Throughout my time in the field, managers at NPower worked closely with professional program evaluation consultants to continuously refine their collection of metrics as the organization implemented them and then evaluated the system of evaluation. One director at the national office told me: "We started with three years of evaluation. I think Joan was smart in thinking that we could not continue to be who we are unless we could show it. In the next three years, we will be doing more and more, like *social return on investment*. I think we are really looking to see what is [the] impact of our services on the community" [42; emphasis added]. At times, staff felt the drive toward quantitative metrics consumed too much attention at NPower. The director of outreach, who managed NPower's national expansion, explained, "My god, at one point we got up to 176 categories that staff could use to report their time, not including billable client engagements" [35].

Metrics and Market Making

Metrics provide the tools of commensuration that make market competition possible. Consumers rely on satisfaction metrics when making purchases (e.g., J.D. Power and Associates' automobile satisfaction ratings). Investors rely on performance metrics when determining stocks and bonds to purchase. Internally, metrics are the basis for business accounting[9] (Miller, 2001). Accounts based on quantitative performance metrics appear objective and therefore more legitimate than other accounts, which allows organizations to make and substantiate competitive claims. Because of their obsessive data tracking, NPower was able to make such claims to foundations as well as to corporate sponsors, which gave the organization a competitive advantage in fund-raising. As a manager at NPower conveyed in an anecdote:

> I had an embarrassing meeting with [another NTAP]. We were at Cisco, and I feel bad I put [the executive director] on the spot. I said well, "what is the breakdown of nonprofits that you serve?" Because we were talking about 50% fee-for-service, so we have a profile. He was like, "we do not capture it that way, we do not know." I was like, "how do you not know who you serve?" It was hard because I felt like we introduced that rigor. We have to know what difference we are making in the community. We have to know is there impact that we are making and which groups we are serving. Because capacity building is such a hard case to make and technology is that much more divorced from kids and puppies. [42]

Performance metrics such as percentage of earned revenue signal the importance of market principles at NPower. However, the organization developed metrics for every aspect of its activities. Aside from (earned and donated) income measures, NPower tracked client demographics, consulting hours, training hours, expenditures per consulting hour, employee productivity, volunteer hours, client satisfaction, board satisfaction, board fund-raising, membership goals, and so forth. NPower even had metrics to assess the rate at which affiliates were adopting the organization's system of metrics.[10] The volume of tools the organization produced to produce and track metrics occupied over 6 megabytes of files on the shared servers. Many of the organization's metrics were developed by professional program evaluation consultants. At one point, NPower tapped McKinsey, a multinational consulting firm, to help it develop performance metrics for the entire network. The organization kept track of its metrics in a client-management-system database built by Changepoint. Regional affiliates entered data into a shared system, which allowed managers at the national office to monitor their productivity. They also produced quarterly reports, which they submitted to managers at the national office, and annual reports, which they shared with all affiliate managers at an annual meeting.

Beyond sharing them among affiliates, NPower disseminated key metrics throughout the nonprofit technology assistance field in reports and at conferences. In doing so, NPower was effectively shaping the cognitive-cultural institutions of the field. In 2001, NPower published its first evaluation report, which was produced by a professional program evaluation consultant. The report presented the key metrics NPower developed as well as the results of tracking them. For example, NPower presented data on its members by size, geographic area, and service area. The report broke down all the training and consulting services the organization delivered by client status. Furthermore, NPower was also able to show which organizations were using and satisfied with which services. NPower's 2001 evaluation report was a breakthrough in the NTAP field. No other NTAP had presented such sophisticated metrics to its stakeholders before. NPower shared the report with foundation and corporate donors as a way of garnering legitimacy with them. To disseminate their metrics to the larger field, the report was made available on NPower's website. Executives from NPower also presented their metrics and the findings of their report at the National Technology Conference.

One indicator of the legitimacy of NPower's performance metrics was that they were emulated by other groups, especially Circuit Rider groups. When TechRocks switched to a fee-for-service model, members of the organization began tracking earned income as a performance metric. As Marshall Mayer, one of TechRocks's directors, explained:

> We are moving toward much more of a fee-for-service model. It used to be that we would do all of these engagements purely subsidized by foundations. Sometimes the organizations wanted it and sometimes they did not. You know, "the foundation made me do it, so I am doing it." And now we are moving much more to a fee-for-service model where an organization is going to put down some money—however they raise it is immaterial to us. But our measure is "are they going to put down more money a little later on to go the next step?" "Are they going to go out and raise that money, or are they going to take that out of the general operating funds and actually go the next step?"[11] [11]

NPower's quantitative metrics provided an account of nonprofit technology that aligned with the institutional expectations of corporate sponsors and like-minded independent foundations. With the spread of NPower's metrics, Fanning strengthened her role as an institutional entrepreneur in the field of NTAPs. A leader in the NTAP field, Jillaine Smith, explained: "I would say that the introduction of NPower also has really shifted the community a bit. Joan [Fanning] introduced a level of rigor that has not existed in the sector. . . .

She has introduced a level of business planning and rigor and evaluation that I think is controversial for the [NTAP] sector because it is not comfortable. It is a different way of doing it, but I think it is a good discomfort" [63].

The metrics developed and employed by NPower focused the attention of managers, foundation officers, and corporate sponsors on the market aspects of nonprofit technology assistance. Such metrics justified the account of technology assistance by reference to market values, such as earned income and expenditures per consulting hour. However, not everyone was happy with the spread of NPower's metrics. Michael Gilbert explained: "I am bothered by some of the efforts to create such metrics in the nonprofit sector. I really do believe that the common metrics in the for-profit sector represent a common set of values. It is capital. The values of capitalism are the values inherent in the tool, in the metrical tools that are used to assess performance in an institution. I believe that the nonprofit sector is too diverse for such tools, for such metrics" [40].

NPower Ascendant

Once established, NPower became the model for nonprofit technology assistance in the United States. Fanning's position and competences meant that NPower had access as well as the capabilities of engaging resource holders, such as independent foundations and corporations. NPower's market account helped the organization gain legitimacy in the nonprofit sector and beyond. NPower grew in budget size as it attracted resources from business and nonprofit worlds. The organization demonstrated its worth through the innovative creation and dissemination of performance metrics, which presented the account of the NPower model as superior to competing models of technology assistance.

This produced two outcomes. First, NPower was given grants to expand nationally, which I will discuss in the next chapter. Second, existing NTAPs, such as TechRocks and Compumentor, began to adopt elements of the NPower model, as I will explain in more detail in Chapter 5. To many Circuit Riders, NPower came to represent the future of nonprofit technology assistance. Gavin Clabaugh, who created the Circuit Rider model and later came to fund the movement from his position at the Mott Foundation, explained: "NPower . . . is a terrific organization for a number of reasons, (A) it is very fundable, (B) it has got great pizzazz, or recognition of its name. It has got a great track record. People seem to like it" [16]. In an interview, Carnet Williams, who started a

Circuit Rider organization called Net Corps, described how NPower has transformed the field:

> It was hard to detract from [NPower] because they were doing the great work. They had a very strong business plan that Joan [Fanning] had put together and they were being successful. A good example of this was even in San Francisco, where you had a lot of nonprofit support organizations, like Compasspoint, Compumentor, and a bunch of others. Even they felt very uncomfortable when NPower was talking about doing something in San Francisco. That was how much influence NPower had. I think everyone kind of fell in line quickly with NPower after that. I am not making judgments. That was just the difference in how [NPower was] able to move forward and how others were struggling along. [51]

Bridging Movements and Markets

This chapter presented the rise of Joan Fanning and NPower to show how institutional entrepreneurs bridge movements and markets. Institutional entrepreneurs leverage competences and position to challenge existing institutional arrangements and organize them according to their interests. Fanning's competences included recognizing a critical turning point in the Circuit Rider movement and understanding the desires of key actors, such as resource holders. Her position was that of both insider and outsider, which gave her the knowledge necessary to understand the field as well as access to innovative ideas she could import from other fields. Fanning's choice of organizational form and development of metrics bridged the Circuit Rider movement and the market for technology assistance. Fanning borrowed elements from the institutional landscape, such as components of the Circuit Rider model and the social enterprise organizational form, and combined them with new elements to fashion NPower. Performance metrics supported a market account on which the organization was based. In doing so, Fanning and NPower helped transform the Circuit Rider movement into a market for technology assistance in the nonprofit sector.

To secure the success of her institutional entrepreneurship, Fanning pressed NPower to develop quantitative metrics. By providing seemingly objective measures of performance, NPower's metrics justified the market practices the organization introduced into the nonprofit technology assistance field. Recall

Stuart's attempt at institutional entrepreneurship from Chapter 2. His institutional entrepreneurship failed because his revolutionary account of Circuit Riding did not resonate with resource holders in the field, such as foundation officers. There is nothing innate about either account that led to the success of NPower over the Circuit Riders. Rather, Fanning's account aligned with shifts in the nonprofit sector toward the legitimacy of market solutions. Further, she provided evidence of the effectiveness of her account that aligned with the epistemology of foundation officers and corporate sponsors, something Stuart was unable to offer. By establishing the metrics by which work in the field was evaluated, Fanning's account passed the test that she helped to construct. In this way, metric-making is a form of institutional entrepreneurship that was able to bridge movements and markets.

The institutional entrepreneurial work of combining elements from various institutional environments—for example, market metrics and commitment to the nonprofit sector—created conditions of institutional multiplicity within NPower (Jarzabkowski, Matthiesen, & Van de Ven, 2009). The evidence I presented in this chapter shows how NPower benefited from institutional multiplicity. However, such a condition creates uncertainty among actors in the field, including the institutional entrepreneurs that attempt to take advantage of it. The next chapter turns to the problem faced by actors in the field as they attempt to reconcile the competing demands of institutional multiplicity in moral markets.

WALKING THE VALUES TIGHTROPE

The Moral Ambivalence of Social Enterprise

With NPower, Joan Fanning built a bridge from the Circuit Rider movement to a market for technology assistance services in the nonprofit sector. Fanning articulated an alternative account to that of the Circuit Riders in NPower, a nonprofit technology assistance provider that took the social enterprise organizational form. The social enterprise form allowed Fanning to appeal to the social values important to the nonprofit sector and the market values held by for-profit corporations. Fashioning an account that appealed simultaneously to multiple value systems (or orders of worth) enabled Fanning to access resources and legitimacy from diverse actors in the field. Her entrepreneurial strategy made NPower wildly successful by many measures, especially those measures the organization created. In this way, Fanning's organizational entrepreneurship was also an act of institutional entrepreneurship, which reconfigured the field of nonprofit technology assistance. NPower's success culminated in a formal partnership with Microsoft to expand the organization nationally, thus extending the reach of market principles among NTAPs. Beyond building the market for technology assistance services through their national expansion, NPower also shaped the market through the business-like practices of their affiliates. In particular, NPower NY, the first and most successful affiliate in the national expansion program, embraced market ideals to an unprecedented extent. NPower NY built on NPower's basic model of social enterprise. However, NPower NY had weaker ties to the Circuit Rider movement than NPower, and was therefore less subject to movement influence. Further-more, the practices and structure at NPower NY were profoundly shaped by the affiliate's close ties to for-profit corporations.

To appeal to both sides of the institutional divide, NPower NY attempted to maintain a balance between social and economic values—taking advantage of a situation I call moral ambivalence. Moral ambivalence is the tension re-sulting from the necessary coexistence of competing orders of worth within an organization. The condition is faced by organizations in situations in which the emergence of a single dominant order of worth is impossible or undesir-able. In this chapter I show how NPower NY structured moral ambivalence into its organizational form as a way of maintaining the tension between social and economic values. Taking advantage of moral ambivalence allows organi-zations to produce accounts of worth amenable to stakeholders in multiple institutional domains (Stark, 2009). This facilitates legitimacy while giving the organization in question a competitive advantage in terms of access to re-sources. However, moral ambivalence also leaves the organization vulnerable to moral legitimacy challenges from stakeholders calling for authenticity or moral purity in the field. In NPower's case, moral legitimacy challenges often came from Circuit Riders, who claimed the organization had become too business-like and dependent on the cutthroat competitive strategies of its cor-porate partners, especially Microsoft. I take up the problem of how the Circuit Riders formulated, articulated, and mounted these challenges in the next chapter.

Social enterprises, such as NPower NY, are particularly subject to the con-dition of moral ambivalence. Social enterprises assemble business-like struc-tures and practices to produce social, as opposed to private, returns (Dart, 2004b; Di Domenico, Haugh, & Tracey, 2010). As such they operate simultaneously in at least two moral domains: the business and voluntary sectors. Social en-terprises bring together values from these seemingly incompatible worlds and must find ways to be accountable to each. Straddling two worlds as they do, social enterprises are challenged to produce accounts that can be justified to parties on both sides of an ostensibly intractable chasm. Because people from Wall Street and the voluntary sector are likely to take different moral stand-points (e.g., market versus civic orders of worth [Boltanski & Thévenot, 1991, 1999, 2006]) when judging the value of the organization's activities, social en-terprises face particularly rugged moral landscapes. Social enterprises trade between worlds, a social space that affords economic opportunity at the risk of moral censure (Barth, 2000). Battilana and Dorado (2010) show that success for social enterprises depends on the ability of leaders to reconcile contradictory institutional logics and present their organizations to members of diverse institutional environments as cohesive, coherent wholes. However, in a series of studies, David Stark and his colleagues (Bach & Stark, 2002; Beunza & Stark, 2004; Girard & Stark, 2003; Neff & Stark, 2003; Stark, 1999, 2009) find that the diversity of evaluative frameworks affords the friction necessary for innovation and entrepreneurship.

Market Expansion

In September 2000, a year into its successful growth as a stand-alone NTAP in Seattle, NPower announced a national expansion program in formal partnership with Microsoft. According to the agreement, Microsoft would donate $750,000 in operating support along with software donations and technical assistance, including management support and board members, to each affiliate of the new program. One of the conditions Microsoft set on its funding was for the start-up to identify matching funds from the local community. Jane Meseck of Microsoft's Community Affairs Department explained the conditions: "[Microsoft] would provide substantial capital funding, sort of like seed funding, up to $250 [thousand] per year for three years, plus software, professional support services, connections to our local field offices for volunteers, or board members or whatever is appropriate for that NPower, as long as the local community came together and matched the money" [15]. Fanning described the arrangement: "We entered into an agreement with Microsoft to provide leadership and strategy and direction for a total of five years. The idea was to plant the seeds to help local partners get up and running and then also provide the leadership and strategy for the network as a whole so that we could get up and running" (Fieldnotes 10–16–2002).

The expansion created what NPower management called a "federated network model."[1] Each new affiliate would incorporate as an independent 501(c)(3) organization, but take on the NPower name, logo, and design. Most important, each affiliate would take on the NPower model of technology assistance, including established service delivery models and fee structures.[2] Affiliates also agreed to report standardized metrics to and share knowledge gained while creating and delivering services with NPower National, the newly formed coordinating body for the network. The plan was for each NPower affiliate to keep enough of the original model to maintain a connection to the national network while having the independence to modify the model for local environments and exigencies. The initial plan targeted key cities in which Microsoft had a corporate presence and could readily provide technical assistance and board members to each affiliate, for example, New York, Washington, D.C., and San Francisco. However, the response quickly overwhelmed national expansion staff at NPower. Microsoft donated more money two years later to fund a national expansion to 12 cities across the country.

To enact the renewed expansion plan, NPower and Microsoft published a joint request for proposals. The request outlined two ways to join the NPower network. First, individuals seeking to start an NTAP could apply to become part of the NPower network. If their business plan was approved, NPower National would provide technical assistance in creating the organization, for example, help filing for tax-exempt status, marketing plans, personnel materials, and organizational models. NPower NY, which will be discussed in this chapter, joined the network this way. Second, existing NTAPs could apply to become part of the NPower network. In that case, NPower National would provide technical assistance to facilitate the transition, including marketing and branding materials and access to NPower's knowledge-management database. Several NTAPs in major cities became part of the NPower network this way, including TechBridge in Atlanta and Technology Works for Good in Washington, D.C. At one point, Compumentor, a well-established NTAP in San Francisco, worked toward becoming part of the NPower network, but the relationship quickly soured and the organizations agreed to separate. Compumentor's executive director, Daniel Ben-Horin, told me that "we were the Bay Area affiliate of NPower and we were a very bad match for what they were trying to do" [81]. Originally, existing organizations that joined the NPower network could keep their name. For example, TechBridge in Atlanta became an official part of the federated network and was able to keep its brand name. However, the executives at NPower National decided that such a policy led to watering down the brand. Afterwards, all organizations that joined the NPower Network had to take the NPower name. For example, Technology Works for Good, an organization started by a Circuit Rider named Trabian Shorters, became NPower Greater DC Region. By the end of 2003, 12 of the new NPower affiliates were operational: Arizona, Charlotte, Colorado, Washington, D.C., Indiana, Los Angeles, Michigan, New York, Oregon, Pennsylvania, Seattle, and Atlanta.[3]

With corporate and foundation funding and 12 affiliates in major cities across the country, NPower became the largest nonprofit technology assistance provider and the only one with a truly national presence. According to business plans submitted to NPower,[4] affiliates identified a prospective market of over 50,000 nonprofit organizations (NPOs). Although the total market size identified by NPower affiliates represents a fraction of the 1.5 million NPOs in the United States, the practice reflects a formal attempt to delineate a market for technology assistance. The delineation of a market was a cognitive shift in the field. The Circuit Riders conceived of the field as a movement, consisting of nonprofit and grassroots organizations dedicated to a specific cause. None of the Circuit Rider organizations conducted formal analyses of potential markets. For example, Dirk Slater of the LINC Project defined the potential targets of services as follows: "If they are low-income individuals and they are focusing on social safety net issues, that is the filter we need to work with. There are not that many of those types of groups, [but] there is enough that we have our plates completely full" [30]. The closest Circuit Rider organizations came to delineating a market was identifying the number of organizations constituting a particular movement. For example, Jon Stahl from ONE Northwest told me that he estimated that about 1,200 environmental groups operated in the Pacific Northwest, but it is important to note that he said that this number came from an analysis they were conducting at the time of the interview, in the summer of 2003, three years after NPower launched [36].

The national expansion also created new conventions for the NTAP field. Establishing a presence across the country enhanced the legitimacy of the NPower model of technology assistance by providing not only a template for organizations seeking to do the work but also a formal procedure by which an organization could adopt the NPower model and become an affiliate of the federated network. This legitimacy was reflected by the number of stakeholders that came to support NPower following the national expansion. Fanning explained how Microsoft's funding attracted more supporters:

> Microsoft was interested in funding [the national expansion], being kind of a seed funder, which made all the difference in the world. If there are seed funders, it brings other resources to the table. It makes it real. It puts it in motion. Without that seed funding, it would have happened, but probably not to the extent that it did, not with the same profile. We would probably have maybe one or two [new affiliates] and that would be it. So the partnership with

Microsoft and then the success of the first NPower in New York, that just brought on lots of other supporters. [71]

The additional supporters NPower enrolled included a portfolio of corporate supporters as well as social venture philanthropies. Of the former, the communications giant SBC, the business software company Changepoint, and the antivirus software firm Symantec gave money and in-kind support to NPower. Of the latter, NPower received funding from the Omidyar Network, a foundation started by the founders of eBay, which supports market-based solutions to social problems.

Applying its quantitative rigor and market-based ideals, NPower conceived of the nonprofit sector as an untapped market for technology services. Business plans for NPower affiliates also broke down local markets by budget size and service area (e.g., health care, arts, education, and so forth). For example, according to internal pricing documents, NPower NY divided NPOs into four budget categories: under $500,000, $500,000 to $1 million, $1 million to $5 million, and over $5 million. According to the 2002 Annual Report, 62% of NPower NY's clients had budgets of over $1 million. By comparison, ONE Northwest generally works with organizations from "the $100,000 to the low million range" [72]. Project Alchemy worked with organizations that "have a budget of maybe under $300,000 with just a few staff, and some of them are completely volunteer-led and volunteer-driven" [37]. Thus, managers at NPower NY conceived of the nonprofit sector in different financial terms and targeted more affluent clients. Recall from the last chapter that one of Fanning's innovations was bringing the democracy of the market to the nonprofit sector by offering services to all organizations, regardless of service area. In practice, this meant serving NPOs with large enough discretionary budgets to afford the services on offer.

Beyond reach, market expansion also meant growth among NPower affiliates. By 2003, each of the 12 NPower affiliates was as big or bigger (in terms of staff and budget size) than other competing NTAPs in the country. For example, TechRocks, which was a spin-off of the Rockefeller Family Fund's Circuit Rider program, reached 20 staff members at its biggest in 2002 [80]. According to tax forms, Compumentor had a larger annual budget than any single NPower affiliate, with a $4.8 million operating budget, but most of its revenues ($3.4 million) came from discounted software sales to the nonprofit sec-

ǀ

tor. In contrast, NPower Seattle and NPower NY had operating budgets of over $4 million and over $3 million, respectively, in 2001.

Fulfilling Market Ideals at NPower NY

Incorporated as a 501(c)(3) in 2001, NPower NY was the first and most successful affiliate of NPower's national expansion. Jane Meseck bragged, "In New York, heck, they already had the funders there. Their funding dwarfed what Microsoft was bringing. If someone asks you what has been the most successful start-up [among NPower affiliates], it was probably New York" [15]. NPower NY had auspicious roots and access to corporate funding. Barbara Chang, the founder of NPower NY, was able to secure matching donations from several large corporations and foundations in New York City, including JP Morgan Chase, Flatiron Partners (a venture capital firm), Accenture (a multinational consulting firm), and the Robin Hood Foundation (a social venture philanthropy). It was clear that Chang, in organizing an NTAP, embraced market principles in the nonprofit sector. Chang considered NPower legitimate by virtue of its corporate connections. She recalled in a conversation with another manager at NPower NY: "I knew she [Fanning] was the real deal because she had a reputation out there in the community already, and she was starting this Microsoft partnership. It was already buzzing in the community that this Microsoft/NPower thing was in formation. In fact, one of the people I talked to said that [the founder] was about to launch this partnership, so I knew right away that she was the real deal. She had Microsoft on her side" (Fieldnotes 1–23–2004).

Funding the Social Enterprise: Social Venture
Philanthropy Meets Venture Capitalism

NPower NY had key advantages over many social enterprises in funding its start-up. Being incorporated as a 501(c)(3) meant that it could more easily garner donations from foundations. Key partnerships in the nonprofit sector also afforded NPower NY access to a pool of potential clients. For example, NPower NY attracted both funding and a portfolio of clients from the Robin Hood Foundation. Furthermore, having a strong for-profit presence on the board meant NPower NY could more easily tap into networks of corporate funders. NPower NY's business and service provision model made it difficult to raise money from many nonprofit foundations beyond Robin Hood. As the director of development at NPower NY explained, "Half the time they [foundation officers] do not even understand [technology]. People say they do not understand technology even though it is sitting on their desk and in their pockets" [25]. However, corporate donors understood the importance of information technology for organizations and were willing to support such endeavors. NPower NY was able to leverage its relationships to raise donations similar to a venture start-up. A program officer at the Robin Hood Foundation explained how NPower NY was different from other NPOs he usually funds:

> If you look at this from the perspective of nonprofits generally, one of the unique things about NPower NY is that they raised their start-up capital prior to ever delivering a service, which is very unusual. Most people start out of a storefront delivering services and then go about backfilling the need for money. I think what that has allowed NPower NY to do is to really be very conscious about how soon do they get out there, what they promise, and not letting the delivery of services run ahead of their capitalization. So it is little bit more like a business model. [68]

NPower NY's close ties to for-profit corporations put isomorphic pressures on the organization to adopt business-like strategies. NPower NY was incubated in the offices of Accenture, which also played a role in setting up NPower NY's formal structure as a multitiered bureaucracy. Several pro bono consultants from Accenture helped configure the original organizational chart: an executive director oversaw the organization's operations; on the next level, five managers coordinated the organization's basic internal and external operations; directors of consulting, workforce development, and training managed staffs that worked with clients; directors of operations and fundraising and development managed internal affairs. The organizational chart reflects the administrative focus of NPower NY, which was heavily bureaucratic for such a young and small organization. During its first year of operations, six administrators oversaw a line staff of fewer than ten, including consultants, trainers, and workforce development staff.

Aside from being incubated at Accenture, NPower NY was modeled on high-tech start-ups, with the language of venture capital replacing the more common language of fund-raising in the nonprofit sector. Two of NPower NY's founding board members worked as venture capitalists (VCs) during

New York City's dot-com boom. When I asked whether they considered themselves venture capitalists to this nonprofit start-up, they both said yes. As one board member told me, "I think that our board, which was small and focused, small in number, very focused, very committed, very engaged, to my mind acted very much like a for-profit, venture-backed, start-up board" [27]. He explained the board's approach to raising start-up money:

> We took a very different approach [from traditional nonprofit funding] as you may recall. What we did is we said, "Let us fund this thing as if we were to fund a start-up. Let us cover one year's worth of operations before we have even launched." I think we got some traditional foundation money. . . . But the money that came in from foundations and the money that came in from corporations was nonspecific operating funds, which is really unique and very much like what a VC would do. When a VC puts money behind a company, he does not say "this for your marketing program." What he says is "this is for the business. Now, let us be very engaged and meet on a monthly basis and make sure that we are spending the money appropriately." [27]

The other board member concurred, adding, however, "We are not going to take it public and cash out" [28]. This treatment was reinforced in the nonprofit sector by NPower NY's relationship with the Robin Hood Foundation, a venture philanthropy[5] based in New York City. NPower NY received donations from the foundation, as well as access to its portfolio of nonprofit grantees, to whom it offered its services. Similar to the Circuit Rider model, the Robin Hood Foundation was a third-party payer for the technology assistance services that NPower NY provided.

Sustaining the Social Enterprise: Earned Revenue Models at NPower NY
NPower NY innovated the NPower model in part by moving it further toward the market. At an organizational retreat, one of the board members from the for-profit sector told members of NPower NY, "The idea behind NPower [NY] was to bring some entrepreneurship to the nonprofit sector, using a venture capital model" (Fieldnotes 1–28–2003). From the outset, NPower NY had a large operating budget funded through donations from nonprofit foundations and for-profit partners. However, the board continually pressed the organization to develop revenue models that relied more on earned income and less on donations, often employing terms such as "sustainability" as business rhetoric to express financial independence from fickle foundation support. By the

middle of 2003, NPower NY earned about 35% of its revenue, which the director of finance at the organization thought was "high for a nonprofit organization" [31]. However, she continued, "The board would still like us to be at a minimum of 50–50 [percent earned and donated revenue]." Throughout my time in the field, staff members acknowledged the pressures to generate earned revenue. The rhetoric behind the demand for earned revenue was "sustainability," which meant in practice financial sustainability. Building on the metrics produced at NPower in Seattle, NPower NY expressed its overall organizational effectiveness in financial terms.

NPower NY's business plan outlined three service areas, which they expressed colloquially as the "three legs of a stool": consulting, training, and workforce development. Consulting and training followed the basic NPower model. Consulting was offered as an on-site service by trained and credentialed consultants, preferably culled from the nonprofit sector. Training services consisted of classes offered in the organization's state-of-the-art computer lab or on-site at the client's location. The workforce development program, which was called Technology Service Corps, was NPower NY's modification of NPower Seattle's volunteer-matching service. In the New York affiliate, workforce development was a technology training program for low-income youths. Two of the three main departments in the organization, namely consulting and training, were considered revenue generators because NPower NY charged clients directly for services they provided in these areas. The workforce development program, Technology Service Corps, however, did not generate earned revenue. In fact, despite being the major recipient of restricted[6] donations, the Technology Service Corps drew money from the organization's unrestricted funds as well.

Consultants in particular were pressed to generate revenue for NPower NY, most often by increasing their billable hours (the hours they charged clients for services). During my time in the field, consultants went from largely dictating their own schedules to facing rules about working at least 24 billable hours per week, choosing among three different fixed schedules to accomplish this goal. The director of operations, who was recruited from Accenture, told me that consultants from Accenture work 40 billable hours per week, but that is because they have a support staff to conduct back-end operations, such as producing documentation or keeping track of hours (Fieldnotes 9–4–2001). The push toward increasing consultants' billable hours began early on, as my fieldnotes from September 2001 indicate:

[The director of operations] began the meeting by discussing the new policy of tracking hours that will come into effect. Starting with consultants, NPower employees will be responsible for tracking their hours throughout the day. They will use the Changepoint system to track hours. [She] explained that "this way, they can forecast the time available for consulting as well as the revenue coming in as a result." She said that it may seem overwhelming at first, but she got used to doing it at Accenture. She explained that all consulting businesses do such things. Then she asked the Accenture people to describe the processes they use to make the task easier. There is even a line item in Changepoint for the time spent entering the time data. (Fieldnotes 9–4–2001)

The pressure was reinforced by a host of performance metrics NPower NY collected regarding its consulting practices. These performance metrics were reported back to the consultants at staff meetings as a way to encourage growth in the area. For example, the executive director rallied the consulting department by reporting their earned revenue over the first two years at one consultants' meeting. From my fieldnotes: "In 2001, they had 1,000 hours of consulting. In 2002, they had 5,000. The staff has not grown significantly since then. The business has been steady. Their job is to be out there. Their revenue in 2001 was $154,000. In 2002, it was $500,000. That is 200% growth. They expect to grow 50% in the next year to $750,000. This is ambitious, but she feels they are able to do it" (Fieldnotes 12–17–2002).

By March 2002, the director of consulting was running reports of billable hours and distributing them at consulting meetings as a way of increasing pressure on the consultants to generate more billable hours (Fieldnotes 3–9–2002). The tracking of billable hours indicates the degree to which NPower NY adopted the evaluative criteria of its for-profit partners. The application of these evaluative criteria to the performance of consultants reflects how mechanisms of isomorphism operate on the micro level through organizational practices enacted by managers and staff (Hallett, 2010; Powell & Colyvas, 2008). The consultants were not happy about the changes. At one point, a consultant took me aside and told me he was concerned about his job. "If I continue to not make my hours, I might be fired," he explained. "They have switched their concerns at NPower," he went on. "They are more concerned about making billable hours. It is more like a for-profit now. It is what the board wants. The board is mostly made up of for-profit people. NPower NY is a business. They point to Accenture and say the consultants there have 100% of their hours billable" (Fieldnotes 5–2–2002). The consultant's comments signal a tension within NPower NY between for-profit drives for efficiency and revenue generation and a nonprofit ethos of volunteerism and commitment to progressive social change. The same consultant explained to me that to counter the business-like practices at work he often volunteered to work extra hours at client sites, doing pro bono work and not telling his manager about it (Fieldnotes 1–2–2002).

Yet, despite consultants' concerns, the executive management pressed the department to find new ways to generate revenues. The executive director announced at a consulting meeting that there was "so much we want to do about improving and standardizing work. We have to start standardizing to produce a level of consistency and quality. We have to look at the best practices out there. People are doing things differently. Practices will shift slightly. This will take focused attention, which will call on your time balance against billable hours" (Fieldnotes 5–7–2002). For the executive director, "standardizing" meant routinizing as much of the consultants' work as possible. By establishing routines, NPower NY could make the variable work of consulting more predictable and efficient. The organization took Accenture as its model for practices in consulting service delivery, working with one board member who was a partner at the multinational consulting firm to develop a "two-year plan to scale [up] the [consulting] department" (Fieldnotes 6–4–2002). The executive director later reported at a board meeting that she sought to reap efficiencies from standardizing practices, which would allow the consultants to work on "higher margin" projects (Fieldnotes 6–26–2002).[7] The rhetoric and practices of efficiency and standardization reflected the market values of the organization. By organizing the consulting department according to these values, managers at NPower NY appeased board members and stakeholders from the for-profit sector.

For the first two years, NPower NY charged clients on a sliding scale, based on the budget of the nonprofit organization being served. Sliding-scale fee structures are a standard practice in the nonprofit sector as well as among NTAPs. As of 2002, NPower NY's sliding scale ranged from $75 to $150 per hour, depending on the size of the organization and whether they were a member.[8] By means of comparison, a Circuit Rider for Project Alchemy in Seattle told me: "We have actually recently increased our fee-for-service rates to try to help recover more of the cost of doing [hands-on consulting] work. When we first got started, we were charging very, very low rates. Our initial fee scale ranged from $15 an hour to $65 an hour, depending on the budget size of the organization, and now we are charging a flat rate of $60, regardless of the budget size of the organization" [37]. Jon Stahl from ONE Northwest explained: "We used to have a sliding scale but we decided it was more trouble than it was worth so we collapsed it down. And in addition to that, there are some cases where we have additional subsidy money that is targeted on certain areas. For example, in Portland we have some grants to cover scheduled support services, so that subsidized the cost down even further. We have some grants that cover support and consulting services for certain groups and that subsidizes it down even further. We also apply a certain amount of our support money, so we do a bunch of assessment and planning work at no cost to groups" [36].

With their attention to earned revenue models and access to donations from corporations and independent foundations, NPower NY grew quickly in size and prominence. By the end of their second year, the organization had close to 20 paid employees and about one dozen Accenture consultants working pro bono. Its revenues grew considerably in their first three years of operation. NPower NY reported a budget of over $3 million on their 2001 990 tax form, a number that includes start-up funding from Microsoft and other corporate funders. The organization's budget reached $1.7 million in 2002 (the first year they operated without an influx of start-up funds) and $2 million in 2003. Across that time, their revenue mix shifted from donations to earned sources. According to analysis of 990 tax forms, NPower NY's attention to earned revenue generated $345,000 by the end of 2002. The organization doubled its earned revenue by the end of 2003 to $744,000. The next year, NPower NY broke the $1 million mark for earned revenue. While the percentage of earned revenue stayed at 35% for 2003 and 2004, it jumped to 45% by the end of 2005. By comparison, NPower Seattle never earned more than 33% of its revenue. The IT Resource Center in Chicago, on which NPower's original fee-for-service model is based, achieved only 16% earned revenue throughout the same time period. NPower NY's move toward earned revenue reflects a larger trend in the nonprofit sector of shifting away from donations and toward fees and contracts as sources of revenue[9] (Salamon, 2003).

Measured by budget size, NPower NY was rapidly becoming one of the largest and most influential NTAPs in the country. In 2004, Barbara Chang was named one of New York City's "Top Ten," an award given by the Executive Council of New York to "ten individuals in the greater New York business community who have, through their innovation, significantly impacted their organization and industry" (York, 2004). She was also interviewed in media outlets, including nonprofit outlets and those dedicated to the growing arena of social enterprise. Research has shown that media attention is an important aspect of market emergence, especially for market categories that are not readily recognized by the general public (Kennedy, 2008). For NPower NY, coverage in the business media was particularly important for attracting attention from potential corporate supporters. For example, an article about social enterprise published by Wharton wrote favorably of NPower NY and its leadership: "Like other nonprofits, Chang says NPower NY can only operate effectively if it adopts a certain for-profit mentality. We don't like to use words like 'profit' or 'earned revenues,' but these terms are becoming more a part of what we do. We have to show outcomes. We have to measure our impact and be savvy business people and keep track of revenues and expenses. . . . We're running a business here. I look at my P&L [profit-and-loss statement] and my balance sheet" (Knowledge@Wharton, 2003).

Implications of NPower NY's Rise to Prominence

NPower NY's rise to prominence changed how people in the field thought about how technology assistance ought to be done. The organization legitimated market approaches to the work. Furthermore, NPower NY's rapid success provided the "proof of concept" that NPower needed to legitimate its national expansion. Fanning explained in an interview: "NPower Seattle had a great reputation. People were wondering whether or not this could be duplicated in other places and NPower NY took it and blew us away. Their success enabled the network [of NPower affiliates] to happen. There were funders that had come on board but many were sitting back and just waiting. . . . The cards were stacked in our favor, but New York just really stacked them in our favor, so if anyone was on edge, it took away almost all concern" [71]. The New York affiliate enrolled large corporate supporters, such as Accenture, into the NPower network. Executives from Accenture took seats on NPower National's board. As NPower NY grew in significance, Barbara Chang's reputation also attracted national attention, which facilitated additional support in the form of donations from independent foundations. Several more NPower affiliates began operating in the year following New York's launch.

NPower's national expansion extended the market for technology assistance services in the nonprofit sector. With 12 operating affiliates, NPower was by far the largest nonprofit technology assistance provider in the country. It attracted resources from independent foundations and corporations alike. However, not everyone was happy with NPower's success in creating a market in the nonprofit sector. NPower's success created a "Matthew Effect" (Merton, 1968): the more resources it acquired among corporate and independent foundations, the more it continued to accrue. As one Circuit Rider observed: "[With] NPower, there is a bit of the David and Goliath issue because there was such a small pot of funds that everyone was going for. NPower came in as a massive Goliath. They had all that Microsoft funding, which then spurred additional funding. I think there was a little envy from smaller groups that NPower is coming in and getting so much support and basically sweeping the top levels of funders in this massive wave" [51]. A manager from a competing NTAP described the funding situation he faced, "We were looking for a grant from Microsoft a year ago and basically found out that all the money that Microsoft gives, they give to NPower so there is not anything for other folks" [53]. Circuit Riders concerned that the expansion of the market would displace the movement began to criticize the organization's market values, referring to the organization as "N-Pire" (Fieldnotes 5–1–2003).

Moral Ambivalence

As is clear from the above, NPower NY embraced market values and pushed the market practices of social enterprise. The organization was subject to market pressures from its for-profit partners and board members, who were enthusiastic about plying the market principles that made their businesses successful in the nonprofit sector. Being mostly removed from the Circuit Riders, NPower NY practiced its business-like behaviors largely outside movement influences. However, as a nonprofit organization incorporated under the 501(c)(3) tax code of the Internal Revenue Service, NPower NY had to demonstrate its worth as a charitable organization in order to maintain its tax-exempt status. Beyond meeting these regulatory requirements, NPower NY was subject to multiple and contradictory institutional expectations from various stakeholders. Although corporate supporters lauded NPower NY's commitment to earned revenue models and market-based metrics, these business-like practices were criticized by managers of other NTAPs. For example, the head of a competing NTAP in New York told me: "The language that is used in a lot of NPower material is very corporate in its nature. It makes sense from where it is coming from, but I am not sure how much it connects to certain groups of nonprofits" [53].

As NPower NY engaged with other actors in the field, these contradictory institutional expectations shaped NPower NY as a hybrid organization. One board member, a venture capitalist in New York City's Silicon Alley, explained the organization's hybridity: "I think that in some ways it [NPower NY] is the best combination of the energy and enthusiasm you find in a start-up with the walk-through-walls commitment to mission that you find at the most altruistic of nonprofits" [27]. As a hybrid organization in structure and practice, NPower NY operated under moral ambivalence.[10] Moral ambivalence is the tension resulting from the necessary coexistence of competing orders of worth (or moral bases) within an organization. Moral ambivalence is an organizational response to external and internal pressure to conform to contradictory institutional expectations from members of the field. The condition is faced by organizations in situations in which the emergence of a single dominant order of worth is impossible or undesirable. Under conditions of moral ambivalence, organizations must satisfy the evaluative criteria of various stakeholders simultaneously. Further complicating matters is the fact that such evaluative criteria change or shift depending on the situation. Under conditions of moral ambivalence, actors may appear inconsistent or contradictory across the situations they encounter.

Facing Multiple Institutional Expectations

NPower NY was subject to multiple contradictory evaluative criteria based on its organizational form, practices, and position in the field. Because they combine social and market values, hybrid organizational forms are subject to contradictory institutional norms from various stakeholders (Hasenfeld & Gidron, 2005; McInerney, 2012). Hybrid practices, such as combining earned and donated revenue streams as well as alternately competing and collaborating with peer organizations, followed contradictory institutional logics (Binder, 2007; Rao & Giorgi, 2006). NPower NY's status and relational positions subject the organization to contradictory institutional expectations. What I mean by the organization's status position is NPower NY's relationship to peer organizations, such as Circuit Rider organizations and other NTAPs. The status-based contradiction meant that NPower NY alternately collaborated and competed with peer organizations and that competition and collaboration often happened during the same project, sometimes switching in an instant during a meeting with a funder. By relational position, I mean its position in a network of organizations, which reflects the structure of the organizational field (Powell, White, Koput, & Owen-Smith, 2005). NPower NY's position in the NTAP field was determined by interorganizational collaborations across institutional boundaries, for example, with the organization's many corporate partners, as well as relationships within the nonprofit sector. In either case, NPower NY's status and relational positions meant that various stakeholders evaluated the organizations' practices on different moral bases (or orders of worth). This is common with hybrid organizations as they bridge institutional worlds and evaluative practices.

Managers at NPower NY were aware of criticism about their relationships with for-profit corporations. Even though business-nonprofit partnerships are increasingly common, they remain a moral gray area for many in the nonprofit sector (Galaskiewicz & Colman, 2006). Such partnerships put the nonprofit organizations and their for-profit partners in positions to have their activities judged from multiple and contradictory moral standpoints, rendering both sides vulnerable to criticism from various stakeholders. Partnering with so many large, multinational corporations put NPower NY in the line of fire on several counts. However, most actors criticized NPower NY for adhering to the market order of worth of their partners. For example, one NPower NY consultant, a self-professed Marxist, told me: "I do not necessarily like where we get our money. Our money comes from venture capitalists and investment bank firms who are stealing from everyone else. And I feel like in some ways I am facilitating that theft" [1]. Such comments criticize the market standpoint that NPower NY takes by virtue of its association with its for-profit partners. One manager at NPower NY told me in an interview: "I think [our collaboration with for-profit organizations] makes [NPower NY] a more business-y environment. And I do not think that is bad. I think it is just different. I think also that it could be perceived as such, and I worry about our perception in the community. 'Oh, they are just another business.' People cannot comprehend that we are nonprofit" [23]. Another manager explained in an interview that "because of our relationship with Microsoft, a lot of the perceptions of Microsoft's approach are ascribed to us" [42].

The executive director also recognized that NPower NY was being denounced for its revenue model: "Some of the folks out there say we are getting so bottom-line oriented, where all we care about is the revenue, [that] we do not care about the mission anymore" [62]. She warned staff in a meeting that

NPower NY was "viewed as shilling for these large corporations" (Fieldnotes 1–15–2002). "We have to be careful about what we end up doing," she told the staff. "We can be viewed as making money on [discounted Microsoft products they sold]" (Fieldnotes 1–15–2002). However, the executive director of the organization ultimately justified the relationship with Microsoft. As she told a reporter: "First of all, our relationship is not that we are a sales force for Microsoft. I understand the relationship is strong, but it is also a double-edged sword. The Microsoft-haters will point fingers and say we are a shill for Microsoft. That could not be further from the truth. If you think about the nonprofit community, 90 percent of the software being used is Microsoft. It is not like we sold it to them or encouraged that. There will be skeptics and cynics that will say 'you're just going down the path Microsoft wants you go to down'" (InternetNews.com, 2002).

Demonstrating Charitable Worth

Whereas the Circuit Riders operated primarily from the moral standpoint of a civic order of worth, NPower NY privileged market and industrial moral orders. NPower NY presents itself to the world as an entrepreneurial NTAP and not as an activist organization. Yet, to attain 501(c)(3) status and maintain legitimacy as a nonprofit organization, NPower NY had to prove its charitable worth. One way it did so was through the creation of the Technology Service Corps (TSC). As outlined in its business plan, TSC is a workforce development program for low-income youths. The program enrolls small classes (8–10 students) of young people (from 18 to 24 years old) for a 12-week intensive training in fixing and maintaining information technologies. The first eight weeks of the program take place in the classroom at NPower NY's offices. For the rest of the time, the student is placed in a paid internship at a local nonprofit organization. TSC was designed to solve two problems simultaneously: to provide career ladders for low-income youths and to build an IT workforce for the nonprofit sector.

TSC allowed NPower NY to make claims of worth based on social values (i.e., based on a civic order of worth). Because it served several communities in need (e.g., low-income youths, nonprofits with small budgets), TSC provided the legitimacy of social service to an otherwise commercial organization. The program allowed NPower NY to justify its commercial activities by claiming to use the funds to help communities in need. To provide proof of its justification, NPower NY funded TSC from its general operating budget for the first several years it operated. The program was also supported by foundation grants, making it, as one manager explained, "the only department that we have a restricted grant for" [31]. Yet, in a board meeting, board members found a silver lining in that: losing money on TSC meant they could charge closer to market rates for consulting services without jeopardizing their tax-exempt status (Fieldnotes 12–5–2002).

Throughout my time in the field, NPower NY struggled internally with two aspects of TSC. First, working with students from low-income backgrounds created social work problems that the technology-oriented staff at NPower NY was ill-equipped to manage. This problem was generally limited to staff that had hands-on contact with the students of the TSC program. At times, TSC staff was called on to help students complete applications for food stamps or find temporary housing. This strained TSC staff's time and resources. It also contributed to a second problem: since TSC relied exclusively on donations and did not generate any revenue, staff continually struggled to integrate the program with the rest of the organization. Despite being part of NPower NY's original business plan, in practice TSC did not fit in with consulting and training as directors and board members had envisioned. Aside from the social work aspects of the program, TSC drew resources away from consulting and training. To business-minded directors and board members, TSC diverted funds that could be invested elsewhere in the organization to generate more revenue. During my time in the field, directors and board members floated various schemes to help TSC generate revenues. For example, one idea was to send TSC graduates into the field as junior consultants, charging lower fees for their services. This plan was abandoned when directors realized that the TSC graduates, while technically proficient, lacked many of the customer-service skills that NPower NY demands of its consultants.

Despite the problems with the program's implementation, the directors and board members of NPower NY considered TSC successful, particularly as it generated goodwill for the organization. The media joined in as well. Channel One in New York City spotlighted the program, presenting a five-minute segment on TSC and its graduates during a prime-time newscast. Corporate partners, such as JP Morgan Chase, invited TSC graduates to attend events as representatives of NPower NY and highlight the good work they were doing in the community. One graduate from the TSC program was asked to speak immediately before Steve Ballmer, Microsoft's CEO, at an NPower NY launch event. After the event, the graduate did not join the rest of his cohort at a reunion in the

NPower NY office because as he explained he "had to go to lunch with Steve" (Fieldnotes 7–31–2002). Working with low-income youths provided members of the NTAP field proof that NPower NY was legitimately nonprofit. As a purely charitable endeavor, TSC produced social forms of worth. The executive director explained at a TSC event that "consulting and training are the 'bread and butter,' but TSC is the 'heart and soul' [of NPower NY]" (Fieldnotes 1–21–2003). Aside from foundations that rewarded NPower NY with restricted grants for the program, other actors in the NTAP field responded positively to TSC. Several NTAPs, including the LINC Project, took on TSC students as interns. TSC allowed NPower NY to be socially accountable to foundations and other actors that might evaluate their moral legitimacy from the standpoint of a nonprofit institutional domain.

Structuring Moral Ambivalence

Thus, a key problem that organizations like NPower NY face is how to manage moral ambivalence. In general, all social enterprises face such conditions as they cope with competing institutional expectations and must reconcile contradictory institutional logics. Other organizational forms struggle with moral ambivalence as well. For example, for-profit corporations attempting to act as good corporate citizens must balance the demands of publics for ethical behavior with those of shareholders seeking to maximize the financial value of their investments.

One way organizations cope with moral ambivalence is by hiring staff members with diverse institutional backgrounds.[11] Social enterprises have been shown to employ staff members from the nonprofit and for-profit sectors to successfully meet contradictory institutional demands (Battilana & Dorado, 2010). Staff members at NPower NY came from the nonprofit and for-profit sectors. In the beginning, NPower NY recruited managers primarily from the nonprofit sector, including the executive director and directors of consulting, training, and workforce development. Only the director of operations, who was recruited from Accenture, had exclusively for-profit experience. Most of the rest of the paid staff worked in the nonprofit sector prior to being hired at NPower NY. However, according to my fieldnotes, at least as many pro bono consultants from Accenture worked full-time for NPower NY throughout its first year of operations.[12] As NPower NY matured, the number of pro bono staff on loan from Accenture declined, but the number of paid management recruited from the for-profit consulting firm increased. For example, when portions of the Health Insurance Portability and Accountability Act regarding electronic patient files went into effect, NPower NY recruited a consultant from Accenture who specialized in consulting in the health care industry. As Microsoft's start-up funding began to dry up, NPower NY courted Accenture more forcefully. NPower NY added a managing partner from Accenture to the board who eventually became its chair, and continued to recruit managers from the multinational for-profit consulting firm. In 2003, NPower NY hired a former Accenture executive as its new director of consulting. This meant two of the five director positions came to be occupied with staff from the for-profit sector.

With staff recruited from for-profit and nonprofit sectors and support from for-profit corporations and nonprofit foundations, NPower NY was simultaneously an insider and an outsider among NTAPs. This staffing pattern allowed NPower NY to maintain institutional multiplicity (Hargrave & Van de Ven, 2009). Hiring staff with different institutional backgrounds provided diverse ideas about how the organization ought to operate, what Girard and Stark (2003) call a "heterarchy of values." In such arrangements, the institutional multiplicity represented by staff members of diverse backgrounds is maintained as no single institutional precept becomes a dominant organizing principle. For example, one of the consultants with a sales background in the for-profit sector expressed interest in how he could sell NPower NY's services, "without looking like I am selling." He was rebuked by another consultant with a background in the nonprofit sector: "You have to be careful. With our Microsoft background, people are suspicious of us already" (Fieldnotes 11–5–2002). The example shows that despite pressure from for-profit board members and directors to increase revenues, staff attempted to balance market values with social values reflecting the nonprofit sector.

Responding to Moral Ambivalence

At times, nonprofit clients appreciated NPower NY's professionalism and business-like practices. The executive director of Rhizome, a digital arts organization in New York City, told me that he hired NPower NY because he thought these practices made the organization "more innovative" than other NTAPs (Fieldnotes 10–15–2001). On other occasions, clients pressed NPower NY to be more charitable, especially with pricing. As this excerpt from my fieldnotes demonstrates, prospective clients in the nonprofit sector expected consulting and training to provide heavily subsidized services at rates well below market value: "I met [one of NPower NY's managers] at the airport this morning. Immediately she started discussing a conversation she had with [the executive director] last night. [The executive director] was concerned about criticisms of the organization around how their services were not affordable to small nonprofits. 'They expect services for free,' [the manager] reported. [The executive director] has gestured toward lowering the costs of services, but wondered at what cost to the agency. The board, especially the chair, wants a revenue model yielding self-sustenance" (Fieldnotes 4–11–2002). This conflict produced moral ambivalence between NPower NY and its clients.

To respond to the condition of moral ambivalence, in early 2003 managers at NPower NY implemented a matrix fee structure based on the budget of the client and the level of difficulty of the engagement. The lower end of the fee structure charged small nonprofits fees below-market rates. These fees were subsidized by charging wealthier nonprofit organizations much higher rates. Additionally, the executive director and board strategized that larger nonprofits would likely need more complex services, which would also come at a premium. The executive director explained the fee structure in a consultants' meeting:

> We are moving toward three tiers and three categories for consulting projects. This will be based on the skill sets necessary to get the work done. These are general guidelines for the pricing. Many projects will be priced differently in the future. The lowest level is actually lower than the present pricing; it includes most scheduled support and basic web design. The middle is a step up; it includes low-end networking and database as well as high-end scheduled support. The high level includes strategic planning and complex work—the work that requires higher level skills that we have to pay for. With work that cuts across these tiers, we will have to work out a blended rate. We also added a new category of nonprofit, those organizations with budgets greater than $10M. (Fieldnotes 4–8–2003)

The matrix fee structure allowed NPower NY to structure moral ambivalence into the organization's practices. Higher rates for more complex services, especially to larger nonprofits, generated revenues that could be used to subsidize services to smaller organizations or pro bono work. The matrix fee structure demonstrates that NPower NY did not simply transpose for-profit behaviors into the nonprofit sector. Rather, intersectoral isomorphism is an example of "editing" (Sahlin-Andersson, 1996) institutional behavior, that is, of translating behavior from one institution into another, keeping some elements and changing others to reflect local exigencies. This revenue-generation scheme allowed NPower NY to be socially accountable to the nonprofit sector (providing low-cost or pro bono services to small nonprofit organizations) while also being financially accountable to its for-profit partners (earning revenues by generating higher fees from serving larger nonprofits and delivering more complex services).

The executive director justified NPower NY's matrix revenue model, claiming that the earned revenue from providing more expensive services subsidized their more charitable work:

> The bottom line is that in order to be an ongoing entity, we have to protect the bottom line. If you do not think enough about that, you can shut your doors in a couple of years if you do not watch out. We have got to be very aware of that. I think that we walk that line carefully and I do not ever think that it is mission *or* finances. It is both. In order to have the impacts you want to make, you have to understand how a really good solid grounding of both of those works. And they will interact with each other, but you cannot just think about doing good and not think about whether you are financially viable. . . . All this money allows us to do things like free training weeks and to lower the prices on some of our services. I do not think they [detractors in the NTAP field] make that distinction, they just say all we do is talk about money all day. Well, the money is going to good stuff. If we make it, then we share that. It is not like it is going to the board of directors in the form of bonuses. That, I think people lose sight of, but I think it is important for us to never lose sight of that. [62]

In the end, NPower NY attempted to meet the institutional precepts of the for-profit and nonprofit sectors by recombining the values and evaluative criteria of each. The matrix fee structure allowed NPower NY to justify its practices to audiences from different institutional domains with a single approach. In this way, NPower NY appeared moral and rational to for-profit organizations and nonprofit organizations. Structuring moral ambivalence in this way allowed NPower NY to retain legitimacy and access to resources from for-profit partners as well as nonprofit foundations under a variety of situations. The balance of market and social values was effective in maintaining a diverse set of supporters. Donations continued between for-profit partners and nonprofit foundations alike. In its 2002 annual report, NPower NY counted 21 entities that provided support. Three were corporations, eight were corporate foundations, and seven were independent nonprofit foundations. The remainder consisted of individual donors.

Moral Ambivalence in Hybrid Organizations

NPower's national expansion extended the reach of the market for nonprofit technology assistance in the sector. By creating a formal program, NPower's national expansion provided a template for NTAPs to adopt market practices, which led the way for new market conventions to develop in the field. Forging those new conventions was NPower NY, which took the social enterprise form and recombined it with market values from its for-profit partners and board members. NPower NY's radical embrace and expression of market values created a particularly entrepreneurial social enterprise. NPower NY capitalized its start-up, following venture philanthropy models of funding. A constant drive toward increasing earned revenues sustained the enterprise.

However, as a 501(c)(3) organization, NPower NY was also pressed to demonstrate its charitable worth, that is, that it produced social goods. NPower NY did so by creating a social service program called the Technology Service Corps, which trained low-income youths for technology jobs in the nonprofit sector. The Technology Service Corps allowed NPower NY to demonstrate charitable worth by providing social services institutionalized as appropriate in the nonprofit sector. Yet even these structures remain tenuous. Ambivalence is different from ambiguity (Carolan, 2010). Whereas the latter can be resolved or lessened by the introduction of more or better information, the former cannot. Moral ambivalence reflects the unresolvable tension that results from institutional multiplicity to which many hybrid organizations, such as social enterprises, are subject. Yet, as a social enterprise, NPower NY was subject to contradictory institutional expectations, which gave rise to moral ambivalence.

Solving the problem of moral ambivalence challenges organizations to make and maintain pragmatic compromises. However, such pragmatic compromises are tenuous and may be undermined by sufficiently motivated challenges (Boltanski, 1996). One way of forging stability is building such compromises into the organization's structure, as NPower NY did by hiring staff from diverse institutional backgrounds. Internally, moral ambivalence can help maintain cohesiveness among such a staff, forming the social glue by which hybrid organizations can maintain a coherent organizational identity. For example, in a study about cognitive dissonance among participants in the mass murder and suicide at Jonestown, Mills (1983: 283) writes that sociological ambivalence, of which moral ambivalence is a type, "may be seen as a kind of slack since it legitimates inconsistent behavior by members. In so doing, it both protects the organization from extreme volatility and produces for it a level of collective wisdom not available to fully taut groups with hypercommitted members." In other words, by affording multiple meanings among actors within the organization, moral ambivalence provides an ethnomethodological slipperiness that keeps organizations from moving toward extremes in their environments. In the case of NPower NY, moral ambivalence kept the strong market tendencies among certain staff and board members in check, allowing the organization to maintain legitimacy in a multi-institutional environment. For example, in practice it allowed consultants to justify providing pro bono services in the face of increasing pressure to produce billable hours.

Externally, moral ambivalence challenged NPower NY to produce multivalent accounts. By multivalent accounts, I mean those that several different stakeholders can interpret simultaneously as aligning with their interests. Such accounts are difficult to produce and "hold together." In other words, multivalent accounts produced in response to moral ambivalence—for example, NPower NY's matrix fee structure—work as long as other actors in the environment consider them legitimate. Like all accounts, those deriving from moral ambivalence are only as strong as their weakest links (Latour, 1986). NPower NY offered low-cost services to small nonprofit organizations. In practice, most of NPower NY's clients were medium-sized or large. Board members and executive managers often pressed consultants to target large nonprofit organizations as potential clients, effectively rendering practices such as the matrix fee structure symbolic. Yet some in the nonprofit sector also judged NPower NY on its contribution to social goods, for example, by their willingness to offer low-cost services to smaller organizations with less ability to pay. A motivated Circuit Rider could have challenged NPower NY on the grounds that it claimed to work with all nonprofit organizations, but in reality worked only with the most affluent and was therefore operating exclusively on market principles. As I discuss in the next chapter, in certain situations some Circuit Riders attempted to do just that. Such claims serve to constrain NPower NY's entrepreneurial drives. The organization could have given up its nonprofit status or eliminated resource-intensive programs such as TSC. However, NPower NY sought to justify its charitable worth to actors in the nonprofit sector, including the Circuit Riders.

With pressure from its for-profit partners, NPower NY embraced market practices. NPower NY justified market principles with social values. Appearing reasonable, such justifications led to market expansion in the nonprofit technology assistance field. Foundation support for NPower NY's version of social enterprise further legitimated market principles among NTAPs. This suggests that under conditions of moral ambivalence, not all competing values are held equally or stably. NPower NY was more or less driven by market principles depending on its interactions with members of the field. Among Circuit Riders, NPower NY demonstrated its commitment to social values, for example, by placing TSC students as interns at competing NTAPs. Among extant and prospective corporate sponsors, NPower NY demonstrated its commitment to market principles by producing financial accounts. Thus, the notion of moral ambivalence reflects the situatedness of organizational action. Over time, pragmatic compromises emerged out of NPower NY's need to reconcile social values and market principles, which helped to regulate the influence of the latter more broadly in the field. As such, the market for technology assistance was instilled with social values, such as altruism and volunteerism, which reflected ideals in the nonprofit sector as well as the Circuit Rider movement.

5

THE CIRCUIT RIDERS RESPOND

Conventions of Coordination as Movements
React to Markets

The Circuit Rider movement began in 1997 through the efforts of Gavin Clabaugh, Rob Stuart, and countless organizers. Within three years, the movement had grown from a handful of Circuit Riders to a legion reportedly almost 10,000 strong. Yet, by 2002, NPower had come to dominate nonprofit technology assistance, moving a grassroots movement of largely independent activists toward a market for consulting services consisting largely of formal organizations. The proliferation of hybrid organizations created a diverse organizational field. Yet the rise of NPower and its model of technology assistance had largely transformed the activism around which the Circuit Riders had organized. The value of technology was no longer measured by its contribution to social justice and the environment. Rather, NPower had developed explicit performance metrics that expressed the value of technology by its contribution to cost savings and administrative efficiency at nonprofit agencies. Technology was no longer offered to nonprofit and grassroots organizations based purely on need. Rather, access to technology was effectively based on an organization's ability to pay. Circuit Riders no longer traveled across the country evangelizing for information technology. Rather, NTAPs operated in geographically constrained markets, often cities and regions, though sometimes entire states. It seemed the Circuit Riders' technology revolution was over.

However, the activism of the Circuit Riders lived on in the hybrid models of the NTAP field. Technology assistance never became a pure market. Their social values were integrated into the organizational DNA of NTAPs. For example, NPower NY was awarded a grant from SBC Global to fund a Circuit Rider program of its own. They hired a young woman to travel throughout parts of the country to provide technology assistance at no cost to agencies enrolled in the program. Furthermore, many of the social values expressed in the business plans of NPower affiliates derived from the activism of the Circuit Riders. In this chapter I explain the ongoing influence of the Circuit Rider movement on the market for technology assistance services in the nonprofit sector. I contend that the Circuit Rider movement's counteractivism shaped the market for technology assistance in profound ways, away from a pure market and toward a hybrid market consisting of economic and social values—a moral market for technology. I use the term "counteractivism," a play on the verb "counteract," to describe how the Circuit Riders mobilized new meanings for technology and deployed new tactics to challenge market principles, and to reassert the social values they considered important to maintain in the nonprofit sector.

Circuit Riders responded in various ways to the dominance of NPower and the transformation of a movement toward a market. Many engaged with the market. Of these, some capitulated, forming organizations and either adopting the NPower model or, like Technology Works for Good in Washington, D.C., becoming NPower affiliates themselves. Others developed hybrid models on the movement side of the movement-market spectrum. For example, Media Jumpstart in New York City organized a collective to provide technology services for social justice groups, charging fees like NPower but subsidizing those fees heavily with foundation support, volunteerism, and the use of free and low-cost software. Alternatively, others challenged the market, mobilizing against NPower and the growing marketization of technology in the nonprofit sector, this time organizing their movement around an alternative technology platform, namely free and open source software (F/OSS). The Circuit Riders associated the ideals of the movement, which they felt reflected the ideals of nonprofit and grassroots organizations, with open source. The movement also denounced NPower and its relationship to Microsoft as monopolistic and competitive.

Outlining these three responses to the rise of NPower reifies the categories. In practice, Circuit Riders and NPower alternately collaborated and competed throughout their history. At times, Circuit Riders competed with NPower, especially for resources, such as foundation grants. For example, in 2002 the SBC Foundation launched an initiative to provide technology to nonprofit organizations throughout the country through what was essentially a Circuit Rider program. NPower, NTEN, TechRocks, and Compumentor were all invited to submit proposals (Fieldnotes 2–26–2002). Ultimately, NPower won the grant, which funded Circuit Riders at NPower offices throughout the country. Some in the Circuit Rider movement felt that grant should have gone to a Circuit Rider organization, or at least NTEN [76]. During other times, NPower and Circuit Rider organizations collaborated to produce collective goods. Such was the case when TechRocks and NPower collaborated to produce a technology tool for the NTAP field.

Such examples also risk reifying the distinction between the Circuit Riders and NPower. In reality, the boundaries between organizations like NPower and movement actors such as independent Circuit Riders were often fluid, as they often shared knowledge and personnel. NPower shared many of the technology tools it developed, as well as its performance metrics, with members of the NTAP field. Their consultants and trainers often appeared on panels and gave talks at the Nonprofit Technology Conference and similar regional meetings. After 9/11, NPower NY convened Circuit Riders and other major NTAPs to coordinate donations and organize recovery efforts for the nonprofit sector in New York City. Many from the Circuit Rider movement joined NPower organizations as managers and consultants. Several Circuit Rider organizations, such as Technology Works for Good in Washington, D.C., joined the NPower network as part of the organization's national expansion. NPower also occasionally hired Circuit Riders and other independent consultants to do contract work with clients.

As I mentioned in the introduction, moral markets are complex. Social movements pressure market actors to embrace certain social values. Sometimes this takes the form of activists using their purchasing power and engaging in market activities to express their social beliefs. At other times, social movements organize boycotts, withdrawing from market activities, to make their point. Businesses sometimes respond by developing corporate social responsibility guidelines or creating ethical products and services in response to consumer and activist demands. At other times, businesses countermobilize against social movement demands. Out of these ongoing interactions emerge conventions of coordination, implicit rules of engagement among collective and individual actors in a field or market. Conventions of coordination are guided by institutions, but not determined by them. They are negotiated in practice, not taken for granted. Conventions of coordination arise as organizations in fields attempt to cope with and reduce uncertainty around appropriate ways of interacting. As discussed in Chapter 4, uncertainty in moral markets often arises out of moral ambivalence, as institutional contradictions leave managers with conflicting ideas about what they ought to do.

The Emergence of Conventions of Coordination in Moral Markets

Participants in moral markets operate under conditions of uncertainty stemming from the ambiguous rules of interaction within them. Questions include the practical: Under what conditions should social movements collaborate with market organizations? Should social movements participate in the market economy? Or should they challenge market exchange altogether? What about businesses? What obligations do they have to various publics? How should businesses respond to the social demands of movements? And the profound: Are markets just? Can they ever be made just? Or are they inherently corrupt or corruptible? All are fundamental questions related to the conventions of coordination in moral markets. What are the bases for relations that arise in moral markets—competition versus collaboration, antagonism versus rapport, conflict versus agreement, coexistence versus cooptation? Throughout their history, NTAPs from the Circuit Riders to NPower had to develop answers to these questions. Many times, such answers emerged as the result of continued interaction among actors in the field, rather than from the strategic planning of managers and leaders.

The Complexity of Competition and Cooperation in Moral Markets
Legend has it that the nickname "Windy City" comes not from weather conditions but from how much Chicagoans brag about their city (Bierma, 2004). Yet, Chicagoans often express insecurity when inevitable comparisons to New York arise. "We constantly compare ourselves to New York, our pizza, hot dogs, skylines, and financial markets," the hypothetical Chicagoan says. "What do New Yorkers think of us?" To which the hypothetical New Yorker replies, "They don't." NPower had a similar relationship to the rest of the NTAP field. When I asked leaders and executives at Circuit Rider organizations and other

NTAPs who they considered their "competition," all mentioned NPower. As the executive director of a large NTAP told me in confidence, "I worry a little bit about NPower, even though we have collaborated with them." When I asked managers at local NPower offices as well as the national office who they considered their competition, they often replied, "no one." One manager told me, "At the national level, I do not mean to sound arrogant, but I do not think we have a lot of peers" [35].

When I probed further, I discovered that managers at NPower did consider other organizations competition at times. As a moral market, nonprofit technology assistance was a complex landscape of alternating competition and cooperation (Lane & Maxfield, 1996). Projects that seemed collaborative at first could become competitive or certain facets of them would become competitive. Fanning expressed the complexity: "Right now when we are working with other national providers that do the same work, like Compumentor, for the first time in a real significant way. There has been competition and it has not been at the staffing level or competing for jobs, but just recognizing that we are collaborating, but there is also competition and the tension around that. We are in the middle of just trying to talk through some ground rules and acknowledge it" [19]. A manager at the IT Resource Center, a long-standing NTAP in Chicago, understood the complexity from the other side: "NPower is both a peer and a competitor. It is a peer in that they are based on our business model and they adapted what they do from what we do. They are a competitor in that they are much more successful in seeking and achieving national funding that we have been unable to acquire and so they do a much better job of that. If we go to those funders, [they say], 'we are already funding NPower'" [55].

What these quotes express is the need for "conventions of coordination" in the market for technology assistance. Conventions of coordination are implicit rules about how competition and collaboration ought to take place among members of the field that emerge out of interactions among those members (Storper & Salais, 1997). For example, Neil Fligstein (1996) finds that many market actors are loath to compete on price because it would produce a race to the bottom, which would undermine everyone's profits. In such instances, Fligstein argues that implicit rules about competition arise in such fields that let competitors know the appropriate grounds on which competition may be based. Competition is only one of many possible modes of coordination. Members of the nonprofit sector often are pressured to collaborate, sometimes as a condition of foundation or government funding. In practice, conventions of coordination are shaped by the evaluative criteria associated with modes of coordination. The implicit rules by which competition is judged as the appropriate mode of coordination or by which certain actors are judged winners derive from various orders of worth. The same is true for collaboration as a mode of coordination. In nascent markets, such as the market for technology assistance, conventions of coordination arise out of the interactions of field members as they evaluate the actions of others in various situations. Conventions of coordination emerge to answer the abstract questions: What is the situation? Who are the relevant actors? What can one expect them to do? What should one do in anticipation of their actions? How should one respond to what they do? Conventions of coordination reduce the uncertainty of action by engaging actors in pragmatic evaluation of situations (and the actors present in them as well as their actions) by focusing their competences toward defining situations and producing collective definitions of the situation.

Between social movement and market actors, conventions of coordination involve the tactical repertoires of social movements. Scholars of social movements use the term "tactical repertoire" to describe the toolkit of actions that a social movement deems appropriate for achieving its goals (Taylor & Van Dyke, 2004). When engaging with market actors, tactical repertoires often include market tactics such as ethical consumption and boycotts (Chasin, 2000; Stehr & Adolf, 2010). Alternatively, social movements deploy extrainstitutional tactics, such as protest and public campaigns (Soule, 2009). The tactical choices of movement actors and organizations contribute to the emergence of conventions of coordination in moral markets in which they are active.[1] Market-based tactics, such as ethical consumption, are attempts to shape market action and actors through positive feedback: ethical corporations are rewarded in the market (Sayer, 2006). Such tactics are judged by reference to the evaluative criteria of the market. Extramarket tactics, such as protests, attempt to influence market actions and actors through punishment and public shaming (King & Soule, 2007). Extramarket tactics are judged by reference to evaluative criteria such as contributions to collective goods (i.e., according to a civic order of worth) or by how well they disrupt the market for the target organization (turning a market order of worth on its head). Both market-based and extramarket tactics contribute to conventions of coordination by shaping the modes of coordination that actors in the field deem appropriate.

As noted in Chapter 4, NPower created a hybrid organizational model based on the social enterprise form and combining social and market values. By introducing and legitimating a hybrid form, NPower legitimated market values in a movement space. After NPower, nonprofit technology assistance became a movement–market hybrid, combining and recombining social and market values and ideals into a moral market. NPower's presence as a social enterprise, already a hybrid form, led to the proliferation of hybrid organizational forms and practices. Both TechRocks (a direct descendant of the Circuit Rider movement) and Compumentor adopted hybrid organizational forms following NPower's ascendance. Many of these organizations were supported by foundation and corporate donors, which expected social as opposed to financial returns on their investments. However, foundation and corporate donors also expected NTAPs to be financially sustainable, which promoted such business-like practices as charging fees commensurate with market value.

Pressure to Cooperate

Since NTAPs are part of the nonprofit sector and incorporated as nonprofits themselves, their leaders understood that the institutional expectations of the nonprofit sector pressured them toward cooperation. Daniel Ben-Horin, the founder and executive director of Compumentor, expressed this sentiment: "I know this may sound a little Pollyannaish but I do not see anyone as our competitors. I do not see any competition to provide [services]. Does one homeless shelter compete with another homeless shelter? There is enough business for both, right?" [81]. Similarly, a member of a Circuit Rider organization from Seattle told me: "NPower is great. I really like a lot of the services and a lot of the programs that they offer and I send people to their trainings. I feel like it is a really good, mutually beneficial thing. There are organizations that contact us that really do not qualify for what we do so I will send them to NPower. It is great being able to do that. It is great not having to say, 'Oh, I am sorry, we cannot help you and we do not know who can'" [37].

Directors and managers at NPower held the same sense of collaboration. Throughout my time in the field, NPower NY hosted several receptions and meetings with Circuit Riders and other NTAPs, including the LINC Project, TechRocks, Summit Collaborative, NTEN, and Media Jumpstart. NPower NY also provided technical support in the form of advice and consultation to the founders of Media Jumpstart, helping the latter organization secure their

501(c)(3) status [49]. In one particular instance of collaboration, NPower NY convened NTAPs, foundations, and several technology companies in the days following 9/11 to coordinate their efforts toward the recovery of affected non-profit organizations. For several days, NPower NY's downtown office buzzed with Circuit Riders, foundation officers, and corporate managers, not to mention their own staff. From my fieldnotes:

> 1:00 p.m. About 50 Circuit Riders, foundation officers, nonprofit representatives, and corporate representatives assembled in the main area at the NPower [NY] offices. Staff members assembled a hodgepodge of chairs from different areas in the office. The chairs filled the available space in the main area of the office. They were quickly filled as the people flowed into the office, signing in to a spreadsheet on two computers at the door. The meeting started with a moment of silence to remember the people whose lives were lost in the World Trade Center attack. The meeting was titled: New York City Nonprofit Technology Recovery Project. The agenda was posted on Post-It white board notes as: Welcome, Introductions, What are the needs, Corporate funders, Suggestions for moving forward, Volunteers for keeping the process going, and Timeline and closing. (Fieldnotes 9–18–2001)

On the national level, NPower collaborated with both TechRocks and Compumentor on projects I will describe in greater detail later. Foundations, Circuit Riders, and managers at NTAPs often considered collaboration as the preferred mode of coordination. This reflects broader institutions of altruism in the nonprofit sector (Clohesy, 2000). In educational programs and on the job, managers of nonprofit organizations are encouraged to cooperate with one another to produce social goods (Jeavons, 1992; Stein, 2002). Yet, despite institutional expectations to cooperate, competition inevitably arose, especially around access to resources.

Competition over Resources

Limited resources in the nonprofit sector, especially for technology assistance, meant that competition for foundation and corporate funding was felt acutely among NTAPs and Circuit Riders. Marshall Mayer explained: "The place where the competition really comes into play is the whole grant-making field for nonprofit technology assistance. . . . It is getting more so because there are shrinking resources, there are fewer and fewer dollars being given away. Because of the nature of how foundations are set up to make decisions about which proposals are worthy and which ones are not, it is a competitive situation there" [11].

Data from 990 tax forms confirms these observations. Executives and development managers at NPower claimed that their presence in the field increased donations for technology assistance, by raising awareness, innovating service delivery, and demonstrating the success of their efforts by their use of performance metrics. Foundation support for technology assistance increased at major NTAPs between 1997 and 2002. However, as NPower made the funding pie bigger, it also took a larger slice in absolute terms. For example, total donations to the top three NTAPs in the United States (NPower, Compumentor, and the IT Resource Center) amounted to nearly $2.4 million in 1999, the first year NPower filed a 990 tax form. NPower accounted for almost 70% of donations that year. By 2001, the peak year of foundation support for NTAPs, foundations provided over $6.3 million to the same three NTAPs. At $3.5 million, NPower accounted for almost 60% of foundation funding to the top three NTAPs. NPower NY raised $3 million in funding in 2001, meaning the NPower affiliates in Seattle and New York combined raised $6.5 million of the $10 million (nearly 67%) of foundation support for major NTAPs in 2001. By 2002, when foundations began reducing grants for technology assistance, NPower affiliates in New York and Seattle continued to account for almost half of the funding to the top NTAPs in the country. The Circuit Riders were aware of the disparity. Gavin Clabaugh, from his position at the Mott Foundation, expressed the dissatisfaction of Circuit Riders when NPower began to receive an outsized proportion of donations: "[NPower] has come in and [been] perceived [by many Circuit Riders] like 'we have been doing this forever, why is NPower now getting the money?' So, yeah, there is this new versus old dichotomy there" [16].

Circuit Riders competed with NPower and other Circuit Riders for limited foundation funding. NPower's success in the funding arena signaled the legitimacy of its business-like practices in the nonprofit sector. This meant that Circuit Riders often felt they had to adopt similar practices if they were to compete for such funds. The result was a further push toward the widespread adoption of business-like practices and the embrace of market principles. This took two basic forms: embracing NPower itself and embracing the market more broadly.

Expressions of Moral Ambivalence in the Field

Out of the contradiction between the pressure to cooperate and the competitive reality, many Circuit Riders were ambivalent about NPower's rise to
prominence. They recognized that NPower's success raised awareness among
foundations and nonprofit organizations about the importance of information technology in contributing to their social missions. Increased awareness
generated material and symbolic support from foundations, which legitimated
the movement's goals, if not its explicit methods for achieving them. It also
attracted new clients in the form of nonprofit and grassroots organizations
that recognized the advantages that information technologies afforded.[2] Yet,
the Circuit Riders remained ambivalent about NPower's market values, which
were transforming their movement. The director of an existing NTAP that
considered affiliating with NPower told me in confidence:

> Honestly, their hookup with Microsoft, this is the confidential part, I would
> say it was both attractive and repulsive. We had no illusions about why Micro-
> soft is interested in us. As soon as I came to understand that this NPower
> partnership and the corporate giving piece was located in the corporate struc-
> ture of Microsoft and [the] department headed by their chief legal counsel,
> during the whole Justice Department thing [federal antitrust suit against Mi-
> crosoft], it was obvious what this was all about. There is an irony in deciding
> that you are going to be part of someone's strategy to defend the most horren-
> dous monopolistic practices, but on the other hand we thought "gee, we actu-
> ally use some Microsoft products."

Circuit Riders and leaders of major NTAPs responded to NPower's rise to
dominance with moral ambivalence. As noted in previous chapters, NPower
attracted new and more resources and attention to the field. However, it also
changed the meaning of technology and technology assistance from activism to
market activity. Pervasive moral ambivalence among Circuit Riders and other
NTAPs created uncertainty in the field, especially around situations of cooperation and competition. Circuit Riders faced this uncertainty in several forms:
Should they work with NPower on specific projects? Should they organize the
movement to make it more competitive with NPower? Should they leave the
market altogether and create an alternative vision of technology assistance in
the field? Uncertainty around how to answer these questions in various contexts
highlighted the need for conventions of coordination in the field.

Conventions of coordination emerge out of the interactions of actors (organizations and individuals) in the field as they attempt to overcome uncertainty (Thévenot, 2001). In their groundbreaking study of the rise of industrial districts, Storper and Salais (1997) show how conventions of coordination emerge out of the interactions of producers and other actors, including state agencies, as members of the field cope with the uncertainty of global markets. Moral ambivalence is a key source of uncertainty for actors operating in moral markets. Moral ambivalence makes it impossible to know ahead of time how one's actions will be evaluated. Conventions of coordination reduce the uncertainty of moral ambivalence by constraining the possible modes of evaluation—that is, the orders of worth—that would be considered appropriate and sensible in a given situation. Take the example of a Circuit Rider applying for the same grant as an NPower affiliate. Given the conventions of coordination in play at the particular moment in question, the Circuit Rider has to consider the following questions: How will foundation officers evaluate the relative merits of Circuit Riding? Will they be held to the same performance metrics as NPower? Would they stand a better chance of getting the grant if they collaborate with an NPower affiliate on the project?

However, conventions of coordination are not simply about the mutual orientation of actors and organizations, such as Circuit Riders and NPower. Rather, conventions of coordination among NTAPs arose around orientation to the market: How should Circuit Riders approach the nascent market for technology assistance services? Should they sell their services on the open market, such as by charging clients directly for services? Should they retain close ties to foundations to support their work? How can Circuit Riders maintain a collective identity as activists in the face of market forces?

Circuit Riders Engaging with the Market

Competition over foundation funding pressed Circuit Riders to adopt many of the market practices that foundation officers rewarded. Since NPower and NPower NY were so successful at attracting foundation support, this often meant adopting many of the business-like practices these organizations espoused.[3]

Embracing NPower

NPower's national expansion gave struggling Circuit Rider organizations prospective access to newfound legitimacy and resources. Several such organizations joined the NPower Network, including Technology Works for Good in Washington, D.C., and TechBridge in Atlanta. Perhaps the most dramatic of these mergers was the addition of Compumentor to the NPower network. Founded in 1987, Compumentor predated NPower by over a decade. The organization was started by Daniel Ben-Horin, who sought ways to connect the technology needs of the local nonprofit sector with the skills of the burgeoning high-tech industry in the Bay Area. To that end, Compumentor engaged primarily in volunteer matching,[4] which ultimately inspired NPower's volunteer-matching program. Compumentor also hired consultants to provide direct technology assistance services to local nonprofit organizations. Aligned with the Circuit Rider movement, Daniel Ben-Horin considers himself an "organic intellectual" and "barely reformed Marxist" [81].[5] He started Compumentor to help nonprofit organizations achieve social change, but was also pragmatic about sustaining the organization. Ben-Horin explained: "We have always said that our priority was small- and medium-sized nonprofits and, within that, social change nonprofits. That is not a term of ours: a lot of nonprofits deal with social change. A homeless shelter is a social change nonprofit. . . . But nevertheless, there are organizations that have an analysis of how their work is going to create systemic change. Those are the most interesting organizations. But we are not in a position where we can say we just work with them" [81]. Similar to Fanning, Ben-Horin defines social change broadly, understanding that the market for social justice organizations is too small to sustain an NTAP. In practice, Compumentor works with nonprofit organizations of all types, but encourages his consultants to identify social change organizations for additional assistance, such as pro bono work.

In 2002, Compumentor announced it was joining the NPower Network. In a press release, Ben-Horin explained: "With the NPower affiliation, we raise our support for the local nonprofit community to a new level. We will collaborate with our peers to improve breadth and depth of local technology assistance services; we will directly deliver Bay Area-focused tech information to nonprofits through localized versions of TechSoup and By The Cup, and we will offer new hands-on implementation services. Our local community will greatly benefit from this new partnership, because it addresses nonprofits' needs for affordable and high-quality tech assistance from so many angles"

(Newswire, 2002). Thus, embracing NPower is a form of ongoing collaboration with the institutional leader in the field. In doing so, Compumentor gained access to NPower's accumulated knowledge as well as its pool of national-level funders, including corporations and independent foundations.

Compumentor was already large compared to most NTAPs. Having predated the Circuit Rider movement, the organization was considered well established. However, Compumentor remained focused on San Francisco for the first ten years of operations. Ben-Horin told me that "between '90 and '98 we were pretty solitary and I would not say it was a national discussion" [81]. Compumentor was introduced to the Circuit Rider movement when Ben-Horin was asked to participate in the National Strategy for Nonprofit Technology. The organization worked alongside the movement through the late 1990s. Compumentor launched TechSoup, a web portal for nonprofit organizations interested in technology, in 2000. Through this model, Compumentor increased its earned income dramatically. According to tax forms, Compumentor earned $628,000 in 1999. After launching TechSoup, its earned income doubled to $1.5 million in 2000, doubling again to $3.4 million in 2001. Compumentor's earned revenue continued to grow, reaching $5.3 million with the launch of DiscounTech in 2002, which was an online store selling discounted software with special pricing for the nonprofit sector. TechSoup became so integral to Compumentor's model that the organization formally changed its name to TechSoup Global in 2008. More important, TechSoup and DiscounTech gave Compumentor a national presence that rivaled NPower's in terms of brand recognition and stature.

Compumentor's relationship with NPower was rocky from the start and never settled. Continuing to focus on software sales and their web portal, Compumentor never fully adopted NPower's service delivery model. Managers from each claimed publicly that the organizations were culturally incompatible. One evening after the Orlando Riders Roundup, I had an informal conversation with two directors from NPower National and a manager at Compumentor about the differences between their respective organizations. The discussion revolved around the lack of formal evaluation at Compumentor (Fieldnotes 4–14–2002). The directors from NPower were frustrated that Compumentor was not adopting the performance metrics they had established for the field. The manager from Compumentor explained that the organization's culture was driven by their contributions to social goods, such as alleviating homelessness and social justice. The conversation revealed that technology assistance meant different things to NPower and Compumentor. When faced with a social-justice-driven organization like Compumentor, NPower evaluated technology assistance through the lens of the market. When faced with a market-driven organization like NPower, Compumentor judged the worth of their endeavors based on civic moral principles like social justice and the environment, applying the same criteria often employed by the Circuit Rider movement.

Within one year, managers at the organizations decided they were incompatible and decided to end the formal affiliation. Ben-Horin explained: "We were the Bay Area affiliate of NPower and we were a very bad match for what they were trying to do. They basically wanted to start organizations that would fit in their model. We were much older and wiser. . . . And for all the reasons you can imagine, there was tension within that" [81]. Despite the formal split, NPower affiliates across the country continued to collaborate with Compumentor on localized versions of Tech Soup and with promoting DiscounTech in their markets.

Yet, the split had ramifications for the larger field of NTAPs. The convention of coordination that emerged from the contention between Compumentor and NPower was selective engagement with the institutional leader in the field. Several independent NTAPs embraced NPower by becoming affiliates. TechBridge in Atlanta and Technology Works for Good in Washington, D.C., made the transition successfully. The former retained its name, the latter was rebranded as NPower Greater DC Region. Compumentor was large and more established than other prospective affiliates. The partnership between NPower and Compumentor was dissolved based on claimed differences in organizational culture and perspective. The success of certain affiliations (and failure of others) created conventions around successful engagement with NPower. Although managers at the national office made no formal rule against it, NPower did not attempt to affiliate with older, more established NTAPs after breaking its affiliation with Compumentor. Sheldon Mains, who worked at such an organization in Minneapolis, explained why their application to affiliate with NPower was turned down: "CompuMentor was a part of the NPower network until this last summer, and after one year they basically pulled out. I think part of the problem was there was a cultural issue between NPower National and CompuMentor. CompuMentor had its own national image, its own visibility, and its own way of doing things and just did not work like the NPower network wanted. . . . They were going through those problems right when our application was submitted" [58].

Such conventions did not depend on the location of the NTAP as a desirable market for NPower. San Francisco was a highly desirable location for an NPower affiliate. Furthermore, several similar NTAPs in desirable markets, such as TACS in Portland and the Management Assistant Program in Minneapolis, applied to become affiliates, but were turned down. Others, such as IT Resource Center in Chicago, considered applying for affiliation, but did not do so after recognizing that other, similar organizations had been turned down. As such, the implicit rule, or convention of coordination, for engaging directly with NPower was that only newer, less established organizations would be considered appropriate.

Embracing the Market

NPower's dominance established the legitimacy of social enterprise and concomitant business practices in the nonprofit technology assistance field. Richard Zorza, who has worked alongside Circuit Riders from the beginning of the movement, explained: "NPower, notwithstanding its relationship with Microsoft, very much came out of the National Strategy [for Nonprofit Technology (NSNT)] and made the field different. NPower is the only game in town in terms of any real national network of support providers. And that is not because of Microsoft money, although Microsoft money has helped. It is actually because of the ideas, because they are committed to an open model [of knowledge sharing among their affiliates]" [60]. NPower's account became conventionalized, that is, it no longer required justification (Biggart & Beamish, 2003; McInerney, 2008). Its model was moving toward the taken-for-grantedness necessary for institutionalization to take hold. One response among Circuit Riders and other organizations in the field was the adoption of entrepreneurial and commercial activity. Scholars of organizations use the term institutional isomorphism to describe how organizations in a field come to have the same form and practices over time (DiMaggio & Powell, 1991b). Many in the NTAP field engaged in mimetic isomorphism, which occurs when organizations copy the forms and practices of others perceived as successful in the field.[6] Several Circuit Rider organizations emulated NPower's organizational forms and practices. However, emulation is rarely a case of straightforward adoption. Rather, organizations "edit" as they copy, which means that forms and practices are adapted to their local contexts by managers and staff as they balance the exigencies of the local environment with the situations they encounter in it (Sahlin-Andersson, 1996). One NTAP, TechRocks, provides a clear example of adapting business-like forms and practices into a Circuit Rider organization.

TechRocks emerged from the center of the Circuit Rider movement, which makes the case of its transformation so compelling as an example of the challenges associated with engagement as a convention of coordination. The RFF was an early adopter of the Circuit Rider model. As I described in Chapter 1, Rob Stuart approached the foundation after learning about Circuit Riding from Gavin Clabaugh. Stuart took a fellowship at the RFF, from which he promoted the Circuit Rider model to nonprofit organizations and foundations and organized a movement of activist technologists. To focus more closely on its core funding areas, the RFF spun off the Circuit Riding program, which became known as the Rockefeller Technology Project. The RFF continued to support the Technology Project, but the arrangement gave the latter greater operational independence.

The Rockefeller Technology Project was one of the first organizations to recognize the changing competitive landscape after Kykuit (see Chapter 2). The growing legitimacy of NPower drew resources and attention away from the Circuit Riders. To maintain its competitive standing, the Rockefeller Technology Project merged with Desktop Assistance to become TechRocks. Predating the birth of the Circuit Rider movement by almost a decade, Desktop Assistance was one of the earliest stand-alone technology assistance organizations in the country. Its principal, Marshall Mayer, was one of the earliest adherents of the Circuit Rider movement.

TechRocks became a hybrid Circuit Rider/market organization, continuing to rely on foundation funding for approximately 85% of its budget, but also charging nonprofit organizations fees for services rendered, which raised the remaining 15%. TechRocks borrowed facets of its business model from NPower, but it was also grounded in the practices of open source. In this way, TechRocks combined the forms and practices of NPower (a stand-alone consulting model that charged clients directly for services) with those of the Circuit Rider movement (heavy, if not total, subsidization of services and the volunteerism and activism of open source, as well as traveling consultants). TechRocks took over the development of an open-source database project called Ebase. Developed originally by Mayer at Desktop Assistance, Ebase was a customizable database designed for nonprofit applications, such as client management systems. Following a standard open source model (Weber, 2004), TechRocks made Ebase available to nonprofits at no cost, but charged for customization of the database. Beyond charging fees-for-service, TechRocks adopted a strategy of serving geographically based markets. TechRocks began with a standard Circuit Rider model, with consultants traveling to cities across the United States. They also continued to refer to their consultants as Circuit Riders. However, the organization soon began emulating NPower, shifting its focus to geographically concentrated markets. Marshall Mayer, one of TechRocks's directors, explained: "We are in the midst of changing [our] model so that we are also highly concentrated in two markets that we will be developing over the next couple of years, New York and San Francisco Bay Area markets" [11]. Something else to note in Mayer's comment is the cognitive shift from movement action toward thinking in terms of markets.

Despite a partial cognitive shift to the market, TechRocks remained true to its roots in the Circuit Rider movement, as it continued to serve advocacy organizations almost exclusively. As their website stated their mission: "TechRocks accelerates social and political progress by building technological capacity for community collaboration and citizen engagement. TechRocks encourages and enables foundations, advocacy groups, and leading activists to use technology to achieve their mission goals, to increase participation from interested constituencies, and achieve change more quickly than by traditional organizing and advocacy methods alone." The organization also continued to employ the rhetoric of the movement, describing its consultants on its website as "Evangelist, organizer, technician, and teacher," the same words Gavin Clabaugh used to explain the role of the Circuit Rider in early presentations (see Chapter 1). Amy Luckey worked for TechRocks during its peak. She described the organization's approach: "I think that Rob [Stuart] and Marshall [Mayer] really infused the organization with an enthusiasm and an excitement for we can do things differently. There is something new and exciting here. Technology can radically transform the way that nonprofits work. In particular, we all were active in terms of progressive political issues. . . . We wanted to change the world and use technology to help do that" [80]. Luckey's comment reflects how TechRocks attempted to channel the ethos of the Circuit Rider movement in a new format. Recall from Chapters 1 and 2 that the Circuit Riders used similar language to establish the worth of their endeavor and mobilize adherents.

Despite the adoption of some market practices, TechRocks struggled to maintain its operations. Rob Stuart left in 2002 to start a consulting group to help progressive and Democratic political campaigns use communications technologies more effectively. He also took a board position at NPower PA (Pennsylvania). From there, Mayer took over sole directorship of the organization, focusing its efforts on Ebase. According to Michael Ward, who worked at TechRocks as well as the Rockefeller Technology Project, the open source software focus made it difficult to raise foundation funding [64]. His explanation is borne out by the data. In 2001, the first year the organization reported revenue, TechRocks had raised close to $400,000 in contributions. The level of funding they received is evidence of foundations rewarding their market focus. After Stuart left and Mayer shifted the focus toward open source, foundations reduced funding to TechRocks precipitously. That year, TechRocks raised only $150,000 and reported only $115 in assets. By 2003, TechRocks reported only $20 in contributions and no assets, closing its doors for good later that year. By December, a person searching for TechRocks online would be met with a 404 File Not Found error message at their former URL. The Circuit Riders employed by TechRocks splintered off into other aspects of technology and technical assistance. Michael Ward left to work with political advocacy groups. Amy Luckey went to work for a nonprofit consulting firm. Marshall Mayer worked to found the Nonprofit Open Source Initiative (described in detail below) before leaving the field entirely and starting a collaborative website about modern homes and sustainability. Michael Ward summarized: "What happened to TechRocks? It went bye-bye. It suffered from a lot of the same problems that the dot-com world did" [64].

TechRocks attempted to engage with the market, but on movement terms. Rather than shedding the social justice ideals of the Circuit Rider movement, TechRocks attempted to make a market virtue of them through supporting open source software and working exclusively in a single market niche, politically progressive advocacy groups. In the end, TechRocks's version of the movement-market hybrid failed. Several reasons for the failure are apparent. First, TechRocks did not embrace the market fully enough to generate sustainable revenue. In the world of social enterprise, which the NTAP field had embraced, earned revenue was a sign of fiscal sustainability. Insufficient earned revenue makes it difficult to generate donated revenue from entrepreneurial-minded foundations (Frumkin, 2003), which included the major funders of nonprofit technology assistance. Second, TechRocks's movement-market hybrid may have been too far toward the movement end of the spectrum, rendering it unrecognizable and illegitimate in the eyes of foundation officers. Publicly traded firms that fall outside of standard categories recognized by analysts suffer lower stock prices as a result (Zuckerman, 1999). A similar process was likely at play in the NTAP field. As a social enterprise, NPower was a hybrid organization as well. However, NPower solved its hybridity problem by tapping into existing accounts of social enterprises (a legitimated form) and ultimately creating a category unto itself through the institutional entrepreneurial work of Joan Fanning and Barbara Chang. The proliferation of hybrids in the NTAP field made it difficult for foundation officers to support organizational forms that fell outside of their experience or understanding of what a successful social enterprise is and does. Third, TechRocks's close ties to the RFF may have crowded out additional independent foundations. Compounding the lack of access to foundation funding, the open source model may have alienated technology companies such as Microsoft.

Engaging with the Market as an Emergent Convention of Coordination
Engaging with the market reflects a convention of coordination rooted in pragmatic, moderate tendencies within the Circuit Rider movement. Seemingly radical Circuit Riders and sympathizers, such as Stuart and Ben-Horin, respectively, engaged with the market rather than attempting to challenge it. Instances such as these challenge the pervasive view within sociology of reifying categories of activist versus market or even subcategories within those groups, such as moderates versus radicals (Den Hond & De Bakker, 2007; Haines, 1984). Conventions of coordination therefore arise out of situations in which actors find themselves and the opportunities to express their competences within them. Both Stuart and Ben-Horin brought certain competences to the table. Stuart considered himself a visionary and organizer and attempted to engage with a market on those competences. He also had close ties to resource holders in the RFF. Ben-Horin took a more pragmatic approach to markets, following from a post-Marxian worldview predicated on deploying the tools of capitalism, such as the modern bureaucratic organizational form, to facilitate incremental social change. Their modes of engagement arose out of these competences to create models of action within the field. Both leaders and their organizations were highly respected within the NTAP community, which facilitated the legitimacy of their models of action.

The failure of Compumentor and NPower's merger and the early success and rapid demise of TechRocks illustrate the challenges and uncertainties when movement actors engage with market actors. Compumentor and NPower were unable to reconcile their approaches to technology and technology assistance. However, Compumentor embraced the market in its own way, through retail software sales, and found commercial success as a result. Foundations rewarded TechRocks's move toward the market, but withdrew their support as the organization shifted back toward the movement with its adoption of open source. TechRocks remained rooted in the movement and its members were unable or unwilling to embrace the market to the degree foundations and other stakeholders deemed necessary.

As I noted in the previous chapter, NPower continued to grow, expanding to 12 affiliates throughout the United States. Affiliates in Atlanta and Washington, D.C., were the result of successful alignments between NTAP and Circuit Rider organizations and the logic of NPower. Other affiliates absorbed former Circuit Riders to work for the organization[7] or serve on its board.

Counteractivism Against the Market

NPower nudged nonprofit technology assistance toward the market, while maintaining certain aspects of its movement roots. Charging fees, branding, and service delivery models reflected the adoption of market practices. The recording and reporting of performance metrics ensured that NTAPs would be evaluated according to market-like criteria, which provided a market-based justification for nonprofit technology assistance. This market-based justification displaced some of the social movement justification of the Circuit Riders— for example, social justice and environmentalism—in determining the worth of technology assistance as a legitimate activity.

Despite NPower's legitimacy among corporations, independent foundations, and some in the Circuit Rider movement, not everyone was happy with their presence in the field. One Circuit Rider who was instrumental in organizing the movement early on said:

> Use NPower as your sample and watch how Compumentor, Compass Point, probably IT [Resource Center] have all changed. It would be interesting to go back and look over the last three to four years how the products, the services, the mission have all started looking like NPower. It is good to have NPower,

just as long as everyone is not NPower. They have this Microsoft mentality to make everyone look like us. Again, you cannot blame people. NPower is so successful at raising money. You are a nonprofit. The bottom line is that you need to raise money and NPower works. They have got funders and maybe we should go after the same funders with a very similar way. But it is making for a very homogenous sector [among NTAPs]. And I cannot blame them. I have been there raising money. I have been there when I cannot pay people a certain amount. Then you are like, what do I need to do? Again, it goes back to the power of the funders. You have to fit what the funders want and what the funders want is NPower. They want something like NPower. It is safe. It is very down the middle. It shows progress. It fits what you want to do. [51]

Circuit Riders criticized NPower for focusing on the market while neglecting the social aspects of their work. The executive director of a competing NTAP group explained: "I was very interested in spending most of the time focusing on much, much more progressive operations and services than technology. NPower was never that way. It was, in my mind at least, from what I understand about the original NPower in Seattle, technology was the issue and that was the beginning and the end of it. There was not really an overt social mission that was associated with it, as I understand it" [57]. NPower's attachment to the democracy of the market created a tension when managers attempted to reconcile it with their social mission and personal political inclinations. This anecdote from my fieldnotes illustrates this tension:

On the way to the station, I asked [NPower's director of consulting] if they have ever had to deny an organization services because of political reasons. He said that they have not yet, but it was a subject of angst in the office. He said that NPower Seattle also feels angst about it. They have had discussions about it, but it has not come up in practice. The closest it has, is with religious organizations. NPower does not work with schools or churches, two possibly contentious groups of clients. That keeps them in the clear from most problems. But, since most of the NPower staff has liberal or progressive politics, an organization like the NRA would pose a problem for them. Hal said that he would actually take pleasure in telling off a conservative client. He said that the nonprofits on the right are generally large and well funded and do not consider themselves nonprofits. While they have not had to deal with the issue, it does concern them. (Fieldnotes 12–20–2001)

The Circuit Riders' commitment to social justice is a defining feature of the model. They do not experience the tension between the market and their social values. Jamie McClelland of Media Jumpstart, a member of the Circuit Rider movement, explained:

> We are not like NPower. We are not like groups that have a big public reputation as being an independent, neutral NTAP. There is one guy I met from NPower that is like "we will work with the NRA. We are here not to be ideological and to do that." Media Jumpstart is a political organization. It is explicitly so. There is no wavering or doubt. NPower is afraid that the NRA is going to say that NPower is a bunch of lefties and they do not want to work with us. If they say that about us, great. [49]

A Circuit Rider expressed it more bluntly: "[NPower's] model was great and it fit into Seattle very well and it began replicating. I guess to a lot of social advocates [Circuit Riders], it felt much more like a corporate entity coming through" [51]. Most starkly, one Circuit Rider told me in confidence that she considered NPower "the Wal-Mart of nonprofit technology assistance providers," which is a powerful critique coming from a movement committed to social justice. As noted in earlier chapters, the Circuit Riders justified their accounts based on the contribution of their work to promoting progressive social causes, what I have been calling social values or social movement values. Now, these groups were criticizing NPower for justifying its account based on the technical aspects of its work, for example, promoting efficiency among nonprofit organizations by implementing information technology solutions.

Resisting Microsoft, the Evil Empire

Many Circuit Riders saw the incursion of Microsoft into the nonprofit sector as particularly problematic. Organizations that collaborated with the software giant became targets of criticism for doing so. On the national level, NPower's partnership with Microsoft made it the target of criticism for the software giant's competitive strategies.[8] The leader of one Circuit Rider organization explained starkly, "NPower is a Microsoft organization. It killed me early on that they were so Microsoft-centric in what they did" [51]. In a social world that considers itself "collaborative, voluntary, and 'non-territorial'," being called "Microsoft-centric" was criticism for being competitive, corporate, and monopolistic. NPower recognized that it was being criticized. The national coordinator for NPower explained to me: "I just think that sometimes NPower is confused for being a for-profit because of our approach to certain things. . . . I think we are seen as less of a nonprofit and more of a vendor, some sort of conduit for these organizations that invest in us. Microsoft would be a good example. . . . I get e-mails on the national level that say 'we are really excited to hear about you. It is too bad that you are partnering with the evil empire'" [24]. The sentiment was felt throughout the field. In a focus group I conducted with several independent nonprofit technology assistance consultants in Seattle, respondents accused Microsoft of "greenwashing"[9] with their funding of NPower [41].

NPower was not the only target of criticism for its collaboration with Microsoft. Compumentor was denounced for their market activities as well. Michael Gilbert, a self-professed "gadfly" in the nonprofit technology assistance world, challenged DiscounTech publicly and vociferously. Gilbert had already posted criticisms of NPower's cozy relationships with Microsoft on his blogs and in e-mails to LISTSERVs. Gilbert publicly denounced DiscounTech at the Nonprofit Technology Conference in March 2003. As a plenary speaker, Gilbert told the audience that he believed Microsoft was flooding the market with low-cost software in order to stifle competition from other software providers, particularly open source providers. Gilbert reiterated this criticism on his blog: "At the opening plenary of the NTEN conference, I raised questions about the potentially damaging nature of Microsoft's donations of software to the nonprofit sector. Although I'm not a lawyer, I also suggested that, as a monopoly, their below market price distribution of software might very well be a form of illegal competition for a particular market" (Gilbert, 2003). The comment was picked up and published in a *New York Times* article questioning Microsoft's motives for donating software to the nonprofit sector (Markoff, 2003). Gilbert told me in an interview: "I know that I insulted the people at DiscounTech but I stood up and said publicly that I believe that Microsoft and DiscounTech could conceivably be taken to court by a properly motivated antitrust attorney around the low market dumping of product within the nonprofit market. I believe that when it is done by a monopoly, it is not a donation" [40].

The resistance to Microsoft reflected a more general animosity to the software giant, as it faced federal monopoly charges. However, it is important to note the context of the Circuit Riders denunciations. In the early stages of the movement, the Circuit Riders welcomed Microsoft's software and monetary donations. Recall from Chapter 2 that Microsoft provided financial support for the National Strategy for Nonprofit Technology. Jane Meseck, Microsoft's community affairs director, was invited to the planning table. She invited Joan Fanning, who was working on the white paper that would eventually become NPower. What changed? Why did the Circuit Riders welcome Microsoft in the beginning and denounce it several years later? I contend that the rise of NPower introduced market values into the movement space, which allowed certain Circuit Riders, such as Michael Gilbert, to draw attention to the implicit contradictions of having Microsoft support the Circuit Riders. Many of the Circuit Riders were not opposed to capitalism or the market. Michael Gilbert himself was a social entrepreneur with a techno-libertarian streak. His organization, Social Ecology, was a for-profit cooperative owned by the nonprofit organizations it served. Rather, what united techno-libertarian and socially progressive Circuit Riders was an opposition to monopoly capitalism that Microsoft represented in the larger world and that NPower represented among NTAPs and the Circuit Rider movement.

Mobilizing Open Source

Criticism of monopoly capitalism in the market led many Circuit Riders to reorganize the movement and remobilize adherents. However, the old account around which the Circuit Riders movement had formed could not be resurrected because it was no longer legitimate to many in the field. NPower's account had displaced the Circuit Riders as the dominant one in the field. New entrants were more likely to emulate NPower's organizational form and practices than those of the Circuit Riders. To challenge the direction of the market, a group of Circuit Riders began to mobilize free and open source software in the service of revitalizing the movement. Mobilizing F/OSS made sense as a tactic. Scholars have shown that social movements choose tactics based on the vulnerabilities of their institutional targets (Walker, Martin, & McCarthy, 2008). Microsoft's proprietary software regime made them a target for technologists, hackers, and even the federal government. F/OSS programmers defined themselves against proprietary software regimes, Microsoft's in particular (Gallaway & Kinnear, 2004). As one Circuit Rider explained the reason for mobilizing F/OSS, "The idea of an operating system that was not controlled by a big corporation was a great idea to me" [54].

F/OSS is a set of programs, programming platforms, and operating systems that are developed by communities of users who make limited or no ownership claims over what they produce and make available the source code underlying their products (McInerney, 2009).[10] Unlike proprietary software, which is designed and developed by a group of professional programmers often working for a single company, a distributed community of independent programmers continuously develops F/OSS programs (Von Hippel, 2005). F/OSS allows and encourages users to change the code that makes programs, platforms, and operating systems work. There are several licensing schemes governing the specific legal rights that users have over F/OSS. The most liberal require all modifications to be made available to the larger community. Under this legal regime, if I add a feature to OpenOffice, a F/OSS productivity suite, I have to upload my code to a central location for other users to download. Less liberal licensing schemes allow users to maintain some rights over their modifications.

Technologies often express the political inclinations of their designers, especially when inscribed in physical artifacts. Scholars of technology often cite the design of the bridges along the Wantagh Parkway, which connects New York City to the beaches of Long Island, as an example of politics inscribed in artifacts. The bridges along the highway are too low to allow passage by bus, effectively preventing the poor and minorities from reaching recreation spots at the newly finished Jones Beach (Caro, 1975). The design reflected the politics of their designer, Robert Moses (Winner, 1986). Bruno Latour (1991) argues that designers of technologies build their interests into artifacts in ways that shape users' behaviors in accordance to them. In a clever example, Latour (1988a) explains how the overlooked technology of a door closer contains within it the interests of building administrators, who carefully balance the needs of their budgets, the safety of the property in their charge, and the needs of the people who come and go.

Physical artifacts such as bridges and door closers create durable expressions of interests. Software is more problematic. Digital technologies like software are malleable. Companies such as Microsoft use closed architecture when designing their products to prevent "misuse" or "inappropriate" use, such as illegal copying. As such, software expresses the interests of its designers, but in ways that are problematic for inscription regimes (McInerney, 2009). Neff and Stark (2003: 186) observe, "If, as has been said, architecture is politics set in stone, then information architecture is politics in code." To that, I would add:

If information architecture is politics in code, then open source is a prescription for political action. Ron Braithwaite, who works for an NTAP called Free Geek, explained the most radical version of F/OSS: "Free software says there are no encumbrances. You get the source code, but I cannot restrict in any way what you do with it. Not only can I not restrict, I cannot limit what you can do with it, you cannot limit what you can do with it when you give it away, too. . . . Microsoft said that open source is like a cancer. It infects everything" [77].

F/OSS programmers are generally politically agnostic in the traditional Left/Right sense (Coleman, 2004; Lawton, 2002; S. Weber, 2004). However, they do see themselves as a movement challenging proprietary software regimes (Lessig, 2005). As a movement, F/OSS programmers have an ideology that tends toward techno-libertarianism (De Landa, 2001) and an infrastructure of advocacy organizations.[11] Among these advocates, the Free Software Foundation (FSF) is at the cutting edge of intellectual property disputes, providing intellectual and material support for the F/OSS movement (O'Mahoney, 2005). After making a large donation to the FSF, Eben Moglen, professor of law and legal history at Columbia University and FSF board member, told reporters, "We are a small organization running a big revolution and we have big adversaries" (Bray, 2002: F3). Moglen could have been speaking for the Circuit Riders.

F/OSS transforms software from a mass product into a custom service, providing the Circuit Riders with a critique of monopoly capitalism that justifies capitalism on a smaller, more individualized scale. Michael Gilbert expressed it this way: "There is a charitable spirit and that appeals to people [with F/OSS]. There is a way in which the open source model values labor over property. And I believe that nonprofits are labor-intensive. They are not property-intensive organizations" [40]. By mobilizing F/OSS in this way, the Circuit Riders are able to criticize NTAPs like NPower, which concentrate service provision into an indomitable market force, while justifying their own approach, which treats technology assistance as a set of intimate relationships between activists and movement organizations. At the same time, mobilizing F/OSS restores the decentralized network around which the Circuit Riders initially organized. Yet, to mobilize F/OSS, the Circuit Riders had to engage in counteractivism against the market, which meant organizing once again.

Growing Dissatisfaction with the Trade Association
Recall from Chapter 2 that one of the outcomes of the Kykuit meeting was that foundation officers insisted that Fanning rewrite the National Strategy

document and organize the trade association outlined in it. That trade association became the Nonprofit Technology Enterprise Network. The creation of NTEN reflected a pragmatic compromise between market and movement forces, as represented by NPower and the Circuit Riders, respectively. However, the Circuit Riders did not want NTEN to become a trade association. Daniel Ben-Horin, who was at the later NSNT meetings, explained how one particularly radical Circuit Rider tried to shape NTEN: "It was not [going to be the] Socialist International but he said one thing this cannot be is a trade association. We thought that would be a total undoing of the [NSNT] principles" [81]. Richard Zorza, who worked alongside the Circuit Rider movement, observed: "I think, for some of us, we had a broader vision of what we would have seen NTEN being as more about focusing on the transformative nature of this and less just serving the people as individuals, which is a lot of what has happened. We used to say at the National Strategy [for Nonprofit Technology that] what we do not want is a trade organization and in a certain sense that is exactly what has happened. We wanted something that would be much more transformative, but it has not happened" [60]. Another Circuit Rider who was instrumental to the movement, Carnet Williams, said:

> I think the founding board members, I truly to this day think we still had very differing interpretations of what NTEN was going to do. I think that myself and a couple of other founding board members envisioned NTEN as an organizing entity to help drive forward new ideas, new directions, and to coalesce folks who are kind of on the fringes of nonprofit technology, be it those doing open source work. I always envisioned NTEN to be an organizing entity. We were going to bring people together, really bring new ideas, almost, not so much like a think tank, but more of an incubator. Someone comes forward and says, "Hey, I have got this great product. It is an open source time tracking thing that can be used in social service organizations. I want groups to use it." Then NTEN would jump in and help incubate that. . . . So we envisioned NTEN really being that kind of entity. [51]

Several Circuit Riders took seats on NTEN's board in an attempt to instill what they considered the "transformative ideals" of the movement into the organization. According to Rob Stuart, "We used the [Circuit] Riders as the venue through which a lot of the organizing of NSNT and subsequently NTEN would happen because we wanted to instill those values, the [Circuit] Rider values into those subsequent organizations" [14]. However, despite their attempts to maintain movement ideals, NTEN became a trade association. Some blamed foundations for being fundamentally conservative. Again, Carnet Williams:

> Funders are more conservative. Funders were looking at NTEN as more of an organization that brings credibility to the field and is acting as more of a trade association. So it is something that has members and the members vote on things and it maybe holds a couple of conferences, maybe publishes a couple of articles. [It's] kind of a much more middle of the road organization. I think that is where the split occurred right after it was formed. The funders won out because the funders on the board were also the initial funders of the organization, which I many times raised my hand and said that was an issue. But, the way things work in the nonprofit world is, without the funders, you do not have an organization. [51]

However, the Circuit Riders also knew that Joan Fanning and NPower had a hand in shaping NTEN, especially as they were given the task of leading the formulation of NTEN as well as its fiscal stewardship. As Deborah Strauss of the IT Resource Center explained, "Joan Fanning basically stepped in and pulled the [NSNT] document into shape and carried it further. And she had extremely good Microsoft relationships so she was the savior, and NTEN came out of that" [57].

As I explained in Chapter 2, the NSNT meetings were a turning point in the Circuit Rider movement. In particular, the meeting at Kykuit afforded an opportunity for Fanning to act as an institutional entrepreneur, taking advantage of her position in the movement as well as access to resource and legitimacy holders to push the movement toward the market. According to the Circuit Riders, NTEN failed to achieve its transformative intentions because the NSNT planning process was subverted by the market-friendly forces of NPower and fundamentally conservative foundations. The Circuit Riders felt that NTEN no longer represented their ideals and, in cases such as the Nonprofit Technology Conference, actually worked against them.

Organizing NOSI, the Anti-NTEN

To provide organizational infrastructure necessary to remobilize the movement, the Circuit Riders founded an alternative coordinating body based on the principles of open source, calling it the Nonprofit Open Source Initiative

(NOSI).[12] Reuben Silvers was charged with pulling together resources, writing a business plan, and organizing NOSI into a full-fledged entity. As a condition of a debt forgiveness program that reduced his student loans in exchange for working in the nonprofit sector, Silvers worked to develop NOSI, an otherwise volunteer-driven organization. Marshall Mayer, another member of the steering committee, gave Silvers a desk and a small stipend at TechRocks to incubate the fledgling open source advocacy organization. Silvers spent the next six months organizing conference calls, driving e-mail discussions, and writing the business plan for NOSI. Members of the steering committee saw NOSI's primary task as advocacy for open source technology. Silvers explained: "What really needs to be happening is that nonprofits do not know about the open source software tools that are already out there. The basic stuff, like Linux, Open Office, and stuff like that. And that we [NOSI] need to be advocating and educating nonprofits and the NTAP community about Linux and how to use it and when to use it, how to even think about using it" [75]. The decision to become an advocacy organization was not always clear. Silvers also explained to me that they considered acting as a software development group, building open source technologies for the nonprofit sector. However, TechRocks failed after attempting to support an open source model. Other NOSI members, such as David Geilhufe, a Circuit Rider and F/OSS programmer, complained in meetings and over e-mail lists of the difficulty he experienced raising donations to support his work. Learning from these lessons, the members of NOSI's steering committee decided to focus on advocacy efforts.

NOSI was an attempt to return to the Circuit Rider ideals as articulated in the original National Strategy for Nonprofit Technology. It mobilized F/OSS in the service of those ideals. The NSNT organizing document outlines four "core principles" of the movement: reciprocity, continual learning, fair compensation, and open standards (Partners, 1999).[13] According to the Circuit Riders, the monopoly capitalism of Microsoft and NPower undermined these principles in the field, even as they implemented them internally. By creating and maintaining an internal knowledge management system and only selectively sharing knowledge with the rest of the field, NPower prevented reciprocity and learning in the nonprofit sector and among NTAPs. Through adherence to market-based pricing and taking advantage of economies of scale from their national operations, NPower made it difficult for Circuit Rider organizations, which had higher overhead costs, to attract foundation resources and stay solvent. By implementing proprietary software solutions,

NPower and Microsoft practiced the opposite of open standards. Carnet Williams, a Circuit Rider who was instrumental in organizing the movement and served on the founding board of NTEN, explained: "NOSI was [an outcome of] my frustration with not seeing the ideals that we talked about early on in the formation of NTEN being pushed forward: the ideals of using open source technology, looking for innovative technologies to push forward" [51].

To the Circuit Riders behind NOSI, F/OSS reinforced the core principles and reinvigorated the ideals of the movement. The NOSI strategic plan invoked ideological alignment strategies: "The open source and nonprofit communities share many norms and values, including the volunteer ethic, integrity, generosity, practicality, and excellence" (Silvers, 2002: 3). In their evangelism, NOSI sought to align their interests with the broader Circuit Rider community, the F/OSS developer community, foundations, and ultimately the nonprofit sector writ large.

Forging New Associations and Fashioning New Accounts

With infrastructural support from NOSI, many Circuit Riders began advocating for the "natural affinity" between the ideals of the technology platform and those of nonprofit organizations. According to "The NOSI Manifesto," an appendix to the organization's strategic plan: "NOSI aims to bridge the gap between the nonprofit and open source communities. We envision a world in which nonprofits are an integral part of the open source community and in which technology development for the nonprofit sector is open, interoperable, useable, sustainable, and minimizes the total cost of ownership" (Silvers, 2002: 18). In an interview, Marshall Mayer expressed NOSI's purpose, "NOSI exists to make connections between the open source community and the nonprofit sector" (LStechie, 2002).

The Circuit Riders' new mobilizing account began by associating the ideals of the technology with the ideals of the nonprofit sector, at the same time redefining and reframing each in order to revitalize the movement (McInerney, 2009). The strategy entailed producing normative claims such as "collaborative," "cooperative," "voluntary," and even "anti-capitalist" to describe the common values they theorized that members of F/OSS community and the nonprofit sector held. Their attitude was driven by what Silvers, the organization's first director, called "a natural philosophical affinity between the nonprofit sector and open source" (Silvers, 2002: 1). In an interview, Jamie McClelland of Media Jumpstart described the relationship:

I think there are a number of different connections between nonprofit and activist organizations and open source software on both ideological and practical levels. On an ideological level, I think it makes a lot of sense especially in anticapitalist organizations working for social justice. The whole ethic of open source software is very conducive to that type of work. It is saying there are two economies here. There is a capitalist economy and it is selling software and buying software, and there is an alternative economy of people coming together and working on software together. I think that, ideologically, is a very powerful incentive to do open source software. [49]

At the same time, the F/OSS account challenged monopoly capitalism in the NTAP market. Michelle Murrain, a Circuit Rider with a self-professed "very serious socialist streak," explained: "The values of open source development are about volunteerism, collaborative development, and that the good of intellectual property is that it is public and the people think it is better to share. That really reflects the values of the nonprofit sector. The nonprofit sector is about volunteerism and collaboration and working together for the greater good" [54].

Taking a page from NPower, NOSI conducted a "total cost of ownership" study of F/OSS for nonprofit organizations. The research, which was funded by IBM, sought to bolster the Circuit Riders' account of F/OSS with the quantitative metrics popularized by NPower. Like the original Circuit Rider report, NOSI articulated a formal account through their *Open Source Primer*. The *Primer* was an attempt to introduce the logic and method of F/OSS to managers of nonprofit and grassroots organizations. In it were ideological appeals, such as the claims of volunteerism, cooperation, and the collaborative spirit of F/OSS. The authors wrote: "The philosophical underpinnings of OSS (community-based development, volunteer effort, freely available software, community support) are very much in line with the mission of organizations in the nonprofit sector. . . . In general, we would argue that all other things being equal, making a choice to implement OSS in a nonprofit organization would add more mission-based value" (Murrain, Cowan, Silvers, Schneiderman, Hickman, & McClelland, 2004: 11). However, as an account of worth, the *Primer* also made claims based on market values. The *Primer* includes several pages on the total cost of ownership metrics for F/OSS, including the cost of implementation, training, software and hardware acquisition, maintenance, upgrades, and administration. It also includes worksheets for managers to calculate total cost of ownership and a sample worksheet demonstrating the long-term cost savings of adopting F/OSS. Thus, the account of worth articulated in the *Primer* was also predicated on an industrial order of worth, similar to that which was put into play by NPower.

Counteractivism Against the Market: To What End?

In interviews and at conferences, Circuit Riders admitted that their attempts to implement F/OSS in the nonprofit sector proved difficult. Of the many obstacles, one major impediment was the ubiquity of Microsoft's platform. Technical issues, such as compatibility, and cultural issues, such as comfort with particular technology platforms, made it difficult to mobilize F/OSS with Circuit Riders not already familiar with it. William Lester, who organizes international Circuit Rider projects, explained:

> Ideally, we would love to be working with the free platforms like Linux. The reality is we work with Microsoft probably 95% although we are really encouraging the growth of Linux as an operating system and of open source as a methodology for building applications. We are really embracing the people that are doing that and supporting them. We would like to see more and more of it but the reality is in the developing world, the people we run into, those who have learned these skills on their own, look at Microsoft as being the be-all and end-all of computer knowledge and so the reality is we deal with what people know, what people are comfortable with. In the few cases where we do plop down Linux solutions, we get looks like "you want us to do what?" There is a lot of learning and training to be done. [74]

Additionally, the Circuit Riders found it difficult forging the last link in the chain of association. The nonprofit and grassroots organizations that were the target of their efforts were already primarily committed to Microsoft products. Jon Stahl, a Circuit Rider with ONE NW, explained the breakdown at his clients in the Pacific Northwest: "The environmental movement is currently running about 80% Windows desktops and 20% Macs and we also have a couple Linux servers. I do a fair amount of Mac consulting but most of the demand was for Windows consulting. Most of the groups you work with are not running their own servers in-house of any kind. When they are running servers, they tend to be just basic file servers that tend to be running Windows" [36]. On the East Coast, Joshua Peskay of the Fund for the City of New York roughly agreed, "I would say it is about 90% Microsoft products and the next 8% Apple and then maybe 2% open source is the honest breakout" [53]. Microsoft's market penetration in the nonprofit sector roughly reflected the broader market penetration of the technology platform. The Circuit Riders faced a steep uphill march in mobilizing F/OSS.

What undermined the Circuit Riders' efforts to forge the last link in the chain of association was that for nonprofit and grassroots organizations the claimed "natural affinity" with F/OSS was never realized, that is, made real. The account of worth articulated in the NOSI *Primer* did not sufficiently align the interests of the movement with those of managers in nonprofit and grassroots organizations. Furthermore, most managers were uninterested in the politics of the technology. Studies have shown that many nonprofit organizations lack the expertise to work with information technologies at all (Robertson, 2001; Seley & Wolpert, 2002: 75). F/OSS presented a technical challenge for these organizations that was made insurmountable by their indifference to the politics of technology platforms and indifference to Microsoft. At a conference organized to advocate for F/OSS called "Demystifying Open Source," one Circuit Rider described the typical attitude from the perspective of a hypothetical client:

> I am often in disagreement about the economic system, but this is how it works. I think about what I use software for and that [the battle between open source and proprietary solutions] is not my fight. I do not need to control the software. I buy the software that I need to accomplish the task I need to accomplish. Whether Microsoft owns it or I own it, I do not care, as long as it works and does what I need it to do. *Technology is not my mission.* For me, it is just a tool. It is not an ideology. It is like a pen. I can buy a Bic or I can buy a Paper Mate and it does not matter, as long as they both write. (Fieldnotes 10-8-2003; emphasis added)

This reflects a misalignment of interests between the Circuit Riders and managers at nonprofit and grassroots organizations. Recall from Chapter 1 that Circuit Riders were bolstered by the imprimatur of foundations, which supported their account of technology assistance. The support of foundations helped align the interests of the Circuit Riders with those of managers at nonprofit and grassroots organizations. This time, foundations remained agnostic in relation to F/OSS. Jonathan Peizer, the chief technology officer at the Soros Foundation,[14] explained the state of the field:

If you track open source now, related to the nonprofit environment, it is not the nonprofits that are pushing it. It is the intermediaries; because there is not anyone in the nonprofits for the most part that is a leader in this. You do not have the expertise that is pushing this. It is left to the intermediaries. This creates an interesting dichotomy. What you really should be doing is looking at what the demand is in the nonprofit, rather than pushing an ideology. This is where I have some issues and concerns with some of my peers [in the Circuit Rider movement]. Some people look at it very much as an ideology. Many of those have never really implemented before or really had to maintain a systems operation. They just see it conceptually as very sexy. . . . I am and will always be a technology agnostic when it comes to how something is implemented. The focus always has to be on meeting the business requirements. [73]

Circuit Riders' attempts at challenging the market by mobilizing F/OSS met with limited success. On the one hand, the movement struggled to align its interest in F/OSS with those of managers at nonprofit and grassroots organizations. The problem was exacerbated by the Circuit Riders' inability to gain access to material resources and legitimacy from foundations, officers of which considered the push for F/OSS as ideologically driven. Without foundation support, several key organizations embracing F/OSS ceased operation in subsequent years. Many forces combined to put these organizations out of business. The point here is that the mobilization of F/OSS by members of the Circuit Rider movement could not resist these forces to revitalize NTAPs embracing the alternative technology platform. The largest of these, TechRocks, had combined a market approach with the volunteerism of F/OSS. As mentioned above, it closed its doors in 2003. The May First Technology Coalition ceased operating as an entity in 2005, when it joined forces with People Link to provide Internet hosting for grassroots organizations in the United States and abroad. The LINC Project ceased operations in 2006.

On the other hand, NOSI continues to operate. In 2003, the organization began hosting Penguin Days, a conference for Circuit Riders and NTAPs interested in F/OSS, as an alternative to the Nonprofit Technology Conference. Each year, the Penguin Day event takes place at the same city and weekend as the Nonprofit Technology conference, assembling Circuit Riders with F/OSS programmers in an attempt to forge mutual interests. As one observation from my fieldnotes shows: "Allen Gunn [from Aspiration Tech] said that the initial idea behind the [Penguin Day] conference was to bring together people from the open source community with people from the Circuit Rider community to start a dialogue. He said he wanted to foster an air of 'serendipitous chaos,' which he described as having a lack of structure and a lack of hierarchy, like the open source movement" (Fieldnotes 3–30–2004). In recent years, NOSI has attracted funding and interest from large corporations, such as IBM and Google, to support these events. F/OSS–Circuit Rider advocacy organizations have emerged to help connect programmers and activists. Aspiration Tech is the largest among these organization, though it remains small compared to NPower. Aspiration Tech absorbed NOSI in 2008, though both organizations have been relatively quiet since then (aside from organizing Penguin Days).

Despite these efforts, the Circuit Riders failed to revitalize the movement or enroll legions of F/OSS programmers into it. As a challenge to the market, the strategy fostered competition between Circuit Riders working with proprietary solutions and those espousing F/OSS. More important, mobilizing F/OSS ultimately contradicted the original mobilizing strategy of the Circuit Rider movement, that is, leading with the cause, not the technology. By leading with the technology (F/OSS), the Circuit Riders had to create associations and accounts that attempted to backfill the interests of nonprofit managers. Recall from Chapter 1 that Gavin Clabaugh established the worth of technology assistance by associating it with the causes to which independent foundations were committed. Now, Circuit Riders were attached to a specific technology platform and attempting to enroll others to accept a new account of worth that was not strong enough to overcome the existing account, that of NPower. In other words, NPower was already established as the market leader. For most in the sector, the challenge was not worth it.

Conventions of Coordination Between Movements and Markets

Members of the Circuit Rider movement had long considered technology assistance as a form of activism in the worlds of social justice and environmentalism. However, as NPower and its affiliates grew in number, size, and significance, the Circuit Riders increasingly found themselves operating in a market. The Circuit Riders expressed ambivalence about the presence of NPower and its market values. At times, many considered NPower an important part of the development of nonprofit technology assistance, bringing much-needed rigor and resources into the field. At other times, Circuit Riders were unnerved by NPower's growing dominance and what that meant for the activism around which their collective identity had been built and the movement had been mobilized.

This ambivalence shaped interactions between the Circuit Riders and NPower, leading to uncertainty on how the sides ought to orient to each other. Conventions of coordination emerged out of this uncertainty as two general types: engaging with the market (either directly with NPower or abstractly by adopting market practices) and mobilizing against monopoly capitalism in the market. However, as this chapter has demonstrated, mobilizing against the market did not last as a convention of coordination in any meaningful way. This is due in large part to the tactics the Circuit Riders used to counteract the market, specifically those efforts geared toward mobilizing F/OSS to create an alternative market. The Circuit Riders' attempted to mobilize F/OSS as a way to enroll legions of untapped computer programmers into the fold. These efforts failed because they could not enroll end users, such as managers from nonprofit and grassroots organizations, or resource holders, such as independent foundations. Missing links in the chain of association meant that the Circuit Riders' new account could not take root and a new market could not emerge. With a dominant convention of coordination established, engaging with the market became institutionalized as the appropriate form of interaction among NTAPs.

The Circuit Riders could have deployed other tactics to challenge the market for technology assistance established by NPower. For example, the Circuit Riders could have mounted a campaign against the marketization of technology assistance by organizing boycotts of NPower affiliates. However, the overwhelming number of prospective clients relative to NTAPs would have rendered such a tactic ineffective. The choice to mobilize F/OSS made sense in the context of the contemporary organizational field. Microsoft had just faced a federal antitrust lawsuit. IBM, which had long competed with Microsoft, began supporting F/OSS platforms, programs, and projects. However, support from key independent foundations, which was necessary to launch the Circuit Rider movement in 1997 as well as NPower in 1999, was lacking for reasons I explained above.

However, through their counteractivism the Circuit Riders did have an effect on NPower and ultimately the market for technology assistance in the nonprofit sector. The adoption of F/OSS by many Circuit Riders forced NPower to engage with the alternative technology platform on certain occasions, such as at the Nonprofit Technology Conference. More significant, the Circuit Riders tempered the market forces introduced by NPower by providing alternatives organizations and services. This was especially important for small nonprofit and grassroots organizations that did not have the financial resources to enter the market for technology services or those in rural areas and small cities that did not have access to an NPower affiliate. For the former, the presence of the Circuit Riders forced NPower to develop low-cost service delivery options, such as Technology Service Corps and volunteer matching. For the latter, NPower either ceded that portion of the market or developed Circuit Rider programs of its own.

The case of the Circuit Riders suggests that, under certain conditions, social movements' tactical repertoires may be severely constrained as they attempt to challenge a market that emerged out of their actions. This is certainly true in the case of the organic movement, in which activists are unable to mount meaningful challenges to dominant market values (Fromartz, 2006; Guthman, 2004). With the widespread acceptance of market conventions across the globe (Boltanski & Chiapello, 2005), social movements are increasingly finding themselves engaging in counteractivism against markets. Antimarket tactics, such as protests, have had limited and highly localized success (Bartley & Child, 2011; King & Soule, 2007). However, activists can press their demands through institutionalized means, such as stockholder tactics, or by organizing movements that create markets, such as the recycling industry (Lounsbury, 2005).

6

PATTERNS WORTH NOTING

Markets Out of Movements

Much of contemporary everyday life is organized by and around markets. This book relies on a case of a market that originated in an arena of the social world once thought impervious to market forces: the nonprofit sector. Markets are increasingly how society meets human needs. However, scholars and citizens should resist the urge to treat markets as abstractions. They remain constituted by people and organizations and continue to be shaped by groups of people, such as those organized in social movements. Social movements are a vital check on the abuses of market actors. Even as NPower established a market for technology assistance services in the nonprofit sector, pressure from the Circuit Riders shaped that market and ensured that NTAPs continued to serve nonprofit and grassroots organizations of all sizes and dedicated to all causes.

The Circuit Riders built a movement that was reportedly 10,000 strong in the late 1990s and early 2000s. In that time, they convinced independent foundations and nonprofit organizations that information technologies were worth adopting. The movement grew its ranks, forged a collective identity, and mobilized adherents by organizing a series of meetings. The Circuit Riders had much of what social movement scholars deem necessary for success: strong mobilizing structures, access to resources, an overarching ideology to guide their activities, and a strong collective identity. Yet, in just fifteen years the Circuit Rider Movement went from being the future of nonprofit technology to almost complete obscurity in the United States.[1] This shift led to this 2010 exchange on the Circuit Riders e-mail list, which continues to operate to this day:

Deborah Elizabeth Finn, who considers herself a "broker" [67] among NTAPs, wrote to an e-mail to the Circuit Riders LISTSERV about the Nonprofit Technology Conference she had just attended: "I had a wonderful time at the NTEN Nonprofit Technology Conference in Atlanta <http://nten.org /ntc>. It was not only very enjoyable but also very informative. . . . However, I missed seeing many of my esteemed colleagues from the Riders movement, and this has prompted me to ask what conference you all are attending these days? Perhaps I should think of attending them as well" (E-mail to Riders list 4–12–2010). One Circuit Rider from the MAP Program in Minneapolis responded: "I also attended [the NTC] and sat at the table labeled 'Circuit Riders' at the Friday Lunch. Only one other person at the table identified as a Circuit Rider and nobody else even knew what it meant. I ended up explaining the origin etc. many times" (E-mail to Riders list 4–12–2010).

What happened? The Circuit Rider movement, which held the promise of information technology for organizations helping those in need, had inadvertently created the conditions for a market. As they did, market actors appealed to resource holders to secure support for their way of doing things. The fate of the Circuit Riders reflects the fate of many social movements in the contemporary commercial era, in which a new spirit of capitalism has become the dominant organizing principle for our society and social problems are increasingly being confronted with market solutions. Social movements are often the first to identify social problems and frame themselves as solutions (Snow & Benford, 1992). However, market actors have become increasingly adept at reframing such problems and asserting their activities as solutions (Lounsbury, Ventresca, & Hirsch, 2003).

As the movement accepted new members, the meaning of Circuit Riding began to change. Technology assistance shifted from activism to professional consulting as an entrepreneurial spirit took hold in the movement. Taking advantage of shifts in the nonprofit sector as well as individual competences, Joan Fanning organized NPower and convinced for-profit corporations and independent foundations to support her social enterprise. NPower bridged the Circuit Rider movement and the market by recombining elements of each into an account that appealed to multiple audiences simultaneously. The organization grew a market for technology assistance services by expanding nationally. NPower NY became the first and most successful affiliate of the national expansion by embracing market values in unprecedented ways. The case of the Circuit Riders shows how social movements and market actors engage in intricate interactions over time to create "rules of engagement." Such rules of engagement, which I call conventions, emerge to reduce the uncertainty of action in interactions between social movement and market actors. Understanding this process contributes to scholarship on institutionalization and the social origins of markets. It also contains lessons for social movement activists and corporate managers.

From the Rise of Movements . . .

Social movements often grow from inauspicious roots. As I show in Chapter 1, the Circuit Riders were launched by the formation, articulation, and legitimation of an account that established that technology assistance was worth doing. In formulating an account, movement leaders such as Gavin Clabaugh and Rob Stuart associated sets of actions with justifications for doing them. The account of Circuit Riding mobilized other activists to join the movement as well as foundations and resource holders to support it. Through the efforts of movement leaders, stakeholders such as independent foundations and nonprofit managers came to realize that technology assistance was worth doing. In other words, Circuit Riding made sense as a way of providing technology assistance to nonprofit and grassroots organizations.

When prospective adherents are convinced that the cause is worth doing, social movements begin to enroll the worthy. This is followed by three concurrent and recursive processes: collective identity formation, mobilization, and organizing. Collective identity formation is the means by which actors come to recognize themselves as members of a movement and supporters of the cause. Mobilization consists of getting adherents to act on behalf of the movement. Organizing is bringing people together according to a certain structure or formation to facilitate more efficient or effective mobilizing and collective identity formation (Skocpol, Ganz, & Munson, 2000). Mobilization reinforces collective identity formation as actors come to identify themselves as members of the movement (Munson, 2008).

Organizing often leads to the creation of formal organizations. Social movement organizations vary in their degree of formalization—from anarchist affinity groups to institutionalized political parties. Sociologists of social movements and organizations have long held that formal organizations tend toward bureaucracy over time (Michels, 1959), though the process is neither linear nor inevitable (Zald & Ash, 1966). Recent scholarship has also pointed toward the development of professional social movement actors and the professionalization of social movement organizations as a trajectory of the bureaucratization process (Staggenborg, 1988). Bureaucratization and professionalization facilitate access to resources and provide stability to the movement, making it easier to maintain over time. Yet, as Chapter 2 shows, the very same forces may challenge core members' notions of authenticity. The form social movement organizations take reinforces the movement's collective identity as well as enables and constrains its efforts at enrollment and mobilization (Clemens, 1993, 1996; Clemens & Cook, 1999). In this way, collective identity formation, enrollment, mobilization, and organizing are recursive. Ways of doing any of these activities enable and constrain ways of doing any of the other activities. By organizing as a loosely coupled network, the Circuit Riders allowed the meaning of their work to be translated to various contexts, but in doing so they lost some control over their collective identity. This allowed professional consultants to gain a foothold in the movement at Riders Roundups.

. . . To the Creation of Markets

When the Circuit Riders organized their first Roundups, they could hardly have known that their actions would spawn a market for technology assistance services in the nonprofit sector. Yet, their work establishing the worth of technology and expressing it through portable accounts began a process that would unfold over time into the institutionalization of market practices in place of the movement they set out to build. Like social movements, market actors must establish the worth of their activities. In moral markets, such as that for nonprofit technology assistance, market actors must combine social and market values and find ways to reconcile two seemingly incompatible moral orders.

Economic sociologists have long been interested in the social origins of markets. In the early 1980s, Harrison White (1981) revitalized economic sociology by asking the question "where do markets come from?" Using complex mathematical models, White showed that markets emerge as producers monitor one another and adjust their behavior accordingly. In this book, I argue that movement actions create markets as individual and collective actors compete to establish accounts of worth that justify their practices and organizational form while blocking the legitimacy of competing actors. Similar to White, I find that the creation of markets is inherently relational. Groups of producers monitor each others' behaviors and adjust them accordingly. This was demonstrated most clearly in Chapter 3, in which I explain how Fanning, in creating a market-based NTAP, translated values and practices from the Circuit Rider movement into values and practices that aligned with the interests of her corporate and independent foundation supporters. The result is akin to what Fligstein and McAdam (2012) call a "strategic action field." Like them, I build on Bourdieu's notion of fields as social arenas in which agents with differential access to resources and capital compete for position (Bourdieu, 1990; Bourdieu & Wacquant, 1992). Markets are fields insofar as they are self-reproducing structures constituted by competing actors (incumbents and challengers) that jockey for position by deploying the resources they have at their disposal (Bourdieu, 2005). As members of a field, NPower and the Circuit Riders alternately competed and collaborated while reconciling institutional expectations with their desire to access more resources and gain better position in the field.

The hybridization of values and actors adds a layer of complexity to the creation of markets. Treating market and social values as discrete reifies them and masks how they are deployed in practice. In moral markets, actors of all kinds engage in innovative combinations of social and market values as they reflect different moral orders. In the field of NTAPs, market and social values were reconciled in hybrid organizational forms, such as social enterprises, and practices, such as charging subsidized rates for services. Hybrid organizations emerge from the attempt to stabilize compromises among competing moral orders. Organizations reflect institutions (Scott, 2008b). However, they are also constituted by fields (Bourdieu, 2004), which Fligstein and McAdam (2012) conceive of as fields within fields, like nested dolls. As fields, organizations are centers for pragmatic compromises among moral orders (Thévenot, 2001). By creating internal structures and routine practices, hybrid organizations stabilize the compromises among moral orders. For example, Chapter 3 showed how NPower combined the social values of the Circuit Riders (e.g., a commitment to nonprofit organizations) with the market values of corporate partners (e.g., charging fees directly to client organizations). To do so, NPower created formal structures, the aggregate of which constituted its organizational form. As a social enterprise, NPower was able to channel the resources it acquired through donations and earnings toward reproducing and ultimately replicating its hybrid organizational form. Chapter 4 demonstrated how organizations are constituted by and embedded in fields. NPower NY reconciled NPower's hybrid practices with pressures to be more business-like. I showed how the organization coped with the condition of moral ambivalence through internal compromises directed toward external moral legitimacy challenges.

A market of hybrids produces moral ambivalence as a particular form of uncertainty. Moral ambivalence is the tension resulting from the necessary coexistence of competing moral orders within an organization. Hybrid organizations, such as social enterprises, experience this tension as they attempt to meet contradictory institutional expectations from other actors in the field. Organizations make pragmatic compromises among moral orders in attempts to cope with the uncertainty generated by moral ambivalence. The result is hybrid forms of organizational structures or practices, such as NPower NY's matrix fee scheme. Similarly, the market for life insurance overcame the moral barrier of putting a monetary value on life by stressing the obligation of providing financial security for one's family (Zelizer, 1979). The resolution combined the market moral order (the value of a life as stated in a policy) with the moral order of the family (ensuring their financial security). More recently, Quinn (2008) has shown how viatical settlements—that is, selling a policy owner's existing life insurance policy to a third party—overcame moral ambivalence by combining the market moral order (the market value of existing life insurance policies) with a domestic order (ensuring that the policyholder lives in dignity and comfort, including the financial comfort of having his or her debts paid).

Conventions of coordination emerge from the interactions of actors in a contentious field. These are the rules of engagement that constrain behavior to what members consider appropriate and in doing so reduce the uncertainty of interaction. Conventions of coordination provide stability to fields while preserving the agency of actors that constitute them. As I showed in Chapter 5, conventions of coordination emerged from ongoing interactions between Circuit Riders and NPower. In some situations, Circuit Riders attempted to engage with the market or with NPower directly. Attempts to engage with the market and NPower were met with limited success as some Circuit Rider groups were unable to overcome the constraints on activism (like the rejection of TechRocks's adoption of an open source practices) or barriers to market access (like Compumentor's uneasy collaboration with NPower). Circuit Riders taking the more radical tack of challenging the market and reinvigorating the movement by mobilizing free and open source software were stymied by a lack of resources and inability to build competitive infrastructure. Attempts to challenge the market might have been more successful if done before NPower could establish market conventions or if the Circuit Riders were able to once again forge an account of worth that aligned their interests with resource holders, such as independent foundations or corporations like IBM and Google, which sponsored F/OSS projects.

Toward a Sociology of Movements and Markets

Not every movement is destined to become a market. However, under capitalism markets pervade many areas of everyday life, including the polity. This concern gave rise to the discipline of sociology. Classical sociological theorists, including Karl Marx, Émile Durkheim, Max Weber, and Georg Simmel, were concerned with the effects of capitalism on individuals, communities, and society. They all thought markets make social relations less personal. Marx feared that relationships among people would be reduced to commodity relations. Durkheim worried that unfettered markets undermined social solidarity and caused pathologies in society. Weber was the most pessimistic among them. For him, capitalism was an inexorable drive toward calculative rationality, which spread throughout the economy, but came to dominate all facets of an individual's life. Because of this, Weber argued that capitalism required a powerful moral justification, which was rooted in the Protestant Reformation (Weber, 1992).

The need to justify capitalism continues today. Boltanski and Chiapello (2005) argue that capitalism is under constant critique and so requires constant justification. Social movements provide many contemporary critiques of capitalism, pressing market actors to adopt practices that align with social values. However, market actors translate the demands of social movements into actions that align with the interests of their managers and shareholders (and sometimes their consumers). For example, the antisweatshop movement has been one of the most successful in challenging markets and reforming labor practices (O'Rourke, 2005). However, their activities ultimately spawned new markets for ethical consumption (Ross, 2008). In this way, social movements become engines of market change and innovation in capitalism. Thus the irony: in challenging capitalism, contemporary social movements produce unintended changes in capitalism that undermine their larger goals.

Sociologists are beginning to pay attention to this dynamic. Economic sociologists are taking social movements seriously. And social movement theorists have begun to study market activism. Yet much work remains to be done. The overlap between economic sociology and sociological studies of social movements can offer new insights into understanding the role of competing accounts of worth in collective action problems. Social movements and markets are arenas in which actors must find appropriate ways of coordinating their behaviors in order to accomplish their mutual goals. Social movements and markets alike rely on accounts of worth, collective identity, evaluative criteria, and conventions of coordination to solve collective action problems in their respective domains.

Markets and Movement Outcomes

Social movements have produced varied outcomes (Giugni, 1998). For example, they have successfully pressed for hate crime reporting (McVeigh, Welch, & Bjarnason, 2003), influenced corporate stock prices (King & Soule, 2007), and overthrown governments (Tilly & Wood, 2009). However, outcomes often vary from the goals social movements seek to accomplish. Freedom Summer did not produce civil rights for African Americans directly, but it did change the way participants understand their role in social change (McAdam, 1990). The goal of the Black Power movement was not to establish the academic discipline of African American studies, which ended up being one of its major outcomes (Rojas, 2007). The policy process is messy and requires compromise, making causal connections between movement action and policy outcomes difficult for scholars to establish (Soule, McAdam, McCarthy, & Su, 1999). Sometimes, the outcome of collective action is simply to forge connections among social movement members (Diani, 1997).

In this book, I show how social movements can also produce unintended outcomes, like the formation and shaping of a market. The Circuit Riders set out to create new ways of championing social justice and environmentalism through the use of innovative technologies. In organizing a movement, they provided times and places for a market to take hold and grow. However, the Circuit Riders continued to shape the market for technology assistance as it evolved. This has implications for the study of social movement outcomes.

First, scholars cannot treat social movement outcomes simply as successful or unsuccessful. Rather, they must trace the long-term trajectories of social movement outcomes to understand the various forces that shape them. Although the Circuit Riders' explicit goal of facilitating social justice and environmentalism was not achieved, the movement did draw attention and funding to the use of technology in the nonprofit sector. Only in understanding the long-term trajectory of the Circuit Riders' movement can one connect its early goals with the outcome of its actions. Second, scholars cannot impose artificial time limits on success. What may appear as success at one point in time (e.g., the establishment of Circuit Riding as a legitimate activity) may prove unsuccessful at a later point in time (e.g., the showdown at Kykuit). Rojas's (2007) exemplary study shows how the Black Power movement of the 1960s and 1970s was transformed through a series of pragmatic compromises into the academic discipline of African American studies. Such scholarship must be tempered with an understanding of the limits on movement activity over time. For example, a movement may go into abeyance when the environment is not amenable to its goals (Taylor, 1989).

More directly, this book has had much to say about markets as movement outcomes. I have traced the early trajectories of the Circuit Rider movement to show how early compromises among moral orders allowed for bigger shifts later. The Circuit Riders justified their work by combining social and market values, though relying more heavily on the former. NPower justified its work in similar ways, but tilting toward the market. As NPower expanded nationally and in significance, it advanced further market justifications to promote its model of technology assistance in the nonprofit sector. The establishment of market justifications set the ideological stage for a market to take hold.

Movements and Market Outcomes

This book examines the case of a single movement that gave rise to a market to understand how social and market values intertwine in the creation of markets. I build on the situational pragmatics of Boltanski and Thévenot (2006) as well as the microfoundational approach in new institutionalism (Hallett & Ventresca, 2006; Powell & Colyvas, 2008) to present a bottom-up, actor-driven theory of market creation and institution building. I have shown how social movements, which are often invoked in the organizations literature to explain institutional change, can produce settlements that are the basis for markets. Settlements are the tenuous periods of stability that occur in fields, such as markets (Fligstein & McAdam, 2012: chap. 4). The stable social relations of settlements reduce uncertainty and allow actors to engage in legitimate modes of cooperation and competition. Once a field is settled, incumbents (those actors that have an interest in the current field arrangement) seek to reproduce the settlement by creating formal rules, for example, through governing bodies such as certifying boards or by appealing to the state to create laws stabilizing relations in the field, both of which limit and constrain new entrants. In the case of NPower and the Circuit Riders, settlement was achieved through the establishment of worth (the account of technology assistance as marketable service), the organizing of fields and formal organizations (which combine movement and market principles and practices), and the emergence of conventions of coordination (the rules about when competition or cooperation was the appropriate mode of engagement). This was reinforced by formal relationships between formally organized NTAPs, such as NPower, and nonprofit foundations and for-profit corporations. The settlement produced a stable market for technology assistance in the nonprofit sector.

Settlements are temporary. The market for technology assistance changed in recent years. The field has shrunk, as many NTAPs have consolidated, merged, or ceased operations altogether. As noted in Chapter 5, many Circuit Rider programs folded, unable to compete in the market. TechRocks and the LINC Project ceased operations in 2003 and 2006 respectively. Media Jump-Start changed its name to the May First Technology Collective before merging with an organization called People Link and shifting its focus to providing technology support and infrastructure for international development projects. Not long after I left the field, the NPower network began to unravel (Mills-Groninger, 2011). Microsoft reduced its support for the national network in 2006. A year later, NPower NY became the national office. Since then, almost half of NPower's 16 affiliates have ceased operations or ended their formal relationship with NPower. Affiliates in Seattle and Portland merged to form NPower Northwest. One of the first affiliates in the national network, NPower Michigan, ended its affiliation in 2010 and changed its name to Highway T. Affiliates in Colorado, Arizona, and Los Angeles ceased operations altogether. NPower and it affiliates remain the largest and most dominant NTAPs in the field. However, the smaller size and significance of the technology assistance field means NPower's influence over the technology choices in the nonprofit sector as a whole has also lessened considerably.

Scholars have likened the creation of markets to social movement activity (Carroll & Swaminatham, 2000; Rao, 2008; Rao, Monin, & Durand, 2003; Swaminatham & Wade, 2001). This book has taken a literal case of a social movement that has created a market to explain parts of the process in greater detail. In doing so, I have highlighted how actors alternately compete and collaborate in market fields. Scholars have already begun to take seriously the contentious nature of markets (King & Pearce, 2010). But they should also be aware that markets are not simply competitive arenas. Businesses and movements alike develop implicit and explicit rules of engagement to help them reduce the uncertainty of action over time. Future research should begin to analyze the conditions under which collaboration and competition take place.

Caveats

The research presented in this book is not a template for the transformation of social movements into markets. Nor do I intend to present a stage theory of the process. Rather, this book presents several of the elements that are necessary, but not sufficient, for the transformation of movements into markets. In doing so, I demonstrate how movements shape markets, sometimes in unintended ways. Although the Circuit Riders and nonprofit technology assistance is an illustrative case, several caveats must be heeded.

Nonprofit technology assistance was a nascent field in the late 1990s and early 2000s. Without the constraints of extant institutions, movement leaders, such as Stuart, and institutional entrepreneurs, such as Fanning, had outsized influence in shaping the field and ultimately the market. More established fields and markets will likely require more organizing and resources to institute transformations on similar scales.

The nonprofit technology assistance field began as a movement with close ties to the nonprofit sector, including financial support from independent foundations. Few social movements begin with access to similar resources, not only in amount but also in kind. Independent foundations supplied money for the creation of Circuit Rider programs across the country, which facilitated the growth of the movement. They also provided financial support for Circuit Rider conferences, such as the Riders Roundups, which helped shape the movement by providing a locus for organizing and collective identity building efforts. More important, independent foundations provided institutional linkages to the nonprofit sector, which created a mainstreaming effect on the Circuit

Riders. Although some Circuit Riders engaged in radical politics, most were technologists that wanted to help nonprofit and grassroots organizations better achieve their missions. As activists, the Circuit Riders were not engaged in the kinds of contentious politics in which many more radical or aggressive social movements engage. In other words, the Circuit Rider movement emerged from institutionalized settings.

The market for technology assistance services never became a pure market. As the movement shifted toward a market, most new entrants into the market retained the nonprofit form. Even individual consultants entering the market considered themselves "NPIs" or nonprofit individuals [41]. Many of these consultants worked occasionally as freelancers for NPower affiliates. None of the organizations in my sample came close to financial sustainability based exclusively on earned revenue. Even NPower NY, which came the closest, could only ever achieve about 50% earned revenue. No one entered the market for technology assistance services in the nonprofit sector to become rich. Rather, all had an affinity for the nonprofit sector, which was often expressed through incorporation as a 501(c)(3) where appropriate.

Finally, the ethnographic lens deployed in this study has focused on the bottom-up mechanisms of market development. Although a strength of this approach is the depth of focus one gains from being where the action is, a weakness is the challenge of observing the large-scale social forces that shape that behavior. In other words, by showing how micro-level behaviors scale up to produce macro-outcomes (Callon & Latour, 1981), I have not paid as much attention to how macro-level structures shape the conditions for them to do so. Throughout the research and writing of this book, I have collected some structural-level data to help understand how the field of nonprofit technology assistance has been shaped by forces in the economy. However, all research involves trade-offs. To understand the microfoundations of institutions, I have had to focus more on micro- and meso-level constructs, such as individual actors, organizations, and fields, and less on macro-level constructs, such as the economy.

What Is to Be Done?

One of the practical implications of this book is highlighting the need for a human-scale capitalism, one in which businesses respond to the legitimate demands of social movements without undermining them. Too often, businesses have the resources and access to decision makers to undermine democratic processes. Major corporations and trade groups lobby, donate to political campaigns, and court politicians. They create "super-PACs" and use their influence to shape policies that benefit their bottom lines. CEOs and corporate representatives have access to politicians that ordinary citizens can only dream of. This scenario contributes to apathy among citizens, who feel that their voices cannot be heard over the din of corporate influence and dollars.

However, when people organize, they can influence business and markets. Brayden King (2008) shows that social movements can shape corporate policies through boycotts and media campaigns. Although many corporate social responsibility policies do not go far enough, they are steps in the right direction. Throughout this book, I have illustrated the pervasiveness of market values in arenas of social life previously considered immune to them, such as the nonprofit sector. Market values gain traction when justifications for market actions become taken for granted.

Lessons for Activists

With various tactics at their disposal, social movements can provide powerful critiques of market actors and actions. Activists should consider their strategies and tactics carefully. Growing a movement of committed adherents takes work. Forging collective identities requires careful deliberation to balance the need to grow ranks with the need to maintain authenticity. At times in their history, the Circuit Riders allowed this balance to tip toward growing their ranks, which caused contention among the core group of activists in the movement.

Activists also need to deliberate carefully over how to frame their message. Framed narrowly or radically, it will appeal to too few potential adherents and sympathizers. The Circuit Riders created an opportunity for Joan Fanning to become an institutional entrepreneur by adopting a "radical" stance regarding information technology. By framing their movement ideals as "chaordic," Stuart and other leaders of the movement alienated many resource holders at a critical time in the movement. Framed too broadly, the message will have little meaning and impact. Creating multivalent accounts that achieve their intended result is difficult. It entails a deep understanding of the stakeholders as well as the rules of engagement in the given situation.

Social movements should be wary of how they engage with markets. The tactical repertoire available to them is broad. Some tactics are more useful than others. Their strategic deployment requires an awareness of the situation in play. Who are the relevant actors? What are their interests? How will one align or diverge their interest with one's own? Boycotts work in some situations. In others, they fail to register on the target's balance sheets or raise the awareness they intend to raise. The Circuit Riders engaged with markets using various tactics and with various outcomes. They were unsuccessful in attempting to replicate the market practices of NPower. This was due in part to their unwillingness to embrace the market completely. Other organizations, such as Compumentor, found success in turning their attention to an untapped, but related, market in discounted software sales to the nonprofit sector. The Circuit Riders also attempted to create an alternative economy by mobilizing free and open source software. This strategy was ultimately unsuccessful because the movement was unable to secure the resources and legitimacy necessary to launch an alternative, particularly at a time when resource pools were shrinking and the primary market, that of NPower, was taking hold.

Lessons for Managers

Managers and other corporate decisions makers often have access to resources that can be used to make a difference in the lives of publics beyond their shareholders and consumers. Corporate social responsibility programs channel corporate resources into activities that provide positive outcomes for communities and the environment. However, to many activists, such activities are public relations stunts, window dressing, or greenwashing. In order to overcome potential criticisms for their good works, managers must be deliberate and thoughtful about how they apply corporate resources to public goods.

First, managers should listen to the legitimate demands of activists that target their corporation. They might find that both parties have stakes in the same outcomes. For example, in one chapter of the documentary *The Corporation* (Achbar & Abbott, 2003), activists stage a sit-in at Sir Mark Moody-Stuart's cottage to protest the environmental and human rights record of the company he chaired, Royal Dutch Shell. Moody-Stuart listens to their concerns and comments: "In the end, what we found out through the conversation was that all the things that they were worried about, I was worried about as well: climate, oppressive regimes, human rights. The big difference between us was that I feel that I can actually make a contribution to this. These people were frustrated because they felt they had nothing to do." Royal Dutch Shell does have a tremendous amount of resources at its disposal. It uses a tiny fraction of those resources to remedy the problems that its corporation creates around the world. When a corporation makes so much money and gives so little of it back to publics beyond its shareholders and CEOs, activists may rightly denounce any of its corporate social responsibility policies as public relations stunts.

Second, managers should engage with members of the communities in which their companies operate. Philanthropy scholars have shown that corporations give more in cities in which they are headquartered (Useem, 1987). Such an uneven distribution of their largesse only reinforces inequalities, especially when their contributions are so small, relative to their earnings. Many large companies engage in corporate philanthropy. The problem with such schemes is that they distribute funds with little regard to public needs. Listening to activists and working with community organizers can better channel corporate philanthropy to doing the most good.

Finally, corporate decision makers should consider taking on some hybrid forms and practices, particularly those that would contribute to a more equitable distribution of wealth. According to a recent *New York Times* article, earnings for large corporations are at an all-time high and workers' wages as a percent of national income are decreasing (Norris, 2011). However, according to the Giving USA survey, donations from corporations and their foundations decreased in 2011 by 3.1% in inflation-adjusted dollars (Clorery & Hrywna, 2012). If corporations are serious about social responsibility, they should consider policies that tie their giving to their profits. Corporations receive many benefits operating in the United States. They should also bear some of the obligations to the public good.

REFERENCE MATTER

APPENDIX A

Methods

Many years ago, I became intent on conducting research among the fast-paced dot-com start-ups of Silicon Alley in New York City. I worked in the sleepy world of nonprofit organizations to support myself throughout those years, first as a research associate then as a program evaluator. In my intellectual immaturity, I thought high-tech start-ups were where the action was, especially if one was interested in organizational and institutional change. After all, companies such as Razorfish were taking on IBM and rewriting the rules of business. However, I found a similarly compelling story among the Circuit Riders and NPower.

The Fieldwork Story

In December 2000, David Stark invited me to a meeting with Barbara Chang, the founder of a fledgling nonprofit technology start-up. He reasoned that my experience in the nonprofit sector would prove useful in understanding the constraints the organization faced. My task was to take notes. As I did, I became increasingly interested in the problems this new organization, NPower NY, faced. They had to raise capital, but lacked access to the capital and equity markets that supported dot-coms. They had to hire talent, but could not compete with the salaries of the high-tech sector. They had to find workers that understood technology in a sector where many came to work with people, not machines. They had to gain material support where old foundations did not understand what they were trying to do and new foundations did not want to gamble on an organization without a record of success. In sum, NPower NY faced a set of constraints that would challenge the savviest of high-tech firms. At the same time, the organization offered a completely new service and model for delivering it. NPower NY was a natural laboratory for studying innovation under constraint, a specialty of Stark's students at the Center on Organizational Innovation at Columbia University.

I began researching the world of nonprofit technology after that meeting. Despite my attempts to meet with her again, Chang was too busy organizing NPower NY to do so. My opportunity came later in the spring of 2001. NPower NY had a skeleton staff and was putting together its programs. I came across a paper by Stephanie Creaturo, who was working for NPower NY creating a workforce development program for nonprofit technology. I contacted her and began a dialogue. I offered to volunteer for her in exchange for access to the organization. I began my ethnographic fieldwork in earnest on May 25, 2001, only a month after NPower NY began delivering services.

NPower NY was the best field site an ethnographer could ask for. The organization provided me with a desk, a connection to the internal computer network, and a company e-mail address. The staff members were friendly, helpful, and always willing to answer my simplistic questions about their everyday work lives. I brought my own laptop, which made for more accurate transcription of fieldnotes as well as of the informal interviews and conversations I had with employees around the office. From my vantage point, I witnessed the growth of a social enterprise. I could observe the microfoundations of institutions in action as managers and subordinates grappled with the twin challenges of rapid growth and contradictory institutional expectations.

I volunteered between 15 and 20 hours per week at NPower NY, spread across two to four days per week, depending on what was happening. During that time, I helped Creaturo and a small staff of employees and pro bono consultants create a workforce development program called Technology Service Corps. Creaturo put my research skills to work benchmarking similar programs and my program evaluator experience to work developing and implementing performance measurement tools for the program as well as writing reports based on them. My work with Technology Service Corps put me close enough to the main action of NPower NY to observe the organization's growth, but far enough from the center to avoid influencing key facets of the organization. This is a key challenge for ethnographers of organizations, especially nonprofit organizations—balancing closeness and distance, observation and participation. I did so by exercising judgment when it came time to contribute. I limited my opinions and expertise to the creation and management of Technology Service Corps, which was never fully integrated into NPower NY's operations while I was in the field. Rather, Technology Service Corps often worked as supplemental to the consulting and training that provided all of the organization's earned revenue.

The staff at NPower NY was friendly and cooperative. Everyone I asked agreed to be interviewed. Only three staff members requested that I not record interviews with them. During summer 2001, I interviewed all of NPower NY's original staff and management. Most of the interviews took place off-site at nearby cafes and restaurants. Some took place in conference rooms at the NPower NY office. Placement depended on the comfort of the respondent. These early interviews focused on the staff members' work life, background, approach to technology, and relationship to the organization and its members.

Throughout my time at NPower NY, space was at a premium. The organization's first office had been formerly occupied by small high-tech firm. Because of space constraints and my low status as volunteer (or intern as I was sometimes called), I was shuffled around the office. Being moved frequently gave me the advantage of access to new perspectives on the office and its inhabitants. Sitting near the training staff, I could see how they worked. I spent time near the consulting staff, observing how they solved technical and organizational problems. This continued through summer 2002, when NPower NY moved to a larger office in midtown.

From there, I began exploring the organizational field in which NPower NY was a member. Taking inspiration from Bruno Latour (1987, 1996), I followed the network. The network first took me to NPower NY's corporate partners, then to NPower National. I interviewed board members as well as key staff from NPower National. When Joan Fanning, who founded the NPower network, visited the New York office, I introduced myself and made an appointment to interview her over the phone. I did the same for Jane Meseck, NPower's key supporter at Microsoft. As I explored further, I uncovered a world of nonprofit technology assistance providers scattered throughout the city as well as the nation. I first learned about the Circuit Riders when talking to the director of consulting at NPower NY. I began researching the movement, following the network back in time.

The next spring, I took a trip to Orlando, Florida, the site of the 2002 Riders Roundup. I applied for, and received, travel support from the Nonprofit Technology Enterprise Network. There, I met many of the Circuit Riders who would provide interviews and other support for the project. My sampling strategy for collecting interviews combined network sampling methods with purposive sampling. Network sampling methods entail constructing a network map of the field (as complete as one can make it) and interviewing people who occupy key nodes (Howard, 2002). The network map was drawn based on previous interviews, archival work, and lists of Roundup attendees as well as membership lists from NTEN, the technology assistance trade association. This sampling method ensured that I spoke with respondents who had played key roles in the development of the movement or had good purchase on the field based on their position in the network or on having been a part of it for a long time. I came away from the Roundup with copious fieldnotes and a list of contacts.

I began phone interviews with Circuit Riders that summer. A rich history began to emerge from these early interviews, one that begged further investigation. It was at that point that I decided to expand the study to account for the Circuit Rider movement not only as key to understanding the organizational field in which NPower NY was embedded but also to understand the temporal development of that field. I had many intense methodological discussions with Bill McAllister about the role of temporality in social science research. One of the strengths of longitudinal ethnography is capturing social processes over time (Van de Ven & Huber, 1990). Bringing the Circuit Riders into the study allowed me to capture the social processes by which the social movement emerged as well as the historical structures that gave rise to NPower and eventually NPower NY. My research was now extended in time and space (Burawoy, 1998; Eliasoph & Lichterman, 1999).

In interviews and fieldwork, I paid close attention to the construction of accounts, stories actors gave to justify their actions and sometimes denounce the actions of others. As Lazega and Favereau (2002: 8) describe the approach: "First, attention is directed towards the verbal arguments produced by the agents themselves, in case of conflict, to justify their attitude and the situations where all agents themselves are led to agree about the relative strength of their respective arguments . . . ; second, research is centered on the rules followed by economic agents, but the rules should be understandable by the agents themselves . . . , which means that the researcher tries to be faithful to the variety of the systems of interpretation, in which economic agents are trained, from their childhood."

I continued to conduct fieldwork at NPower NY through the summer of 2002. That fall, I became acquainted with Mitch Duneier, who encouraged me to immerse myself fully in the worlds I was studying. On his recommendation, I traveled to Seattle in October 2002 to observe the NPower National Summit. The Summit provided intimate insight into the partnership between NPower and Microsoft, allowing me to witness the work of justification firsthand as speakers from their respective organizations discussed the collaboration as beneficent to the nonprofit sector. Back in New York, I interviewed the next wave of hires, including new managers and two key board members.

The following summer (2003), I received a grant from the Department of Sociology at Columbia University to conduct fieldwork and interviews at several NTAPs in the Pacific Northwest, including ONE NW, Project Alchemy, Technology Assistance for Community Services, and NPower Seattle (as well as the national office). I spent several weeks in Portland and Seattle interviewing key personnel from these organizations as well as independent Circuit Riders. I interviewed one Circuit Rider at an anarchist coffeehouse in Portland. I was fortunate enough to have a contact, Phil Klein, offer me his guest room and arrange for a focus group of independent technology consultants in Seattle.

I returned to New York later that summer to continue fieldwork at NPower NY. With insights from the entire field as part of my data set, I interviewed the key executive managers at NPower NY once again. By fall 2003, I withdrew from fieldwork at the organization to focus on collecting interview data and observations at other NTAPs in New York City. I worked with Dirk Slater at the LINC Project on a case study about technology applications for civic engagement. I attempted to conduct participant observation at a Circuit Rider organization called Media Jumpstart, but was turned down. Media Jumpstart operated on a pure consensus model. After meeting with the entire staff and pitching my participation, the staff voted against taking part in my research project. Their reason was that, as a small and busy organization, they were concerned that my presence would interfere with getting their work done. I settled for several interviews with two of the main organizers of the collective, both of whom were active at the national level, especially in the open source movement among the Circuit Riders.

I spent the remainder of the winter deep in my fieldnotes and interview transcripts doing the preliminary analysis and checking my interview list against the network map that had evolved throughout the project. I identified several key respondents that could potentially fill gaps in my data. I also recognized that I needed second interviews with other key respondents, such as Joan Fanning and Rob Stuart. I spent the spring tracking down the final respondents and arranging follow-up interviews with these key respondents. By the end of summer 2004, I had collected all the data for this project: 81 formal interviews, over 500 pages of fieldnotes, two file cabinet drawers full of physical documents, and several gigabytes of electronic documents.

Methodology

Ethnography is an umbrella for a host of qualitative research methods. I took my ethnographic cues from courses I took with Terry Williams and Mitch Duneier as well as guidance and advice from my advisors, especially Nicole Marwell, Sudhir Venkatesh, and David Stark. The result of these influences helped me produce what Van Maanen (1988) calls a "realist" tale, in which the role of the ethnographer is to capture, analyze, and report social worlds based on how inhabitants experience them. In this, I was heavily influenced by Stanley Aronowitz's approach to the sociology of everyday life. Throughout my ethnography, I paid careful attention to the mundane details of organizational life. For this project, I combined participant observation, formal interviews, and archival research. I describe those methods and the logic behind them in detail below.

Participant Observation

My research began as an organizational ethnography, but quickly turned multisited. Organizational ethnography is well-suited to understanding intraorganizational dynamics and change (Barley, 1990; Schwartzman, 1993). Contemporary organizational theory acknowledges the importance of the environment, including the field, population, and network, in shaping organizations (Scott & Davis, 2007). Therefore, any comprehensive study of organizations requires an understanding of the environment in which it is embedded (Schneiberg & Clemens, 2006).

My participant observation was rooted in the phenomenological tradition of ethnography (Schatzman & Strauss, 1973). The logic behind the approach was to understand social worlds from the perspective of their inhabitants. This requires a balance of participation and observation. For me, participation entailed volunteering for NPower NY, but also writing reports and shadowing consultants and Circuit Riders. I spent many afternoons following NPower NY's consultants to clients' sites. I listened as they communicated with clients. I crawled under desks with them and ran diagnostic tools on computers when they asked me to. I went to bars after hours and heard about feats of technical heroism (Orr, 1996). I shadowed managers and executives to clients' organizations as well as meetings with other NTAPs. I did the same with Circuit Riders. I offered to write case studies and help them work on grant proposals. I was fortunate to have a little background in computing, which helped me perform competently as a technician when called upon to do so. At the very least, it allowed me to talk competently with consultants and Circuit Riders about computers and technology. Along the way, I engaged participants in many conversations and informal interviews, which took place in various venues inside offices as well as during subway and bus rides and events at bars and restaurants. These informal interviews allowed me to follow up with respondents about their interpretations of the many events and situations at which I was present.

Formal Interviews

Throughout my time in the field, I conducted 81 formal interviews (see appendix B for the complete list) either in person or over the phone. I interviewed several key respondents—Rob Stuart, Joan Fanning, and Barbara Chang—twice. Almost all interviews were tape-recorded. Three respondents at NPower NY refused to be taped out of concern for their privacy. Tape-recorded interviews were transcribed. I transcribed many of the interviews on a Dictaphone machine I bought used online. The remainder of the interviews were professionally transcribed.

Interviews ranged from 45 minutes to over four hours in length. Most were about an hour long. Interview questions varied based on the respondent's position in the field or in their organization as well as the historical role they had played in the movement. Historical interviews focused on how the respondent understood his or her role in the movement or organization in question. I attempted to corroborate factual information provided by respondents through other interviews, participant observation, and document analysis. Otherwise, I treated responses as perceptions of events from the standpoint of the respondents (Kvale, 1996). Interviews were semistructured and attempted to engage respondents in conversations in which they were active coconstructors of the data (Holstein & Gubrium, 1995). I often asked respondents to reflect on events in which they had participated. This was especially useful when I also witnessed the event. In this way, my participant observation and formal interviews were synergistic.

Document Collection

I collected many documents related to the Circuit Riders and NPower affiliates. Key historical respondents, such as Gavin Clabaugh, Rob Stuart, and Dirk Slater, provided conference agendas, memos, reports, and published stories on the Circuit Rider movement. Sean O'Brien gave me a short video of interviews he had conducted at the second Riders Roundup. I conducted document research about the Circuit Rider movement and affiliated organizations and foundations on the Internet Archive (http://www.archive.org). I also collected agendas and other documents at Riders Roundups and other Circuit Rider events I attended.

Managers at NPower provided internal and external reports, prospectuses, memos, and drafts of other documents related to the organization. I benefited greatly from access to the file servers at NPower and NPower NY, where I could peruse the organization's formal documentation related to almost every aspect of operations (sensitive information, such as personnel data, was protected on a separate part of the server to which I did not have access). I also collected documents about NPower, such as agendas and reports, at meetings, events, and summits I attended.

Documents were both physical and electronic. Items such as meeting agendas and published reports were often distributed in physical form. These I collected and stored in file cabinets. Electronic documents included e-mails (directly to me and on LISTSERVs), reports, prospectuses, and web pages. Since web pages are ephemeral, besides relying on the Internet Archive, I used software to capture the websites of key NTAPs in my sample, recording them in total on my hard drive.

Analysis

Longitudinal qualitative research, like my historical-institutional ethnography, produces unwieldy amounts of data. By the end of my time in the field, I had accumulated several thousand pages of fieldnotes, interview transcripts, and documents. Additionally, I collected artifacts, such as images, photographs, and physical objects (e.g., a computer toolkit from a Riders Roundup I attended, a pen and keychain set from an NPower Summit) that were not easily amenable to text-based analyses.

To analyze these data, I engaged in iterative coding and memo writing (Emerson, Fretz, & Shaw, 1995; Hodder, 2000; Lofland & Lofland, 1995; Ryan & Bernard, 2000). Iterative coding begins with an initial set of codes, which emerge from intimate interaction with the data. Initial codes are a rough cut based on themes that arise as one reads transcripts, fieldnotes, documents, and so forth. Once I had a set of initial codes, I recoded the data according to themes and categories that emerged from them. I conducted this procedure once more before settling on a complete set of coded data. This iterative coding scheme produced many documents of coded text, which was organized thematically and encoded with hyperlinks to connect themes across codes. This allowed me to generate connections across codes, which helped me avoid reifying analytical categories.

From these codes, I wrote theoretical and empirical memos. Memo writing produced the first drafts of ideas, which I then organized thematically to produce chapter outlines. I discarded most of the memos I wrote as untenable (some were theoretical dead ends, others seemed to make sense when I wrote them but not on reflection). The remaining memos formed the bases for the sections of each chapter. This procedure helped produce a historical-institutional ethnography that reflected the concerns and understandings of respondents.

I chose the methods outlined above to produce a historical-institutional ethnography that would capture multiple levels of analysis. Day-to-day participant observation and interviews captured the micro-level interactions. Interviews and documents captured meso-level phenomena. And the combination of these methods over time captured certain aspects of the macro level. If there is fault with my combination of methods it is that they do not focus sufficiently on the macro level. Capturing phenomena at the macro level requires methodological and analytical tools I did not employ in this study. This was due in large part to the nature of the field under study. The Circuit Rider community began as a relatively small network. The emergent NTAP market remained relatively small. Despite fluctuations in population size, a theoretical focus on institutional development meant the best course of action was a methodological focus on the key players—those leaving institutional traces on the field. As Fligstein and McAdam (2012: 169) describe the methods of field analysis: "To accurately capture the dynamics of any given field the analyst must, in our view, understand the internal structure and workings of the field *and* the broader set of relationships that tie any given field to a host of other strategic action fields (including various state fields). . . . The key is understanding the crucial relationships that shape the field, rather than neatly differentiating those that are internal and external to the strategic action field."

APPENDIX B

List of Interviews

Interview	Respondent	Date	Medium	Affiliation
1	Ronen Kaufman	7/30/2001	In-Person	NPower NY
2	Alison Marano	7/31/2001	In-Person	NPower NY
3	Hal Allen	7/31/2001	In-Person	NPower NY
4	Stephanie Creaturo	7/31/2001	In-Person	NPower NY
5	Barbara Chang	8/30/2001	In-Person	NPower NY
6	Matthew Kershnar	10/12/2001	In-Person	NPower NY
7	Lystra Batchoo	11/29/2001	In-Person	NPower NY
8	Arissa Sidoti	12/12/2001	In-Person	NPower NY
9	Angela Russell	12/18/2001	In-Person	NPower NY
10	Dayna Graham	3/19/2002	In-Person	Accenture
11	Marshall Mayer	5/14/2002	Telephone	Desktop Assistance/ TechRocks
12	Beth Kanter	5/17/2002	In-Person	Independent
13	Jeff Susor	5/22/2002	Telephone	Independent
14	Rob Stuart	5/31/2002	In-Person	TechRocks
15	Jane Meseck	6/6/2002	Telephone	Microsoft
16	Gavin Clabaugh	8/6/2002	Telephone	TCN/W. Alton Jones Foundation/ Mott Foundation
17	Sean O'Brien	8/14/2002	Telephone	W. Alton Jones Foundation
18	Jeremy Edes-Pierotti	8/23/2002	Telephone	W. Alton Jones Foundation
19	Joan Fanning	9/16/2002	Telephone	NPower National
20	Gregg Bishop	12/17/2002	In-Person	NPower NY
21	Hal Allen	1/2/2003	In-Person	NPower NY
22	Denis Petrov	1/9/2003	In-Person	NPower NY
23	Theresa Stroisch	2/27/2003	In-Person	NPower NY
24	Nikki Roberg	3/5/2003	Telephone	NPower National
25	Stephanie Hyacinth	4/10/2003	In-Person	NPower NY

Interview	Respondent	Date	Medium	Affiliation
26	Steve Mortimer	4/22/2003	In-Person	NPower NY
27	Jerry Colonna	5/6/2003	Telephone	NPower NY
28	Jeff Walker	5/16/2003	Telephone	NPower NY
29	Amanda Hickman	6/5/2003	In-Person	LINC Project
30	Dirk Slater	6/5/2003	In-Person	LINC Project
31	Alison Marano	6/19/2003	In-Person	NPower NY
32	Kay Sohl	7/8/2003	In-Person	Technical Assistance for Community Services
33	Tanya Zumach	7/9/2003	In-Person	Independent
34	Allen Poole	7/11/2003	In-Person	Independent
35	Jennifer Bright	7/15/2003	In-Person	NPower National
36	Jon Stahl	7/15/2003	In-Person	ONE Northwest
37	Samantha Moscheck	7/16/2003	In-Person	Project Alchemy
38	Steve Albertson	7/16/2003	In-Person	ONE Northwest
39	Denise Joines	7/17/2003	In-Person	ONE Northwest
40	Michael Gilbert	7/17/2003	In-Person	Independent
41	Seattle 501 Tech Club	7/17/2003	In-Person	Independent
42	Jaime Green	7/18/2003	In-Person	NPower National
43	Christine Stearn	7/24/2003	In-Person	NPower NY
44	Frank Ordway	8/13/2003	Telephone	NPower National
45	Dean Erikson	8/21/2003	In-Person	ONE Northwest
46	Eugena Harrington	8/27/2003	In-Person	NPower NY
47	Paul Brainerd	9/3/2003	Telephone	Bullitt Foundation
48	Cassandra James	9/5/2003	In-Person	NPower NY
49	Jamie McClelland	9/5/2003	In-Person	Media Jumpstart
50	Franklin Rosado	9/8/2003	In-Person	NPower NY
51	Carnet Williams	9/16/2003	Telephone	NetCorps/NTEN
52	Mark Bailey	10/2/2003	In-Person	NPower NY
53	Joshua Peskay	10/10/2003	In-Person	Fund for the City of New York
54	Michelle Murrain	10/13/2003	Telephone	NOSI/Independent
55	Tim Mills-Groninger	10/14/2003	Telephone	IT Resource Center
56	David Ritchie	10/21/2003	In-Person	Tech Foundation/ NPower NY
57	Deborah Strauss	11/4/2003	Telephone	IT Resource Center
58	Sheldon Mains	11/4/2003	Telephone	MAPS
59	Dirk Slater	11/6/2003	In-Person	LINC Project
60	Richard Zorza	11/6/2003	Telephone	Independent

Interview	Respondent	Date	Medium	Affiliation
61	Theresa Crawford	11/17/2003	In-Person	Independent
62	Barbara Chang	12/8/2003	In-Person	NPower NY
63	Jillaine Smith	12/10/2003	Telephone	Independent
64	Michael Ward	12/10/2003	In-Person	TechRocks
65	Michael Stein	12/16/2003	Telephone	Groundspring
66	Art McGee	12/30/2003	Telephone	Independent
67	Deborah Elizabeth Finn	1/22/2004	Telephone	Independent
68	Michael Park	1/27/2004	In-Person	Robin Hood Foundation
69	Stephanie Creaturo	1/29/2004	In-Person	NPower NY
70	Marc Osten	2/24/2004	Telephone	Summit Collaborative/ NTEN
71	Joan Fanning	4/9/2004	Telephone	NPower National
72	Todd Koym	4/12/2004	Telephone	W. Alton Jones Foundation
73	Jonathan Piezer	4/29/2004	In-Person	Open Society Institute/Soros Foundation
74	William Lester	5/4/2004	In-Person	Engender Health
75	Reuben Silvers	5/18/2004	Telephone	NOSI
76	Rob Stuart	5/21/2004	In-Person	TechRocks
77	Ron Braithwaite	6/30/2004	Telephone	Free Geek
78	Vince Stehle	7/20/2004	In-Person	Surdna Foundation
79	Todd Cohen	7/27/2004	Telephone	Philanthropy News Network
80	Amy Luckey	8/18/2004	In-Person	Independent
81	Daniel Ben Horin	8/19/2004	In-Person	Compumentor

NOTES

INTRODUCTION

1. Some companies market their environmentally sound cleaning products as safer for children and pets, offering some immediate benefits for their consumers.

2. The Circuit Riders took their name from nineteenth-century traveling clergymen who served a circuit of congregations, usually in rural areas. In their contemporary form, Circuit Riders travel across the country serving technology to nonprofit and grassroots organizations.

3. The numbers in brackets refer to specific interviews conducted for this research project. See Appendix B for a complete list of interviews with corresponding numbers.

4. I draw my ideal types of values from collapsing "regimes of worth" found in the works of Boltanski and Thévenot (1991, 1999, 2006). I do this here for the sake of simplicity and clarity, especially for those unfamiliar with these theories. These categories will be treated in their expanded form in subsequent chapters.

5. Things such as arts, crafts, and music are often sold. However, I differentiate between art as commodity (produced to be sold) and art for arts sake (the social ideal). Again, these distinctions rarely appear so discrete in practice.

6. Locavores are also concerned with maintaining small farms and sometimes address working conditions on farms as well.

CHAPTER 1

1. Dirk Slater, a Circuit Rider with the LINC Project and leader in the movement, explained it in colloquial terms: "I think beer is very important for us. I mean going out and having beer after the day and having some social time is really important" [30].

2. Carnet Williams, one of the early leaders in the Circuit Rider movement.

3. Ego and alter are sociological terms used to explain social action from the frame of reference of a particular subject. Ego is the person whose frame of reference is being considered at the time. Alter is the person (or persons) who is interacting with ego. In this passage, Padgett and Ansell explain how the identity of ego varies across alters as each has a different understanding of who ego is.

CHAPTER 2

1. Stuart told me during an informal interview that he invited Circuit Riders, members of Circuit Riding programs, and leaders of nonprofit technology assistance providers of which he was aware during his time at the Rockefeller Technology Project (Fieldnotes 3–27–2004).

2. This shift reflected broader changes in the nonprofit sector. Many professional managers and consultants were turning their attention toward "capacity building" in the sector throughout the early 2000s (Eisinger, 2002). Capacity building refers to efforts made to enhance the infrastructure of an organization. In the nonprofit sector, capacity building was most often directed toward supporting and training administrators, though some efforts were also geared toward board selection, recruitment, and management. Capacity building reflects an industrial order of worth rather than the civic order around which the original Circuit Rider account had been forged (Boltanski & Thévenot, 1991, 1999, 2006). An industrial order of worth is one that privileges efficiency and productivity over other modes of evaluation. In a practical sense, this meant that nonprofit organizations were increasingly judged by their ability to serve more people in need rather than contribute solutions to broader social problems. For example, homeless shelters were evaluated by increases in the number of beds they made available (their capacity) rather what actions they took to help solve the problem of homelessness.

3. This statement is based on comparisons of Riders Roundups attendance lists I acquired in the course of my fieldwork. The attendance lists in my data set include the years 1997 through 2003.

4. The penguin is the mascot of Linux, a major F/OSS operating system.

5. Information technology was at the periphery of capacity-building discussions. Therefore, Stuart was not only trying to recruit foundation officers to support Circuit Riding, he was also trying to get information technology on the capacity-building agenda.

CHAPTER 3

1. Social enterprises are organizations and entrepreneurs that apply market solutions to social problems. Social enterprise gained legitimacy as an organizational form throughout the late 1990s and early 2000s (Dart, 2004b), which coincided with NPower's rise to prominence.

2. Competences, such as practical sense, are not innate. Rather, actors acquire competences as they interact with others.

3. The latter problem is called the "paradox of embedded agency" (Seo & Creed, 2002), referring to the contradiction inherent in conceiving of action that subverts the structures that shape it.

4. Though scholars have tried to differentiate between social enterprise and social entrepreneurship, I use the terms interchangeably. The differences in the literature are technical and taxonomical and are not relevant for my discussion throughout the chapter.

5. This irony stems from the fact that Circuit Riders were often funded by donations from foundations. Serving more clients did not necessarily mean securing more donations to do their work. Because of this, successful evangelizing might mean access to more clients without the commensurate financial resources to service them.

6. An unfortunate side effect of this benefit was that client organizations would often become members solely to secure these discounts, letting their memberships lapse when they were no longer in contract with NPower for services. However, membership did allow NPower to demonstrate success to their supporters, including Microsoft and other foundations that provided them with resources.

7. Brainerd made his fortune developing Aldus Pagemaker, a desktop-publishing program. He later sold his company to Adobe for over $50 million. Brainerd established an eponymous foundation that supported environmental causes, including several Circuit Rider organizations that were involved in the movement, such as ONE Northwest. He also organized Social Venture Partners, a consortium of funders committed to social-venture philanthropy and social enterprise.

8. Social ventures, such as social entrepreneurs, do not have to use the nonprofit legal form. Case studies throughout business literature describe for-profit social entrepreneurships (Bielefeld, 2006). Goldman Sachs also hosts a social entrepreneurship competition each year, awarding start-up funds to the most "scalable" social venture, regardless of legal organizational form.

9. Such accounting reflects the calculative rationality that classical sociologist Max Weber considered so important for the development of Western capitalism (Collins, 1980; Weber, 1978, 1992).

10. This is not hyperbole. NPower managers kept a spreadsheet called the "Network Evaluation Tool Grid" to track whether specific affiliates had implemented metrics developed at the national office.

11. Unfortunately, TechRocks would not make it to the next step. As I will explain in more detail in Chapter 5, TechRocks faced difficulties emulating NPower. The organization ceased operations in 2003.

CHAPTER 4

1. The federated network model as an organizational form was the outcome of an analysis by the consulting firm McKinsey & Company, which was underwritten by Boeing. McKinsey worked with NPower for several months on planning their national expansion.

2. At the 2002 Summit, Fanning described the national organization of NPower: "We define the network now as a federation of independent, locally based, nonprofit technology assistance providers who come together or who are bound together by a common mission, visions, values, and service philosophy" (Fieldnotes 10–16–2002).

3. NPower affiliates operated across cities or entire states depending on the size of the potential markets available to them. To be considered for affiliation, markets needed to be large enough to justify the capital investment by Microsoft and technical investment by NPower National.

4. Prospective affiliates were required to submit a formal business plan as part of their application to NPower. Included in the business plan was a detailed market analysis demonstrating the prospects' potential for financial sustainability through earned revenue as well as access to foundation support for matching start-up funds.

5. As discussed in Chapter 3, venture philanthropy is a model of foundation funding based on venture capital models. Venture philanthropists evaluate potential funding recipients based on business-like criteria, such as financial sustainability and managerial expertise (Brainerd, 1999).

6. Donations to nonprofit organizations take two forms. The use of restricted donations is defined or expressed by the donor. Unrestricted donations can be used for any purpose. Although nonprofit organizations prefer unrestricted funds, most of their donations are restricted.

7. To increase revenues, NPower NY began pressing consultants to seek "higher margin" projects, like technology planning and strategy with clients. Such projects would allow the organization to bill at higher rates and generate future work by "aligning organizations with what we do at NPower" (Fieldnotes 7–9–2002). Higher-margin projects were also more technically challenging and therefore more interesting. NPower NY experimented with dividing labor among consultants to facilitate revenues. Higher- margin projects were often assigned to higher-paid, experienced senior consultants with formal credentials, leaving the more routine work to less-qualified, lower-paid consultants.

8. When applying for its 501(c)(3) designation from the Internal Revenue Service (IRS), NPower NY was able to negotiate its pricing structure. The IRS claimed that, in order to meet the criteria for a charity under the law, NPower NY would have to set its prices at 15% of the full-market *cost* of services. NPower NY's lawyers negotiated that upward to 45% of full-market *price* of services. Therefore, NPower NY was able to charge 45% of what their Accenture partner charged to deliver consulting services in the nonprofit sector.

9. However, most studies of revenue mix in the nonprofit sector are based on analyses of 990 tax forms, which treat government contracts as earned revenue. With the transfer of many services from the government to the private sector, many nonprofit organizations receive the bulk of their earned revenue from government sources (Boris & Steuerle, 2006; Jossey-Bass, 2002). This was not true for NTAPs for whom earned revenues came from fees-for-services collected from client organizations, or, in the case of the Circuit Riders, from foundation third-party payers.

10. This ambivalence is structured into the social relations that constitute economic organizations, making it a "sociological ambivalence" (Merton & Barber, 1963).

11. Evidence of this strategy has been found in other organizational settings that face moral ambivalence. For example, during New York City's Internet boom, many technology companies hired senior executives from the publishing and banking industries to give them legitimacy in the respective institutional domains (Indergaard, 2004).

12. Accenture experienced a decline in demand for its services in New York City in 2000–2001. Consultants that were not under contract with clients were encouraged to seek out opportunities to volunteer or provide pro bono services in the community. Working pro bono at NPower NY was a good way for consultants to impress the Accenture partners serving on NPower NY's board.

CHAPTER 5

1. Extreme extramarket tactics may bring unwanted and negative public attention to social movements, undermining their cause. Boycotts may simply prove ineffective. As such, tactical repertoires are connected to the strategic aims of social movements. Furthermore, market actors may respond to social movement actions in ways that undermine the latter's goals. For example, Wal-Mart has been shown to gauge community resistance to their store openings as a market probe, meaning that the company locates stores where activists are less likely to target them (Ingram, Yue, & Rao, 2010).

2. A case study I conducted for the Low-Income Networking and Communications (LINC) Project demonstrated the power of databases for political advocacy efforts at the state level that produced outcomes at the national level (McInerney, 2004).

3. As I show in Chapter 3, business-like practices and forms existed in the NTAP field before NPower. For example, the IT Resource Center in Chicago, which emerged from the management support organizations field of the 1980s and early 1990s, followed a subsidized consulting model that predated NPower. Fanning knew Deborah Strauss, the executive director of IT Resource Center, from the NSNT meetings. NPower emulated IT Resource Center's consulting model in the development of its service offerings. However, Fanning's institutional entrepreneurship popularized the model and was often given credit for it, to the chagrin of principals at the IT Resource Center.

4. Volunteer matching entails connecting volunteers with certain technical skills to nonprofit organizations in need of those skills. Compumentor's volunteer matching program connected technology volunteers with nonprofit organizations that needed technology assistance.

5. Ben-Horin began our conversation with references to French sociological analyses of the May 1968 movement and the works of Marxian scholar Antonio Gramsci.

6. Normative isomorphism was also in evidence as foundation officers pressed managers of NTAPs to adopt practices established and legitimated at NPower. For example, foundations often required NTAPs to employ performance metrics created by NPower when reporting the outcomes of the grants they received.

7. For example, when Tech Foundation closed its New York City office, two of its employees, a manager and a consultant, came to work at NPower NY.

8. It is important to note that during the time period of the NPower partnership, Microsoft was undergoing a trial brought by the U.S. attorney general for violating the Sherman Antitrust Act. The case was brought in 1998. The judge ruled that Microsoft

had violated the Sherman Antitrust Act in 2000. Microsoft appealed in 2001, settling the case one year later, with the settlement not fully approved until 2004.

9. "Greenwashing" is a pejorative term used by activists to describe corporate environmental policies and actions that they think are being done for public relations rather than as a sincere commitment to environmental stewardship. In a broader context, it refers to any corporate policies or actions taken to appease public demands for social responsibility that are not driven by a sincere commitment to the particular cause they attempt to address.

10. Members in the software community draw a technical distinction between free and open source software. In general, open source refers to the practice of making available the "source code" underlying software. The opposite of open source is proprietary code, which users are legally not allowed to access. A good analogy for understanding the difference is a car. An open source car enables the user (driver/owner) to look under the hood, tinker with the engine, and replace parts with ones of their own design or modification. A proprietary car would have its hood welded shut so the user could not change the design or operation of the vehicle.

11. In the F/OSS milieu, grantmaking foundations support intermediaries and the nonprofit organizations receiving their services as well as making financial contributions directly to F/OSS foundations. According to the Foundation Search database, between 2000 and 2004 grantmaking foundations made eight grants explicitly related to open source technology, totaling $2.25 million. Major grantmaking foundations supporting F/OSS include Ford, Soros, and the Omidyar Foundation, as well as corporate foundations such as IBM.

12. The name "Nonprofit Open Source Initiative" was a riff off the existing Open Source Initiative, an open source advocacy group and information clearinghouse (see http://www.opensource.org).

13. These principles come from the last draft of the NSNT that Rob Stuart and his collaborators produced. Joan Fanning revised the planning document, rearticulating how these principles would be built into NTEN. The contrasts between the language used in the two drafts is telling. Stuart's draft reads like a movement manifesto, full of ideals and expressing a deep need for social change, but it is short on details on how to achieve their goals. Fanning's draft reads like a business plan, complete with marketing terminology and plans for building and implementing NTEN. It compromises many of the transformational movement's ideals, but makes practical suggestions for how to promote technology in the nonprofit sector.

14. The Soros Foundation, through its Open Society Institute, is a major funder of information and communications technology programs throughout the world. Working through networks of intermediaries in recipient countries, the Open Society Institute's technology program supports open source development in Eastern Europe and Africa. In the early 1990s, following the collapse of the Soviet Union, program grants provided between $50,000 and $125,000 for intermediaries to develop information and communication technology infrastructure in Eastern Europe (Peizer, 2006).

CHAPTER 6

1. Several Circuit Rider programs have been established in Europe and elsewhere. The largest of these is Lasa's Circuit Rider program in the United Kingdom (see http://www.lasa.org.uk/ict/lasa-circuit-riders/).

REFERENCES

Abbott, A. D. (1988). *The System of Professions: An Essay on the Division of Expert Labor*. Chicago: University of Chicago Press.

Achbar, M. (Director), & Abbott, J. (Writer) (2003). The Corporation (Film).

Anand, N., & Watson, M. R. (2004). Tournament Rituals in the Evolution of Fields: The Case of the Grammy Awards. *Academy of Management Journal, 47*(1), 59–80.

Anderson, E. (1997). Practical Reason and Incommensurable Goods. In R. Chang (Ed.), *Incommensurability, Incomparability, and Practical Reason* (pp. 90–109). Cambridge, MA: Harvard University Press.

Anteby, M. (2010). Markets, Morals, and Practices of Trade: Jurisdictional Disputes in the U.S. Commerce in Cadavers. *Administrative Science Quarterly, 55*, 606–638.

Ashforth, B. E., & Gibbs, B. W. (1990). The Double-Edge of Organizational Legitimation. *Organization Science, 1*(2), 177–194.

Austin, J. E. (2000). *The Collaboration Challenge: How Nonprofits and Businesses Succeed Through Strategic Alliances*. San Francisco: Jossey-Bass.

Austin, J. E., Stevenson, H. H., & Wei-Skillern, J. (2006). Social and Commercial Entrepreneurship: Same, Different, or Both? *Entrepreneurship: Theory and Practice, 30*(1), 1–22.

Bach, J., & Stark, D. (2002). Innovative Ambiguities: NGOs Use of Interactive Technology in Eastern Europe. *Studies in Comparative International Development, 37*(2), 3–25.

Baker, T., & Nelson, R. E. (2005). Creating Something from Nothing: Resource Construction Through Entrepreneurial Bricolage. *Administrative Science Quarterly, 50*, 329–366.

Baker, W. E. (1984). The Social Structure of a National Securities Market. *American Journal of Sociology, 89*(4), 775–811.

Barley, S. R. (1990). Images of Imaging: Notes on Doing Longitudinal Fieldwork. *Organization Science, 1*(3), 220–247.

Barth, F. (2000). Economic Spheres in Darfur. In R. Swedberg (Ed.), *Entrepreneurship: The Social Science View* (pp. 139–160). New York: Oxford University Press.

Bartley, T. (2007). How Foundations Shape Social Movements: The Construction of an Organizational Field and the Rise of Forest Certification. *Social Problems, 54*(3), 229–255.

Bartley, T., & Child, C. (2011). Movements, Markets, and Fields: The Effects of Anti-Sweatshop Campaigns on U.S. Firms, 1993–2000. *Social Forces, 90*(2), 425–451.

Batchilder, M. (1998, September). Circuit Riders Are Hired Guns for Nonprofit Technology. *Nonprofit Times*, 21–22.

Batista, E. (2002). *Welcome to the Roundup.* Paper presented at the N-TEN Roundup, Orlando, Florida.

Battilana, J. (2006). Agency and Institution: The Enabling Role of Individuals' Social Position. *Organization, 13*(5), 653–676.

Battilana, J., & Dorado, S. (2010). Building Sustainable Hybrid Organizations: The Case of Commercial Microfinance Organizations. *Academy of Management Journal, 53*(6), 1419–1440.

Berger, P. L., & Luckmann, T. (1966). *The Social Construction of Reality: A Treatise in the Sociology of Knowledge.* New York: Anchor Books.

Berlinger, L. R., & Te'eni, D. (1999). Leaders' Attitudes and Computer Use in Religious Congregations. *Nonprofit Management and Leadership, 9*(4), 399–412.

Beunza, D., & Stark, D. (2004). Tools of the Trade: The Socio-Technology of Arbitrage in a Wall Street Trading Room. *Industrial and Corporate Change, 13*(2), 369–400.

Bielefeld, W. (2006). Issues in Social Enterprise and Social Entrepreneurship. *Journal of Public Affairs Education, 15*(1), 69–86.

Bierma, N. (2004, December 7). Windy City: Where Did It Come From? Did *New York Sun* Editor Charles A. Dana Coin the Phrase, or Is That Legend Just Full of Hot Air? *Chicago Tribune*, p. 2.

Biggart, N. W., & Beamish, T. D. (2003). The Economic Sociology of Conventions: Habit, Custom, Practice, and Routine in Market Order. *Annual Review of Sociology, 29*, 443–464.

Binder, A. (2007). For Love and Money: Organizations' Creative Responses to Multiple Environmental Logics. *Theory and Society, 36*, 547–571.

Boltanski, L. (1996). *Endless Disputes from Intimate Injuries to Public Denunciations.* Unpublished manuscript, Cornell University, Ithaca, NY.

Boltanski, L., & Chiapello, E. (2005). *The New Spirit of Capitalism.* New York: Verso.

Boltanski, L., & Thévenot, L. (1991). *De la Justification.* Paris: Gallimard.

Boltanski, L., & Thévenot, L. (1999). The Sociology of Critical Capacity. *European Journal of Social Theory, 2*(3), 359–377.

Boltanski, L., & Thévenot, L. (2006). *On Justification: Economies of Worth* (C. Porter, Trans.). Princeton: Princeton University Press.

Boris, E. T., & Steuerle, C. E. (Eds.). (2006). *Nonprofits and Government: Collaboration and Conflict.* Washington, DC: Urban Institute Press.

Borsook, P. (2000). *Cyberselfish: A Critical Romp Through the Terribly Libertarian Culture of High-Tech*. New York: Public Affairs.

Borzaga, C., & Defourny, J. (2001). *The Emergence of Social Enterprise*. London: Routledge.

Bourdieu, P. (1986). The Forms of Capital. In J. G. Richardson (Ed.), *The Handbook of Theory and Research for the Sociology of Education* (pp. 241–258). New York: Greenwood Press.

Bourdieu, P. (1990). *The Logic of Practice*. Stanford, CA: Stanford University Press.

Bourdieu, P. (1996). *The Rules of Art: Genesis and Structure of the Literary Field* (S. Emanuel, Trans.). Stanford, CA: Stanford University Press.

Bourdieu, P. (2004). Principles of an Economic Anthropology. In N. J. Smelser and R. Swedberg (Eds.), *The Handbook of Economic Sociology* (pp. 75–89). New York and Princeton: Russell Sage Foundation and Princeton University Press.

Bourdieu, P. (2005). *The Social Structures of the Economy*. New York: Polity Press.

Bourdieu, P., & Wacquant, L. J. D. (1992). *An Invitation to Reflexive Sociology*. Chicago: University of Chicago Press.

Boxenbaum, E., & Battilana, J. (2005). Importation as Innovation: Transposing Managerial Practices Across Fields. *Strategic Organization, 3*(4), 355–383.

Brainard, L. A., & Brinkerhoff, J. M. (2004). Lost in Cyberspace: Shedding Light on the Dark Matter of Grassroots Organizations. *Nonprofit and Voluntary Sector Quarterly, 33*(3), 32S–53S.

Brainard, L. A., & Siplon, P. D. (2002). Cyberspace Challenges to Mainstream Nonprofit Health Organizations. *Administration and Society, 34*(2), 141–175.

Brainerd, P. (1999). Social Venture Partners: Engaging a New Generation of Givers. *Nonprofit and Voluntary Sector Quarterly, 28*(4), 502–507.

Bray, H. (2002, November 25). Free Software vs. Goliaths: Open-Source Movement Faces Big Adversaries. *Boston Globe*, p. F3.

Brint, S., & Karabel, J. (1991). Institutional Origins and Transformations: The Case of American Community Colleges. In W. W. Powell and P. DiMaggio (Eds.), *The New Institutionalism in Organizational Analysis* (pp. 311–336). Chicago: University of Chicago Press.

Burawoy, M. (1998). The Extended Case Method. *Sociological Theory, 16*(1), 4–33.

Burt, R. S. (2004). Structural Holes and Good Ideas. *American Journal of Sociology, 110*(2), 349–400.

BusinessWire. (2003). 2003 SBC Excelerator National Grant Recipient Improves Nonprofit Technology Capabilities. Retrieved March 4, 2003, from http://www.busi nesswire.com/news/home/20030304005354/en/2003-SBC-Excelerator-National -Grant-Recipient-Improves.

Callon, M. (1986). Some Elements of a Sociology of Translation: Domestification of the Scallops and Fishermen of St. Brieuc Bay. In J. Law (Ed.), *Power, Action,*

Belief: A New Sociology of Knowledge? (pp. 197–233). London: Routledge and Kegan Paul.

Callon, M. (1998). The Embeddedness of Economic Markets in Economics. In M. Callon (Ed.), *The Laws of Markets* (pp. 1–57). Malden, MA: Blackwell.

Callon, M., & Latour, B. (1981). Unscrewing the Big Leviathan: How Actors Macrostructure Reality and How Sociologists Help Them to Do So. In K. Knorr Cetina and A. V. Cicourel (Eds.), *Advances in Social Theory and Methodology: Toward an Integration of Micro- and Macro-Sociologies* (pp. 277–303). Boston: Routledge.

Campbell, J. L. (2005). Where Do We Stand? Common Mechanisms in Organizations and Social Movements. In G. F. Davis, D. McAdam, W. R. Scott, and M. N. Zald (Eds.), *Social Movements and Organization Theory* (pp. 41–68). New York: Cambridge University Press.

Caro, R. A. (1975). *The Power Broker: Robert Moses and the Fall of New York*. New York: Vintage Books.

Carolan, M. (2010). Sociological Ambivalence and Climate Change. *Local Environment, 15*(4), 309–321.

Carroll, G. R., & Swaminatham, A. (2000). Why the Microbrewery Movement? Organizational Dynamics of Resource Partitioning in the U.S. Brewing Industry. *American Journal of Sociology, 106*(3), 715–762.

Cartwright, P., & Strickland, W. P. (1857). *Autobiography of Peter Cartwright, the Backwoods Preacher* (8th ed.). New York: Carlton & Porter.

Castells, M. (1996). *The Rise of the Network Society* (Vol. 1). Malden, MA: Blackwell.

Chasin, A. (2000). *Selling Out: The Lesbian and Gay Movement Goes to Market*. New York: St. Martin's Press.

Chesters, G., & Welsh, I. (2004). Rebel Colours: "Framing" in Global Social Movements. *Sociological Review, 52*(3), 314–335.

Chicago Climate Exchange. (2011). Fact Sheet [electronic version]. Retrieved August 4, 2011, from https://www.theice.com/publicdocs/ccx/CCX_Fact_Sheet.pdf.

Clemens, E. S. (1993). Organizational Repertoires and Institutional Change: Women's Groups and the Transformation of U.S. Politics, 1890–1920. *American Journal of Sociology, 98*(4), 755–798.

Clemens, E. S. (1996). Organizational Form as Frame: Collective Identity and Political Strategy in the American Labor Movement, 1880–1920. In D. McAdam, J. D. McCarthy, and M. N. Zald (Eds.), *Comparative Perspectives on Social Movements: Political Opportunities, Mobilizing Structures, and Cultural Framings* (pp. 205–226). New York: Cambridge University Press.

Clemens, E. S. (1997). *The People's Lobby: Organizational Innovation and the Rise of Interest Group Politics in the United States, 1890–1925*. Chicago: University of Chicago Press.

Clemens, E. S., & Cook, J. M. (1999). Politics and Institutionalism: Explaining Durability and Change. *Annual Review of Sociology, 25*, 441–466.

Clohesy, W. W. (2000). Altruism and the Endurance of the Good. *Voluntas: International Journal of Voluntary and Nonprofit Organizations, 11*(3), 237–253.

Clorery, P., & Hrywna, M. (2012, July 1). 2011 Giving Estimated at $298.42B: Religious Giving Erodes While International Relief Jumps. *Nonprofit Times*, 1–4.

Cohen, T. (1999). Wake-Up Call for National Tech Strategy. Retrieved May 24 2004, from http://www.pnnonline.org/print.php?sid=3752.

Cohen, T. (2004, December 1). Making Assessments. [electronic version] *Nonprofit Times*. Retrieved March 10, 2012, from http://www.thenonprofittimes.com/news-articles/making-assessments/.

Coleman, G. (2004). The Political Agnosticism of Free and Open Source Software and the Inadvertent Politics of Contrast. *Anthropological Quarterly 77*(3), 507–519.

Collins, R. (1980). Weber's Last Theory of Capitalism: A Systematization. *American Sociological Review, 45*(6), 925–942.

Cooney, K. (2006). The Institutional and Technical Structuring of Nonprofit Ventures: Case Study of a Hybrid Organization Caught Between Two Fields. *Voluntas: International Journal of Voluntary and Nonprofit Organizations, 17*, 143–161.

Corder, K. (2001). Acquiring New Technology: Comparing Nonprofit and Public Sector Agencies. *Administration and Society, 33*(2), 194–219.

Czarniawska, B. (2008). *A Theory of Organizing.* Northampton, MA: Edward Elgar.

Czarniawski, B. (2000). Organizational Translations: From Worlds to Words and Numbers—and Back. *Okonomie und Gesellschaft, 16*, 117–142.

Dart, R. (2004a). Being "Business-Like" in a Nonprofit Organization: A Grounded and Inductive Typology. *Nonprofit and Voluntary Sector Quarterly, 33*(2), 290–310.

Dart, R. (2004b). The Legitimacy of Social Enterprise. *Nonprofit Management and Leadership, 4*(14), 411–424.

De Landa, M. (2001). The Politics of Software. *Dissent, 48*(4), 96–99.

Dees, J. G., Economy, P., Emerson, J., & NetLibrary Inc. (2001). *Enterprising Nonprofits a Toolkit for Social Entrepreneurs.* New York: Wiley.

Dees, J. G., Emerson, J., & Economy, P. (2002). *Strategic Tools for Social Entrepreneurs: Enhancing the Performance of Your Enterprising Nonprofit.* New York: Wiley.

DeJean, F., Gond, J.-P., & Leca, B. (2004). Measuring the Unmeasured: An Institutional Entrepreneur Strategy in an Emerging Industry. *Human Relations, 57*(6), 741–765.

Den Hond, F., & De Bakker, F. G. A. (2007). Ideologically Motivated Activism: How Activist Groups Influence Corporate Social Change Activities. *Academy of Management Review, 32*(9), 901–924.

Desrosières, A. (2001). How Real Are Statistics? Four Possible Attitudes. *Social Research, 68*(2), 339–355.

Di Domenico, M., Haugh, H., & Tracey, P. (2010). Social Bricolage: Theorizing Social Value Creation in Social Enterprises. *Entrepreneurship: Theory and Practice, 34*(4), 681–703.

Diani, M. (1997). Social Movements and Social Capital: A Network Perspective on Movement Outcomes. *Mobilization: An International Journal, 2*(2), 129–147.

DiMaggio, P. (1988). Interest and Agency in Institutional Theory. In L. G. Zucker (Ed.), *Institutional Patterns and Organizations: Culture and Environment.* Cambridge, MA: Ballinger.

DiMaggio, P. (1991). Constructing an Organizational Field as a Professional Project: U.S. Art Museums, 1920–1940. In W. W. Powell and P. DiMaggio (Eds.), *The New Institutionalism in Organizational Analysis* (pp. 267–292). Chicago: University of Chicago Press.

DiMaggio, P., & Louch, H. (1998). Socially Embedded Consumer Transactions: For What Kinds of Purchases Do People Most Often Use Networks? *American Sociological Review, 63*, 619–637.

DiMaggio, P., & Powell, W. W. (1991a). Introduction. In W. W. Powell and P. DiMaggio (Eds.), *The New Institutionalism in Organizational Analysis* (pp. 1–38). Chicago: University of Chicago Press.

DiMaggio, P., & Powell, W. W. (1991b). The Iron Cage Revisited: Institutional Isomorphism and Collective Rationality in Organizational Fields. In W. W. Powell and P. DiMaggio (Eds.), *The New Institutionalism in Organizational Analysis* (pp. 63–82). Chicago: University of Chicago Press.

Donaldson, T., & Preston, L. E. (1995). The Stakeholder Theory of the Corporation: Concepts, Evidence, and Implications. *Academy of Management Review, 20*(1), 65–91.

Earl, J., & Schussman, A. (2003). The New Site of Activism: On-Line Organizations, Movement Entrepreneurs, and the Changing Location of Social Movement Decision Making. *Research in Social Movements, Conflicts and Change, 24*, 155–187.

Edwards, B., & McCarthy, J. D. (2004). Resources and Social Movement Mobilization. In D. A. Snow, S. A. Soule, and H. Kriesi (Eds.), *The Blackwell Companion to Social Movements* (pp. 116–152). Malden, MA: Blackwell.

Eesley, C. E., & Lenox, M. J. (2006). Firm Responses to Secondary Stakeholder Action. *Strategic Management Journal, 27*, 765–781.

Eisinger, P. (2002). Organizational Capacity and Organizational Effectiveness Among Street-Level Food Assistance Programs. *Nonprofit and Voluntary Sector Quarterly, 31*(1), 115.

Eliasoph, N., & Lichterman, P. (1999). "We Begin with Our Favorite Theory . . .": Reconstructing the Extended Case Method. *Sociological Theory, 17*(2), 228–234.

Emerson, J., & Twersky, F. (Eds.). (1996). *New Social Entrepreneurs: The Success, Challenge, and Lessons of Non-profit Enterprise Creation.* San Francisco: Roberts Foundation.

Emerson, R. M., Fretz, R. I., & Shaw, L. L. (1995). *Writing Ethnographic Fieldnotes.* Chicago: University of Chicago Press.

Espeland, W. N., & Stevens, M. L. (1998). Commensuration as a Social Process. *Annual Review of Sociology, 24,* 313–343.

Executive Council of New York. (2004). The 2004 New York "Ten Awards" Gala. Retrieved March 21, 2012, from http://www.tenawards.com/2004/index.asp.

Feeding America. (2012). Mission and Values. Retrieved March 28, 2012, from http://feedingamerica.org/how-we-fight-hunger/mission-and-values.aspx.

Fisher, D. R. (2006). *Activism, Inc: How the Outsourcing of Grassroots Campaigns Is Strangling Progressive Politics in America.* Stanford: Stanford University Press.

Fligstein, N. (1996). Markets as Politics: A Political Cultural Approach to Market Institutions. *American Sociological Review, 61,* 656–673.

Fligstein, N. (1997). Social Skill and Institutional Theory. *American Behavioral Scientist, 40*(4), 397–406.

Fligstein, N. (2001). *The Architecture of Markets: An Economic Sociology of Twenty-First-Century Capitalist Societies.* Princeton: Princeton University Press.

Fligstein, N., & Dauter, L. (2007). The Sociology of Markets. *Annual Review of Sociology, 33,* 105–128.

Fligstein, N., & McAdam, D. (2012). *A Theory of Fields.* New York: Oxford University Press.

Forbes, D. P. (1998). Measuring the Unmeasurable: Empirical Studies of Nonprofit Organizational Effectiveness from 1977 to 1997. *Nonprofit and Voluntary Sector Quarterly, 27*(2), 183–202.

Fourcade, M., & Healy, K. (2007). Moral Views of Market Society. *Annual Review of Sociology, 33,* 285–311.

Fromartz, S. (2006). *Organic, Inc.: Natural Foods and How They Grew.* New York: Harcourt.

Frumkin, P. (2003). Inside Venture Philanthropy. *Society, 40*(4), 7–15.

Galaskiewicz, J., & Bielefeld, W. (1998). *Nonprofit Organizations in an Age of Uncertainty: A Study of Organizational Change.* New York: A. de Gruyter.

Galaskiewicz, J., & Colman, M. S. (2006). Collaboration Between Corporations and Nonprofit Organizations. In W. W. Powell and R. Steinberg (Eds.), *The Nonprofit Sector: A Research Handbook* (2nd ed., pp. 180-204). New Haven: Yale University Press.

Gallaway, T., & Kinnear, D. (2004). Open Source Software, the Wrongs of Copyright, and the Rise of Technology. *Journal of Economic Issues, 38*(2), 467–475.

Gamson, J. (1997). Messages of Exclusion: Gender, Movements, and Symbolic Boundaries. *Gender and Society, 11,* 178–199.

Gamson, W. (1991). Commitment and Agency in Social Movements. *Sociological Forum, 6,* 27–50.

Ganz, M. (2004). Why David Sometimes Wins: Strategic Capacity in Social Movements. In J. Goodwin and J. M. Jasper (Eds.), *Rethinking Social Movements: Structure, Meaning, and Emotion* (pp. 177–200). New York: Rowman and Littlefield.

Ganz, M. (2009). *Why David Sometimes Wins: Leadership, Organization, and Strategy in the California Farm Worker Movement.* New York: Oxford University Press.

Garfinkel, H. (1984). *Studies in Ethnomethodology.* Malden, MA: Polity Press.

Garud, R. (2008). Conferences as Venues for the Configuration of Emerging Organizational Fields: The Case of Cochlear Implants. *Journal of Management Studies, 45*(6), 1061–1088.

Garud, R., & Karnoe, P. (2003). Bricolage Versus Breakthrough: Distributed and Embedded Agency in Technology Entrepreneurship. *Research Policy, 32,* 277–300.

Geilhufe, D. (2010). [RIDERS-TALK] Nonprofit Technology Conference—a Query. In riders-talk@npogroups.org (Ed.).

Gertner, J. (2004, June 6). The Virtue in $6 Heirloom Tomatoes. *New York Times Magazine,* 44–47.

Gilbert, M. (1998). Interview with Rob Stuart of the Rockefeller Family Fund [electronic version]. *Nonprofit Online News.* Retrieved October 9, 2002, from http://news.gilbert.org/features/featureReader$3583.

Gilbert, M. (2003). Questionable Microsoft Donations in Europe. Retrieved May 3, 2010, from http://news.gilbert.org/2003/05/news.

Girard, M., & Stark, D. (2003). Heterarchies of Value in Manhattan-Based New Media Firms. *Theory, Culture & Society, 20*(3), 77–105.

Giugni, M. G. (1998). Was It Worth the Effort? The Outcomes and Consequences of Social Movements. *Annual Review of Sociology, 24,* 371–393.

Granovetter, M. (1985). Economic Action and Social Structure: The Problem of Embeddedness. *American Journal of Sociology, 91,* 481–510.

Granovetter, M. (1992). Economic Institutions as Social Constructions: A Framework for Analysis. *Acta Sociologica, 35*(1), 3–11.

Green, S. E., Jr., & Li, Y. (2011). Rhetorical Institutionalism: Language, Agency, and Structure in Institutional Theory Since Alvesson 1993. *Journal of Management Studies, 48*(7), 1662–1697.

Greenwood, R., & Hinings, C. R. (1996). Understanding Radical Organizational Change: Bringing Together the Old and New Institutionalism. *Academy of Management Review, 21*(4), 1022–1054.

Greenwood, R., & Suddaby, R. (2006). Institutional Entrepreneurship in Mature Fields: The Big Five Accounting Firms. *Academy of Management Journal, 49*(1), 27–48.

Guthman, J. (2004). *Agrarian Dreams: The Paradox of Organic Farming in California.* Berkeley: University of California Press.

Haenfler, R. (2004). Collective Identity in the Straight Edge Movement: How Diffuse Movements Foster Commitment, Encourage Individualized Participation, and Promote Cultural Change. *Sociological Quarterly, 45*(4), 785–805.

Hägglund, P. B. (2000). The Value of Facts: How Analysts' Recommendations Focus on Facts Instead of Values. *Okonomie und Gesellschaft, 16,* 313–337.

Haines, H. H. (1984). Black Radicalization and the Funding of Civil Rights. *Social Problems, 32,* 31–43.

Hallett, T. (2010). The Myth Incarnate: Recoupling Processes, Turmoil, and Inhabited Institutions in an Urban Elementary School. *American Sociological Review, 75*(1), 52–74.

Hallett, T., & Ventresca, M. J. (2006). Inhabited Institutions: Social Interactions and Organizational Forms in Gouldner's *Patterns of Industrial Bureaucracy. Theory and Society, 35,* 213–216.

Hansmann, H. (1980). The Role of Nonprofit Enterprise. *Yale Law Journal, 89*(5), 835–901.

Hargrave, T. J., & Van de Ven, A. H. (2009). Institutional Work as the Creative Embrace of Contradiction. In T. B. Lawrence, R. Suddaby, and B. Leca (Eds.), *Institutional Work: Actors and Agency in Institutional Studies of Organizations* (pp. 120–139). New York: Cambridge University Press.

Hasenfeld, Y., & Gidron, B. (2005). Understanding Multi-purpose Hybrid Voluntary Organizations: The Contributions of Theories of Civil Society, Social Movements, and Non-profit Organizations. *Journal of Civil Society, 1*(2), 97–112.

Haveman, H. A., & Rao, H. (1997). Structuring a Theory of Moral Sentiments: Institutional and Organizational Coevolution in the Early Thrift Industry. *American Journal of Sociology, 102*(6), 1606–1651.

Healy, K. (2006). *Last Best Gifts: Altruism and the Market for Human Blood and Organs.* Chicago: University of Chicago Press.

Herman, R. D., & Renz, D. O. (1997). Multiple Constituencies and the Social Construction of Nonprofit Organizational Effectiveness. *Nonprofit and Voluntary Sector Quarterly, 26*(2), 185–206.

Herman, R. D., & Renz, D. O. (1999). Theses on Nonprofit Organizational Effectiveness. *Nonprofit and Voluntary Sector Quarterly, 28*(2), 107–126.

Herman, R. D., & Renz, D. O. (2002). *More Theses on Nonprofit Organizational Effectiveness.* Paper presented at the Midwest Center for Nonprofit Leadership Conference: Nonprofit Organizational Effectiveness and Performance: Challenges and Advances in Theory and Practice, Kansas City, MO.

Hitlin, S., & Piliavin, J. A. (2004). Values: Reviving a Dormant Concept. *Annual Review of Sociology, 30,* 359–379.

Hodder, I. (2000). The Interpretation of Documents and Material Culture. In N. K. Denzin and Y. S. Lincoln (Eds.), *The Handbook of Qualitative Research* (pp. 703–715). Thousand Oaks, CA: Sage Publications.

Hogan, M. (2006, July 31). Whole Foods: A Little Too Rich? [electronic version]. *Business Week*. Retrieved July 31, 2006, from http://www.businessweek.com/stories /2006-07-20/whole-foods-a-little-too-rich-businessweek-business-news-stock -market-and-financial-advice.

Holland, T. P. (1988). The Effectiveness of Non-Profit Organizations. *Journal of Applied Social Sciences, 12*(2), 202–221.

Holstein, J. A., & Gubrium, J. F. (1995). *The Active Interview.* Thousand Oaks, CA: Sage.

Howard, P. N. (2002). Network Ethnography and the Hypermedia Organization: New Media, New Organizations, New Methods. *New Media & Society, 4*(4), 550–574.

Hunt, S. A., Benford, R. D., & Snow, D. A. (1994). Identity Fields: Framing Processes and the Social Construction of Movement Identities. In E. Larana, H. Johnston, and J. R. Gusfield (Eds.), *New Social Movements: From Ideology to Identity* (pp. 185–208). Philadelphia: Temple University Press.

Hwang, H., & Powell, W. W. (2005). Institutions and Entrepreneurship. In S. A. Alvarez, R. Agarwal, and O. Sorenson (Eds.), *Handbook of Entrepreneurship Research: Interdisciplinary Perspectives* (pp. 201–232). New York: Springer.

Indergaard, M. (2004). *Silicon Alley: The Rise and Fall of a New Media District.* New York: Routledge.

Ingram, P., Yue, L. Q., & Rao, H. (2010). Trouble in Store: Probes, Protests, and Store Openings by Wal-Mart, 1998–2007. *American Journal of Sociology, 116*(1), 53–92.

InternetNews.com. (2002). Q&A: Barbara Chang, NPower NY [electronic version]. *Internet News.com.* Retrieved August 15, 2002, from http://www.internetnews.com /bus-news/article.php/1437831/QA-Barbara-Chang-NPower-NY.htm.

Jarzabkowski, P., Matthiesen, J., & Van de Ven, A. H. (2009). Doing Which Work? A Practice Approach to Institutional Pluralism. In T. B. Lawrence, R. Suddaby, and B. Leca (Eds.), *Institutional Work: Actors and Agency in Institutional Studies of Organizations* (pp. 284–316). New York: Cambridge University Press.

Jeavons, T. H. (1992). When the Management Is the Message: Relating Values to Management Practice in Nonprofit Organizations. *Nonprofit Management and Leadership, 2*(4), 403–417.

Jenkins, J. C., & Eckert, C. M. (1986). Channeling Black Insurgency: Elite Patronage and Professional Social Movement Organizations in the Development of the Black Movement. *American Sociological Review, 51,* 812–829.

Johnston, H., Larana, E., & Gusfield, J. R. (1994). Identities, Grievances, and New Social Movements. In E. Larana, H. Johnston, and J. R. Gusfield (Eds.), *New Social Movements: From Ideology to Identity* (pp. 3–35). Philadelphia: Temple University Press.

Johnston, J. (2008). The Citizen-Consumer Hybrid: Ideological Tensions and the Case of Whole Foods. *Theory and Society, 37,* 229–270.

Jossey-Bass. (2002). *The New Nonprofit Almanac and Desk Reference: The Essential Facts and Figures for Managers and Volunteers* (1st ed.). San Francisco: Jossey-Bass.

Kanter, R. M., & Summers, D. V. (1987). Doing Well While Doing Good: Dilemmas of Performance Measurement in Nonprofit Organizations and the Need for a Multiple-Constituency Approach. In W. W. Powell (Ed.), *The Nonprofit Sector: A Research Handbook* (pp. 154–166). New Haven: Yale University Press.

Kennedy, M. T. (2008). Getting Counted: Markets, Media, and Reality. *American Sociological Review, 73*(2), 270–295.

King, B. G. (2008). A Political Mediation Model of Corporate Response to Social Movement Activism. *Administrative Science Quarterly, 53,* 395–421.

King, B. G., & Pearce, N. A. (2010). The Contentiousness of Markets: Politics, Social Movements, and Institutional Change in Markets. *Annual Review of Sociology, 36,* 249–267.

King, B. G., & Soule, S. A. (2007). Social Movements as Extra-institutional Entrepreneurs: The Effect of Protests on Stock Price Returns. *Administrative Science Quarterly, 52,* 413–442.

Kirschenbaum, J., & Kunamneni, R. (2001). *Bridging the Organizational Divide: Toward a Comprehensive Approach to the Digital Divide.* Oakland, CA: PolicyLink.

Knowledge@Wharton. (2003). Many Nonprofits Now Combine Social Mission with For-Profit Mentality. Retrieved March 22, 2012, from http://knowledge.wharton.upenn.edu/article.cfm?articleid=772.

Kvale, S. (1996). *InterViews: An Introduction to Qualitative Research Interviewing.* Thousand Oaks, CA: Sage Publications.

Lampel, J., & Meyer, A. D. (2008). Field-Configuring Events as Structuring Mechanisms: How Conferences, Ceremonies, and Trade Shows Constitute New Technologies, Industries, and Markets. *Journal of Management Studies, 45*(6), 1025–1035.

Lane, D., & Maxfield, R. (1996). Strategy Under Complexity: Fostering Generative Relationships. *Long Range Planning, 29*(2), 215–231.

Latour, B. (1986). The Powers of Association. In J. Law (Ed.), *Power, Action, and Belief: A New Sociology of Knowledge* (pp. 265–280). Boston: Routledge.

Latour, B. (1987). *Science in Action: How to Follow Scientists and Engineers Through Society.* Cambridge, MA: Harvard University Press.

Latour, B. (1988a). Mixing Humans and Nonhumans Together: The Sociology of a Door-Closer. *Social Problems, 35*(3), 298–311.

Latour, B. (1988b). *The Pasteurization of France.* Cambridge, MA: Harvard University Press.

Latour, B. (1991). Technology Is Society Made Durable. In J. Law (Ed.), *The Sociology of Monsters: Essays on Power, Technology and Domination* (pp. 103–131). New York: Routledge.

Latour, B. (1996). *Aramis, or the Love of Technology*. Cambridge, MA: Harvard University Press.

Latour, B. (2005). *Reassembling the Social: An Introduction to Actor-Network-Theory*. New York: Oxford University Press.

Lawrence, T. B., Suddaby, R., & Leca, B. (Eds.). (2009). *Institutional Work: Actors and Agency in Institutional Studies of Organizations*. New York: Cambridge University Press.

Lawton, G. (2002, February 2). The Great Giveaway. *New Scientist*, 3434.

Lazega, E., & Favereau, O. (2002). Introduction. In O. Favereau and E. Lazega (Eds.), *Conventions and Structures in Economic Organization: Markets, Networks and Hierarchies* (pp. 1–28). Northampton, MA: Edward Elgar.

Lessig, L. (2005). Open Code and Open Societies. In J. Feller, B. Fitzgerald, S. A. Hissam, and K. R. Lakhani (Eds.), *Perspectives on Free and Open Source Software* (pp. 349–360). Cambridge, MA: MIT Press.

Levin, P. (2008). Culture and Markets: How Economic Sociology Conceptualizes Culture. *Annals of the American Academy of Political and Social Science, 619*, 114–129.

Light, P. C. (2000). *Making Nonprofits Work: A Report on the Tides of Nonprofit Management Reform*. Washington, DC: Brookings Institution Press; Aspen Institute.

Light, P. C. (2002). *Pathways to Nonprofit Excellence*. Washington, DC: Brookings Institution Press.

Little, A. G. (2004, December 17). The Whole Food Shebang. *Grist Magazine*. Retrieved July 20, 2006, from http://www.grist.org/news/maindish/2004/12/17/little-mackey/.

Lofland, J., & Lofland, L. H. (1995). *Analyzing Social Settings: A Guide to Qualitative Observation and Analysis* (3rd ed.). Belmont, CA: Wadsworth.

Lounsbury, M. (2004, August 14–17). *The New Reformation: Economic Ideas and the Nonprofit Sector*. Paper presented at the American Sociological Association, San Francisco.

Lounsbury, M. (2005). Institutional Variation in the Evolution of Social Movements: Competing Logics and the Spread of Recycling Advocacy Groups. In G. F. Davis, D. McAdam, W. R. Scott, and M. N. Zald (Eds.), *Social Movements and Organization Theory* (pp. 73–95). New York: Cambridge University Press.

Lounsbury, M., & Rao, H. (2004). Sources of Durability and Change in Market Classifications: A Study of the Reconstitution of Product Categories in the American Mutual Fund Industry, 1944–1985. *Social Forces, 82*(3), 969–1000.

Lounsbury, M., Ventresca, M., & Hirsch, P. M. (2003). Social Movements, Field Frames and Industry Emergence: A Cultural-Political Perspective on US Recycling. *Socio-Economic Review, 1*(1), 71–104.

LStechie. (2002). LStechie Q & A: Marshall Mayer [electronic version]. *LStechie eJournal*. Retrieved July 23, 2003, from http://lstech.org/news/journal/02May/Marshall Mayer.htm.

MacKenzie, D. (2008). *An Engine, Not a Camera: How Financial Models Shape Markets*. Cambridge, MA: MIT Press.

MacKenzie, D., Muniesa, F., & Siu, L. (Eds.). (2008). *Do Economists Make Markets? On the Performativity of Economics*. Princeton, NJ: Princeton University Press.

Maguire, S., & Hardy, C. (2009). Discourse and Deinstitutionalization: The Decline of DDT. *Academy of Management Journal, 52*, 148–178.

Maloney, F. (2006, March 17). Is Whole Foods Wholesome? The Dark Secrets of the Organic-Food Movement. Retrieved July 25, 2006, from http://www.slate.com/id /2138176/.

Markoff, J. (2003, May 26). Microsoft Finds Some Doubters for the Motives of Its Largesse. *New York Times*. Retrieved May 26, 2003, from http://www.nytimes.com /2003/05/26/technology/26SOFT.

Martin, J. L. (2003). What Is Field Theory? *American Journal of Sociology, 109*(1), 1–49.

McAdam, D. (1990). *Freedom Summer*. New York: Oxford University Press.

McCarthy, J. D., & Zald, M. N. (1977). Resource Mobilization and Social Movements: A Partial Theory. *American Journal of Sociology, 82*(6), 1212–1241.

McCloud, J. (2007, March 12). Eating Better Than Organic. *Time*, 169.

McInerney, P.-B. (2004). *Working for Equality and Economic Liberation: Using Technology Strategically for Civic Engagement*. New York: LINC Project (TechSoup).

McInerney, P.-B. (2008). Showdown at Kykuit: Field-Configuring Events as Loci for Conventionalizing Accounts. *Journal of Management Studies, 45*(6), 1089–1116.

McInerney, P.-B. (2009). Technology Movements and the Politics of Free/Open Source Software. *Science, Technology, and Human Values, 34*(2), 206–233.

McInerney, P.-B. (2012). Social Enterprise in Mixed-Form Fields: Challenges and Prospects. In Y. Hasenfeld and B. Gidron (Eds.), *Social Enterprises: An Organizational Perspective*. New York: Palgrave Macmillan.

McVeigh, R., Welch, M. R., & Bjarnason, T. (2003). Hate Crime Reporting as a Successful Social Movement Outcome. *American Sociological Review, 68*(6), 843–867.

Mead, G. H. (1995). *Mind, Self, and Society: From the Standpoint of a Social Behavioralist*. Chicago: University of Chicago Press.

Melucci, A. (1989). *Nomads of the Present: Social Movements and Individual Needs in Contemporary Society*. Philadelphia: Temple University Press.

Merton, R. K. (1968). The Matthew Effect in Science. *Science, 159*(3810), 56–63.

Merton, R. K., & Barber, E. (1963). Sociological Ambivalence. In E. A. Tirykian (Ed.), *Sociological Theory, Values, and Sociocultural Change: Essays in Honor of Pitirim Sorokin* (pp. 91–120). New York: Harper and Row.

Meyer, A. D., Gaba, V., & Colwell, K. A. (2005). Organizing Far from Equilibrium: Nonlinear Change in Organizational Fields. *Organization Science, 16*(5), 456–473.

Meyer, J. W., & Rowan, B. (1977). Institutionalized Organizations: Formal Structure as Myth and Ceremony. *American Journal of Sociology, 83*(2), 340–363.

Meyer, M. W. (1994). Measuring Performance in Economic Organizations. In N. J. Smelser and R. Swedberg (Eds.), *The Handbook of Economic Sociology* (pp. 556–578). Princeton: Princeton University Press.

Meyer, M. W., & O'Shaughnessy, K. C. (1993). Organizational Design and the Performance Paradox. In R. Swedberg (Ed.), *Explorations in Economic Sociology* (pp. 249–278). New York: Russell Sage Foundation.

Michels, R. (1959). *Political Parties: A Sociological Study of the Oligarchical Tendencies of Modern Democracy* (E. a. C. Paul, Trans.). New York: Dover Publications.

Miller, P. (2001). Governing by Numbers: Why Calculative Practices Matter. *Social Research, 68*(2), 379–396.

Mills, C. W. (1940). Situated Actions and Vocabularies of Motive. *American Sociological Review, 5*(6), 904–913.

Mills, E. W. (1983). Sociological Ambivalence and Social Order: The Constructive Uses of Normative Dissonance. *Sociology and Social Research, 67*, 279–287.

Mills-Groninger, T. (2003). A History of the TRC (e-mail). Chicago: IT Resource Center.

Mills-Groninger, T. (2004, May 1). Special Report: The Encompassing Approach to the Nonprofit Sector's Utilization of Technology. *Nonprofit Times 18*, 21–22, 25, 33.

Mills-Groninger, T. (2011, May 15). Disconnecting from the Network: NPower Members Deciding Whether to Stay or to Go. *Nonprofit Times 25*, 1, 4, 6–7.

Moody, M. (2008). "Building a Culture": The Construction and Evolution of Venture Philanthropy as a New Organizational Field. *Nonprofit and Voluntary Sector Quarterly, 37*(2), 324–352.

Munson, Z. (2008). *The Making of Pro-life Activists: How Social Movement Mobilization Works*. Chicago: University of Chicago Press.

Murrain, M. (2010). Re: [RIDERS-TALK] Nonprofit Technology Conference—a Query. In riders-talk@npogroups.org (Ed.).

Murrain, M., Cowan, R., Silvers, R., Schneiderman, A., Hickman, A., & McClelland, J. (2004). *Choosing and Using Open Source Software: A Primer for Nonprofits*. Washington, DC: Nonprofit Open Source Initiative.

Murray, V., & Tassie, B. (1994). Evaluating the Effectiveness of Nonprofit Organizations. In R. D. Herman and Associates (Eds.), *The Jossey-Bass Handbook of Nonprofit Leadership and Management* (pp. 303–324). San Francisco: Jossey-Bass.

Neff, G., & Stark, D. (2003). Permanently Beta: Responsive Organization in the Internet Era. In P. N. Howard and S. Jones (Eds.), *Society Online: The Internet in Context* (pp. 173–188). Thousand Oaks, CA: Sage.

Newswire, P. (2002). Compumentor Launches Bay Area Services [electronic version]. *PR Newswire*. Retrieved May 8, 2012, from http://www.prnewswire.com/news-re leases/compumentor-launches-bay-area-services-77169332.html.

Nicholls, A. (2010). The Legitimacy of Social Entrepreneurship: Reflexive Isomor-phism in a Pre-Paradigmatic Field. *Entrepreneurship: Theory and Practice, 34*(4), 611–633.

Nicholls, A. (Ed.). (2006). *Social Entrepreneurship: New Models of Sustainable Social Change*. New York: Oxford University Press.

Norris, F. (2011, August 6). As Corporate Profits Rise, Workers' Income Declines. *New York Times*. Retrieved August 6, 2011, from http://www.nytimes.com/2011/08/06 /business/workers-wages-chasing-corporate-profits-off-the-charts.html.

NPower. (1998). *NPower Prospectus*. Unpublished manuscript, Seattle.

O'Brien, S. (1999). An Ecologist Outside Academia. *NewSource*. Retrieved May 17, 2007, from http://www.esa.org/teaching_learning/webDocs/articlesPerspective.php.

O'Brien, S. (2000). Roundup 2000 and First Day of Service, Kansas City, MO. Char-lottesville, VA: W. Alton Jones Foundation.

Olson, M. (1971). *The Logic of Collective Action: Public Goods and the Theory of Groups*. Cambridge, MA: Harvard University Press.

O'Mahoney, S. (2005). Nonprofit Foundations and Their Role in Community-Firm Software Collaboration. In J. Feller, B. Fitzgerald, S. A. Hissam, and K. R. Lakhani (Eds.), *Perspectives on Free and Open Source Software* (pp. 393–414). Cambridge, MA: MIT Press.

Organic Trade Association. (2011). U.S. Organic Industry Overview. Retrieved Septem-ber 8, 2011, from http://www.ota.com/pics/documents/2011OrganicIndustrySurvey .pdf.

Orbuch, T. L. (1997). People's Accounts Count: The Sociology of Accounts. *Annual Review of Sociology, 23*, 455–478.

O'Rourke, D. (2005). Market Movements: Nongovernmental Organization Strategies to Influence Global Production and Consumption. *Journal of Industrial Ecology, 9*(1–2), 115–128.

Orr, J. E. (1996). *Talking About Machines: An Ethnography of a Modern Job*. Ithaca, NY: ILR Press.

Osten, M. (1999). riders@npogroups.org. Retrieved July 10, 2002, from http://npogroups .org/lists/info/riders.

Padgett, J. F., & Ansell, C. K. (1993). Robust Action and the Rise of the Medici, 1400–1434. *American Journal of Sociology, 98*(6), 1259–1319.

Peizer, J. (2006). *The Dynamics of Technology for Social Change: Understanding the Fac-tors That Influence Results; Lessons Learned from the Field*. New York: iUniverse.

Pfeffer, J., & Salancik, G. R. (1978). *The External Control of Organizations*. New York: Harper and Row.

Planning Committee. (2001). *National Circuit Rider Community: Strategic Direction Overview.* Unpublished manuscript, Denver, CO.

Planning Partners. (1999). *National Strategy for Nonprofit Technology Draft Vision Document* (Web document). Philadelphia: Rockefeller Technology Project. http://web.archive.org/web/20001215145900/www.rffund.org/strategy.

Polletta, F. (2006). *It Was Like a Fever: Stories in Protest and Politics.* Chicago: University of Chicago Press.

Polletta, F., & Jasper, J. M. (2001). Collective Identity and Social Movements. *Annual Review of Sociology, 27,* 283–305.

Powell, W. W., & Colyvas, J. A. (2008). Microfoundations of Institutional Theory. In R. Greenwood, C. Oliver, R. Suddaby, and K. Sahlin (Eds.), *The Sage Book of Organizational Institutionalism* (pp. 276–298). Los Angeles: Sage.

Powell, W. W., White, D. R., Koput, K. W., & Owen-Smith, J. (2005). Network Dynamics and Field Evolution: The Growth of Interorganizational Collaboration in the Life Sciences. *American Journal of Sociology, 110*(4), 1132–1205.

Prasad, M. (1999). The Morality of Market Exchange: Love, Money, and Contractual Justice. *Sociological Perspectives, 42*(2), 181–213.

Quarter, J., Mook, L., & Richmond, B. J. (2003). *What Counts: Social Accounting for Nonprofits and Cooperatives.* New York: Prentice-Hall.

Quarter, J., & Richmond, B. J. (2001). Accounting for Social Value in Nonprofits and For-Profits. *Nonprofit Management and Leadership, 12*(1), 75–85.

Quinn, S. (2008). The Transformation of Morals in Markets: Death, Benefits, and the Exchange of Life Insurance Policies. *American Journal of Sociology, 114*(3), 738–780.

Rao, H. (2008). *Market Rebels: How Activists Make or Break Radical Innovations.* Princeton: Princeton University Press.

Rao, H., & Giorgi, S. (2006). Code Breaking: How Entrepreneurs Exploit Cultural Logics to Generate Institutional Change. *Research in Organizational Behavior, 27,* 269–304.

Rao, H., Monin, P., & Durand, R. (2003). Institutional Change in Toque Ville: Nouvelle Cuisine as an Identity Movement in French Gastronomy. *American Journal of Sociology, 108*(4), 795–843.

Reger, J. (2002). More Than One Feminism: Organizational Structure and the Construction of Collective Identity. In D. S. Meyer, N. Whittier, and B. Robnett (Eds.), *Social Movements: Identity, Culture, and the State* (pp. 171–184). New York: Oxford University Press.

Rifkin, J. (2000). *The Age of Access: The New Culture of Hypercapitalism Where All of Life Is a Paid-For Experience.* New York: Jeremy P. Tarcher/Putnam.

Robertson, B. (2001). *Beyond Access: A Foundation Guide to Ending the Organizational Divide.* Washington, DC: National Committee on Responsive Philanthropy.

Robnett, B. (2005). We Don't Agree: Collective Identity Justification Work in Social Movement Organizations. *Research in Social Movements, Conflicts and Change, 26*, 201–237.

Rojas, F. (2007). *From Black Power to Black Studies: How a Radical Social Movement Became an Academic Discipline*. Baltimore: Johns Hopkins University Press.

Rojas, R. R. (2000). A Review of Models for Measuring Organizational Effectiveness Among For-Profit and Nonprofit Organizations. *Nonprofit Management and Leadership, 11*(1), 97–104.

Roper, J., & Cheney, G. (2005). Leadership, Learning, and Human Resource Management: The Meanings of Social Entrepreneurship Today. *Corporate Governance, 5*(3), 95–104.

Ross, A. (2008). The Quandaries of Consumer-Based Labor Activism. *Cultural Studies, 22*(5), 770–787.

Rotheroe, N., & Richards, A. (2007). Social Return on Investment and Social Enterprise: Transparent Accountability for Sustainable Development. *Social Enterprise Journal, 3*(1), 31–48.

Rottenburg, R. (2000). Accountability for Development Aid. *Okonomie und Gesellschaft, 16*, 143–174.

Rottenburg, R., Kalthoff, H., & Wagener, H.-J. (2000). Introduction: In Search of a New Bed: Economic Representations and Practices. *Okonomie und Gesellschaft, 16*, 9–34.

Ryan, G. W., & Bernard, H. R. (2000). Data Management and Analysis Methods. In N. K. Denzin and Y. S. Lincoln (Eds.), *Handbook of Qualitative Research* (2nd ed., pp. 769–801). Thousand Oaks, CA: Sage Publications.

Ryan, P. W., & Lyne, I. (2008). Social Enterprise and the Measurement of Social Value: Methodological Issues with the Calculation and Application of the Social Return on Investment. *Education, Knowledge, and Economy, 2*(3), 223–237.

Sahlin-Andersson, K. (1996). Imitating by Editing Success: The Construction of Organizational Fields. In B. Czarniawski and G. Sevon (Eds.), *Translating Organizational Change* (pp. 69–92). New York: Walter de Gruyter.

Saidel, J. R., & Cour, S. (2003). Information Technology and the Voluntary Sector Workplace. *Nonprofit and Voluntary Sector Quarterly, 32*(1), 5–24.

Salamon, L. M. (2003). *The Resilient Sector: The State of Nonprofit America*. Washington, DC: Brookings Institution Press.

Salm, J. (2000). *NPower—Putting Technology Know-How in the Hands of Non-Profits Case A*. Unpublished manuscript, Seattle.

Sayer, A. (2006). Approaching Moral Economy. In N. Stehr, C. Henning, and B. Weiler (Eds.), *The Moralization of the Market* (pp. 77–108). New Brunswick, NJ: Transaction Publishers.

Schatzman, L., & Strauss, A. L. (1973). *Field Research: Strategies for a Natural Sociology*. Upper Saddle River, NJ: Prentice-Hall.

Schlosser, J. (2006, April 3). After a Dip, Whole Foods Looks Tasty. *Fortune, 153*, 115.

Schneiberg, M., & Clemens, E. S. (2006). The Typical Tools for the Job: Research Strategies in Institutional Analysis. *Sociological Theory, 24*(3), 195–227.

Schurman, R. (2004). Fighting "Frankenfoods": Industry Opportunity Structures and the Efficacy of the Anti-Biotech Movement in Western Europe. *Social Problems, 51*(2), 243–268.

Schwartzman, H. B. (1993). *Ethnography in Organizations*. Newbury Park, CA: Sage.

Scott, M. B., & Lyman, S. M. (1968). Accounts. *American Sociological Review, 33*(1), 46–62.

Scott, W. R. (1994). Conceptualizing Organizational Fields: Linking Organizations and Societal Systems. In H.-U. Derlien, U. Gerhardt, and F. W. Scharpf (Eds.), *Systemrationalitat und Partialinteresse* [System Rationality and Partial Interests] (pp. 203–221). Baden-Baden: Nomos Verlagsgesellschaft.

Scott, W. R. (2008a). Approaching Adulthood: The Maturing of Institutional Theory. *Theory and Society, 37*, 493–511.

Scott, W. R. (2008b). *Institutions and Organizations: Ideas and Interests* (3rd ed.). Los Angeles: Sage.

Scott, W. R., & Davis, G. F. (2007). *Organizations and Organizing: Rational, Natural, and Open System Perspectives*. Upper Saddle River, NJ: Prentice-Hall.

Seley, J. E., & Wolpert, J. (2002). *New York City's Nonprofit Sector*. New York: New York City Nonprofits Project.

Seo, M.-G., & Creed, W. E. D. (2002). Institutional Contradictions, Praxis, and Institutional Change: A Dialectical Perspective. *Academy of Management Review, 27*(2), 222–247.

Shapin, S. (2006, May 15,). Paradise Sold: A Critic at Large. *New Yorker, 82*, 84–86.

Shorters, T. (2001). *The Circuit Riding Recipe in Washington DC*. Unpublished manuscript, Washington, DC.

Silvers, R. (2002). *NOSI Strategic Plan*. Washington, DC: Nonprofit Open Source Initiative.

Skocpol, T., Ganz, M., & Munson, Z. (2000). A Nation of Organizers: The Institutional Origins of Civic Voluntarism in the United States. *American Political Science Review, 94*(3), 527–546.

Slater, D. (1998). Roundup 2 Evaluation. (E-mail). New York.

Snow, D. A., & Benford, R. D. (1992). Master Frames and Cycles of Protest. In A. D. Morris and C. M. Meuller (Eds.), *Frontiers in Social Movement Theory* (pp. 156–173). New Haven: Yale University Press.

Snow, D. A., Rochford, E. B., Jr., Worden, S. K., & Benford, R. D. (1986). Frame Alignment Processes, Micromobilization, and Movement Participation. *American Sociological Review, 51*, 464–481.

Soule, S. A. (2009). *Contention and Corporate Social Responsibility*. New York: Cambridge University Press.

Soule, S. A., McAdam, D., McCarthy, J. D., & Su, Y. (1999). Protest Events: Cause or Consequence of State Action. *Mobilization: An International Journal, 4*(2), 239–256.

Staggenborg, S. (1988). The Consequences of Professionalization and Formalization in the Pro-Choice Movement. *American Sociological Review, 53*(4), 585–605.

Staggenborg, S. (1991). *The Pro-Choice Movement: Organization and Activism in the Abortion Conflict*. New York: Oxford University Press.

Stark, D. (1996). Recombinant Property in East European Capitalism. *American Journal of Sociology, 101*(4), 993–1028.

Stark, D. (1999). Heterarchy: Distributing Authority and Organizing Diversity. In J. H. Clippinger III (Ed.), *The Biology of Business: Decoding the Natural Laws of Enterprise* (pp. 153–180). San Francisco: Jossey-Bass.

Stark, D. (2001). Ambiguous Assets for Uncertain Environments: Heterarchy in Postsocialist Firms. In P. DiMaggio (Ed.), *The 21st Century Firm: Changing Economic Organizations in International Perspective* (pp. 69–104). Princeton: Princeton University Press.

Stark, D. (2005). *For a Sociology of Worth*. Unpublished manuscript, Columbia University, New York.

Stark, D. (2009). *The Sense of Dissonance: Accounts of Worth in Economic Life*. Princeton: Princeton University Press.

Stark, D., & Bruszt, L. (1998). *Postsocialist Pathways: Transforming Politics and Property in East Central Europe*. New York: Cambridge University Press.

Stehr, N. (2008). *Moral Markets: How Knowledge and Affluence Change Consumers and Products*. Boulder, CO: Paradigm Publishers.

Stehr, N., & Adolf, M. (2010). Consumption Between Market and Morals: A Socio-Cultural Consideration of Moralized Markets. *European Journal of Social Theory, 13*(2), 213–228.

Stehr, N., Henning, C., & Weiler, B. (2006). Introduction. In N. Stehr, C. Henning, and B. Weiler (Eds.), *The Moralization of the Market* (pp. 1–19). New Brunswick, NJ: Transaction Publishers.

Stein, T. S. (2002). *Workforce Transitions from the Profit to the Nonprofit Sector*. New York: Kluwer Academic/Plenum Publishers.

Storper, M. (2000). Conventions and Institutions: Rethinking Problems of State Reform, Governance, and Policy. In L. Burlamaqui, A. C. Castro, and H.-J. Chang (Eds.), *Institutions and the Role of the State* (pp. 73–102). Northampton, MA: Edward Elgar.

Storper, M., & Salais, R. (1997). *Worlds of Production: The Action Framework of the Economy*. Cambridge, MA: Harvard University Press.

Strauss, A. L. (1982). Social Worlds and Legitimation Processes. *Studies in Symbolic Interaction, 4*, 171–190.

Stuart, R. (1998). Foundation Commentary: He Wants to Hold Your Hand. Retrieved August 29, 2002, from http://int1/cof.org/foundationnews/august1998/commentary.html.

Stuart, R. (1999). Computer Camp: About the Camp. Retrieved July 30, 2004, from http://web.archive.org/web/19990508064330/www.rffund.org/camp/about2.html.

Swaminatham, A., & Wade, J. B. (2001). Social Movement Theory and the Evolution of New Organizational Forms. In C. B. Schoonhoven and E. Romanelli (Eds.), *The Entrepreneurship Dynamic: Origins of Entrepreneurship and the Evolution of Industries* (pp. 286–313). Stanford: Stanford University Press.

Swedberg, R. (2009). Schumpeter's Full Model of Entrepreneurship: Economic, Non-Economic, and Social Entrepreneurship. In R. Ziegler (Ed.), *An Introduction to Social Entrepreneurship: Voices, Preconditions, Contexts* (pp. 77–106). Northampton, MA: Edward Elgar.

Tarrow, S. (2011). *Power in Movement: Social Movements and Contentious Politics* (3rd ed.). New York: Cambridge University Press.

Taylor, V. (1989). Social Movement Continuity: The Women's Movement in Abeyance. *American Sociological Review, 54*(5), 761–775.

Taylor, V., & Van Dyke, N. (2004). "Get Up, Stand Up": Tactical Repertoires of Social Movements. In D. A. Snow, S. A. Soule, and H. Kriesi (Eds.), *The Blackwell Companion to Social Movements* (pp. 262–293). New York: Blackwell.

Telecommunications Cooperative Network. (1996). *Circuit Riders: Pioneers in Nonprofit Networking* (Report). Charlottesville, VA: W. Alton Jones Foundation.

Thévenot, L. (2001). Organized Complexity: Conventions of Coordination and the Composition of Economic Arrangements. *European Journal of Social Theory 4*(4), 405–425.

Thévenot, L., Moody, M., & Lafaye, C. (2000). Forms of Valuing Nature: Arguments and Modes of Justification in French and American Environmental Disputes. In M. Lamont and L. Thévenot (Eds.), *Rethinking Comparative Cultural Sociology: Repertoires of Evaluation in France and the United States* (pp. 229–272). Cambridge: Cambridge University Press.

Thompson, J. L. (2002). The World of the Social Entrepreneur. *International Journal of Public Sector Management, 15*(4–5), 412–432.

Thornton, P. H. (2004). *Markets from Culture: Institutional Logics and Organizational Decisions in Higher Education Publishing.* Stanford, CA: Stanford University Press.

Tilly, C. (1978). *From Mobilization to Revolution.* Reading, MA: Addison-Wesley.

Tilly, C. (2006). *Why? What Happens When People Give Reasons . . . and Why.* Princeton: Princeton University Press.

Tilly, C., & Wood, L. J. (2009). *Social Movements 1768–2008* (2nd ed.). Boulder, CO: Paradigm Publishers.

Tracey, P., Phillips, N., & Jarvis, O. (2011). Bridging Institutional Entrepreneurship and the Creation of New Organizational Forms: A Multilevel Model. *Organization Science, 22*(1), 60–80.

Treuhaft, S., Chandler, A., Kirschenbaum, J., Magallanes, M., & Pinkett, R. (2007). *Bridging the Innovation Divide: An Agenda for Disseminating Technology Innovations Within the Nonprofit Sector* (Report). Oakland, CA: Policy Link and BCT Partners.

Tuckman, H. P. (1998). Competition, Commercialization, and the Evolution of Nonprofit Organizational Structures. *Journal of Policy Analysis and Management, 17*(2), 175–194.

Useem, M. (1987). Corporate Philanthropy. In W. W. Powell (Ed.), *The Nonprofit Sector: A Research Handbook* (pp. 340–360). New Haven: Yale University Press.

Van de Ven, A. H., & Huber, G. P. (1990). Longitudinal Field Research Methods for Studying Processes of Organizational Change. *Organization Science, 1*(3), 213–219.

Van Maanen, J. (1988). *Tales of the Field: On Writing Ethnography*. Chicago: University of Chicago Press.

Vasi, I. B. (2009). New Heroes, Old Theories? Toward a Sociological Perspective on Social Entrepreneurship. In R. Ziegler (Ed.), *An Introduction to Social Entrepreneurship: Voices, Preconditions, Contexts* (pp. 155–173). Northampton, MA: Edward Elgar.

Vasi, I. B. (2011). *Winds of Change: The Environmental Movement and the Global Development of the Wind Energy Industry*. New York: Oxford University Press.

Vedres, B., & Stark, D. (2010). Structural Folds: Generative Disruption in Overlapping Groups. *American Journal of Sociology, 115*(4), 1150–1190.

Von Hippel, E. (2005). Open Source Software Projects as User Innovation Networks. In J. Feller, B. Fitzgerald, S. A. Hissam, and K. R. Lakhani (Eds.), *Perspectives on Free and Open Source Software* (pp. 268–278). Cambridge, MA: MIT Press.

Waldrop, M. M. (1996, October). The Trillion-Dollar Vision of Dee Hock: The Corporate Radical Who Organized Visa Wants to Dis-Organize Your Company. *Fast Company* 1, 75.

Walker, E. T., Martin, A. W., & McCarthy, J. D. (2008). Confronting the State, the Corporation, and the Academy: The Influence of Institutional Targets on Social Movement Repertoires. *American Journal of Sociology, 114*(1), 35–76.

Weber, M. (1978). *Economy and Society* (Vol. 1). Berkeley: University of California Press.

Weber, M. (1992). *The Protestant Ethic and the Spirit of Capitalism* (T. Parsons, Trans.). New York: Routledge.

Weber, S. (2004). *The Success of Open Source.* Cambridge, MA: Harvard University Press.

Weerawardena, J., & Mort, G. S. (2006). Investigating Social Entrepreneurship: A Multidimensional Model. *Journal of World Business, 41,* 21–25.

Weisbrod, B. A. (1998). *To Profit or Not to Profit: The Commercial Transformation of the Nonprofit Sector.* Cambridge: Cambridge University Press.

Weitzman, M. S., Jalandoni, N. T., Lampkin, L. M., & Pollak, T. H. (2002). *The New Nonprofit Almanac and Desk Reference: The Essential Facts and Figures for Managers, Researchers, and Volunteers.* San Francisco: Jossey-Bass.

White, H. C. (1981). Where Do Markets Come From? *American Journal of Sociology, 87,* 517–547.

Whole Foods Workers Unite! (2006). Retrieved July 25, 2006, from http://www.whole workersunite.org.

Winner, L. (1986). Do Artifacts Have Politics? In *The Whale and the Reactor: A Search for Limits in an Age of High Technology* (pp. 19–39). Chicago: University of Chicago Press.

Wright, A. L., & Zammuto, R. F. (2012). Creating Opportunities for Institutional Entrepreneurship: The Colonel and the Cup in English County Cricket. *Journal of Business Venturing.*

Wry, T., Lounsbury, M., & Glynn, M. A. (2011). Legitimating Nascent Collective Identities: Coordinating Cultural Entrepreneurship. *Organization Science, 22*(2), 449–463.

Yaziji, M., & Doh, J. (2009). *NGOs and Corporations: Conflict and Collaboration.* New York: Cambridge University Press.

Young, D. R. (2003). New Trends in the US Non-profit Sector: Towards Market Integration. In Organisation for Economic Co-operation and. Development (Ed.), *The Non-profit Sector in a Changing Economy* (pp. 61–77). Paris: Organisation for Economic Co-operation and Development.

Young, R. (2006). For What It Is Worth: Social Value and the Future of Social Entrepreneurship. In A. Nicholls (Ed.), *Social Entrepreneurship: New Models of Sustainable Social Change.* New York: Oxford University Press.

Zald, M. N., & Ash, R. (1966). Social Movement Organizations: Growth, Decay, and Change. *Social Forces, 44*(3), 327–341.

Zaloom, C. (2006). *Out of the Pits: Traders and Technology from Chicago to London.* Chicago: University of Chicago Press.

Zelizer, V. A. (1979). *Morals and Markets: The Development of Life Insurance in the United States.* New York: Columbia University Press.

Zelizer, V. A. (2010). *Economic Lives: How Culture Shapes the Economy.* Princeton: Princeton University Press.

Ziegler, R. (Ed.). (2009). *An Introduction to Social Entrepreneurship: Voices, Preconditions, Contexts.* Northampton, MA: Edward Elgar.

Zilber, T. B. (2011). Institutional Multiplicity in Practice: A Tale of Two High-Tech Conferences in Israel. *Organization Science, 22*(6), 1539–1559.

Zuckerman, E. W. (1999). The Categorical Imperative: Securities Analysts and the Illegitimacy Discount. *American Journal of Sociology, 104*(5), 1398–1438.

Zuckerman, E. W. (2012). Construction, Concentration, and (Dis)Continuities in Social Valuations. *Annual Review of Sociology, 38*, 223–245.

INDEX

Note: Page numbers in *italics* indicate figures and tables.

Printed and bound by CPI Group (UK) Ltd, Croydon, CR0 4YY

23/04/2025